EUROPEAN CENTRAL BANK

THE EUROPEAN CENTRAL BANK

ORY,
E AND
CTIONS

PETER K. SCHELLER

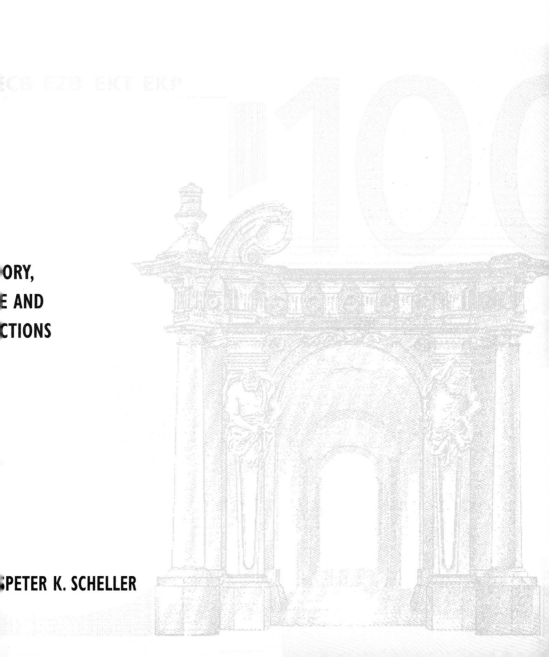

© European Central Bank, 2004

Address
Kaiserstrasse 29
60311 Frankfurt am Main
Germany

Postal address
Postfach 16 03 19
60066 Frankfurt am Main
Germany

Telephone
+49 69 1344 0

Internet
http://www.ecb.int

Fax
+49 69 1344 6000

Telex
411 144 ecb d

*The cut-off date for the data included in
this book was 1 July 2004.*

ISBN 92-9181-505-5 (print)
ISBN 92-9181-506-3 (online)

CONTENTS

CHAPTER 3

CHAPTER 4

CHAPTER 5

CHAPTER 6

ANNEX 1

Excerpts from the Treaty establishing the European Community

ANNEX 2

Protocol on the Statute of the European System of Central Banks and of the European Central Bank

BOXES

TABLES

CHARTS

DIAGRAMS

ILLUSTRATIONS

ABBREVIATIONS AND ACRONYMS

BEPG	Broad Economic Policy Guideline
BIS	Bank for International Settlements
BSC	Banking Supervision Committee
CESR	Committee of European Securities Regulators
CMFB	Committee on Monetary, Financial and Balance of Payments Statistics
EBA	Euro Banking Association
EBC	European Banking Committee
EC	European Community
ECB	European Central Bank
ECJ	European Court of Justice
ECOFIN	Economics and Finance (Ministers)
ECU	European Currency Unit
EEC	European Economic Community
EFC	Economic and Financial Committee
EMCF	European Monetary Cooperation Fund
EMI	European Monetary Institute
EMS	European Monetary System
EMU	Economic and Monetary Union
EPC	Economic Policy Committee
ERM	exchange rate mechanism
ESCB	European System of Central Banks
EU	European Union
GDP	gross domestic product
HICP	Harmonised Index of Consumer Prices
IMF	International Monetary Fund
MFI	monetary financial institution
NCB	national central bank
OECD	Organisation for Economic Co-operation and Development
OJ	Official Journal of the European Union
OLAF	European Anti-Fraud Office
RTGS	Real-time gross settlement
SGP	Stability and Growth Pact
SSS	Securities settlement system
TARGET	Trans-European Automated Real-time Gross settlement Express Transfer system

FOREWORD

The ECB is fully committed to the principles of openness and transparency, and it honours this commitment in particular with a large volume of publications that explain its aims and activities. In addition to the frequent and extensive publications on current developments within its field of competence, the ECB publishes Working Papers and Occasional Papers on specific topics. It therefore devotes a significant share of its resources to communication with the world of banking, market participants, academia and the general public.

The ECB also publishes comprehensive monographs on its role and activities. The first publication in this series was entitled "The Monetary Policy of the ECB", the second edition of which was published in early 2004. The present book focuses on the history, role and function of the ECB itself, approaching the organisation from the legal, institutional and organisational points of view. It describes the processes that led to the establishment of the ECB and the introduction of the euro, the role and the functions that are performed by the ECB as captain of the European monetary team, namely the Eurosystem, and the multiple aspects of its status as a supranational organisation established under Community law. All these elements form the background to the ECB's and the Eurosystem's policies and activities and it is our hope that the fuller knowledge provided by this book will lead to an even better understanding of the ECB's objectives and aims. At the same time, the book illustrates the important role of national central banks (NCBs) within the Eurosystem under the leadership of the ECB. Joint action by the ECB and the NCBs and close intra-system cooperation account for the proper discharge of the Eurosystem's mandate.

The NCBs have had dozens of years to evolve, at least half a century and in some cases two centuries. In comparison, the ECB was developed in "fast motion" mode. Ten years ago the European Monetary Institute (EMI), the forerunner of the ECB, started to prepare, together with the NCBs of the European Union, the future European central banking system and its leader, the ECB. Only five years later, the ECB, as the captain of the Eurosystem team, took over responsibility for the single monetary policy of the euro area, i.e. for one of the world's two most important currencies. The start of Stage Three of Economic and Monetary Union (EMU) in 1999, however, did not mark the end of the ECB's development. Many issues still needed to be settled – in particular, the euro cash changeover in 2002 – before the move towards EMU could be completed; and the ECB had to develop as an organisation itself.

The introduction of the euro has meant a big change for everyone in the euro area. It is also expected to arouse the demand of a large audience for information on the organisation that is responsible for the stability of the euro. As the ECB operates in a highly complex environment, it is all the more important to provide a "guide" and meet the demands of the ECB's multinational audience for information. It is for this reason that the Executive Board commissioned this book from an expert on these issues who, since the beginning of the 1990s, has played a prominent role in the preparation of EMU and the establishment and development of the ECB.

This book is addressed to anyone who wishes to have a greater in-depth understanding of all legal, institutional and organisational aspects of the ECB. EU enlargement has further broadened this audience, and the ECB expects that the demand for information will increase accordingly. At this point I should mention that the governors of the NCBs of the new EU Member States have been members of the ECB's General Council since 1 May 2004 and that, since the same date, these NCBs have been full members of the European System of Central Banks (ESCB). The eventual adoption of the single currency, after due convergence, is a clear prospect for all of the countries concerned, and all have committed themselves to respect the terms of the Maastricht Treaty without reservation. The ECB, which has warmly welcomed the enlargement process, will help to prepare the convergence process with the greatest of care in close cooperation with the NCBs concerned.

I am sure that this book will provide useful information to all those who are interested in the work of the ECB

Jean-Claude Trichet
President of the ECB

ACKNOWLEDGEMENTS

This book has benefited greatly from numerous comments and drafting suggestions from my colleagues at the ECB, to whom I am most grateful. I would also like to express my gratitude to the ECB's Linguistic Services Division for their valuable assistance and to the Official Publications and Library Division for their expertise in dealing with all the technical aspects of this publication. The responsibility for the content of this book, however, remains entirely mine.

Hanspeter K. Scheller
Frankfurt am Main, July 2004

INTRODUCTION

Central banking in Europe always used to be tantamount to issuing and managing national currencies: a national currency became an indispensable ingredient of national sovereignty; national banknotes, which occupied an increasingly important role in the circulation of money and eventually replaced par-value gold and silver coins as legal tender, communicated national cultures and symbols. Concurrently with the increasing role of banknotes as a means of payment in modern economic life, their issuers, the central banks, grew in importance and the conduct of monetary policy became an essential part of a nation's economic politics.

Against this historical background, the realisation of European Economic and Monetary Union (EMU) at the end of the 20th century was unique in that it introduced a new monetary regime with a single currency for a large part of Europe. The 12 Member States of the EU that have so far adopted the euro represent two-thirds of the EU's total population and the extension of the euro area to other EU Member States is expected in due course.

The transfer of monetary policy to the Community level has required substantial changes to the European central banking framework. The establishment of a new supranational monetary organisation, the ECB, and the integration of NCBs into a European central banking system, the ESCB, and its sub-set, the Eurosystem, are representative of the supranationalisation of European central banking. To date, no other policy area of the European Community has reached the same depth of integration as the single monetary and exchange rate policy. Nowhere else has the Community developed its own identity more convincingly than in the euro and the ECB.

The ECB is also the embodiment of modern central banking: the overriding objective of its monetary policy is price stability; it is independent within a clear and precise mandate; and it is fully accountable to the citizens and their elected representatives for the execution of this mandate. These features are not necessarily the result of purely European developments; they are in line with the worldwide trend. However, almost nowhere are these features spelled out so clearly and firmly than in the organic law of the ECB, the Statute of the ESCB and of the ECB. Their embodiment in the EC Treaty, with quasi-constitutional status, underlines their importance in the new monetary regime of Europe. The codification of central bank law in the EC Treaty and the Statute of the ESCB is likely to serve as a benchmark for central bank law outside the EU: Switzerland, for example, has recently revised its National Bank Act along the lines of the Statute of the ESCB.

This book is designed to introduce the reader to the history, role and functions of the ECB within the framework of EMU. It is divided into six chapters dealing with the different aspects of the ECB as a policy-maker, as an organisation of Community law and as the core and leader of the Eurosystem.

Chapter 1 gives a brief overview of the establishment of EMU and the ECB and the changeover to the euro. It also puts the ECB in the context of the objectives and arrangements of EMU under the umbrella of the EU.

Chapter 2 focuses on the legal, institutional and organisational aspects of European central banking which resulted from the realisation of EMU.

Chapter 3 describes ECB policies and their implementation by Eurosystem activities, as well as the intra-Eurosystem financial relationships.

Chapter 4 gives an overview of the ECB's status and role in the institutional context of the European Community. Although the ECB is independent vis-à-vis the Community institutions and bodies, it is a part of the European Community's institutional and political framework and is subject to Community law. It is held accountable by the European Parliament and European citizens for the fulfilment of its mandate, its acts and omissions are subject to legal review by the European Court of Justice and its financial integrity is scrutinised by the European Court of Auditors.

Chapter 5 describes the ECB's involvement in the external representation of the euro area. In the light of growing globalisation, the participation of the ECB in international organisations and fora is of utmost importance for the fulfilment of its mandate.

Chapter 6 presents the ECB as a corporate entity. It shows in particular how the policy mission of the ECB is substantiated in its corporate governance, internal organisation and staff policy.

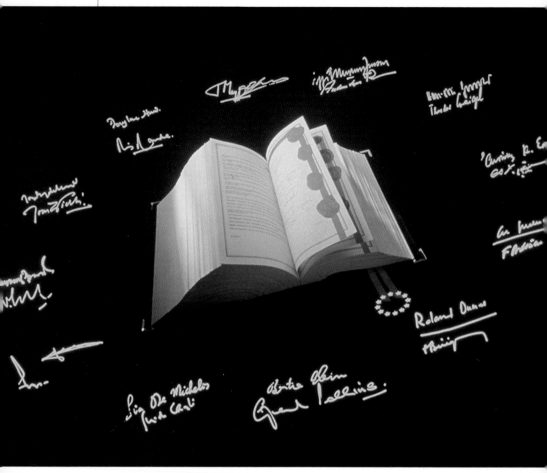

The Treaty on European
Union (Maastricht Treaty)
with the Statute of the ESCB
and of the ECB, signed on
7 February 1992.
Credit: Audiovisual Library of
the European Commission.

I EMU, THE ECB AND THE EURO

This chapter gives an overview of the steps that have culminated in the establishment of EMU and describes its main organisational features.

I.I THE ROAD TO EMU AND THE EURO

So how did it all start? One possible starting point for this chronology of economic and monetary union in Europe might be the Treaties of Rome[1], which entered into force on 1 January 1958. After all, the realisation of EMU is one of the achievements of European integration; indeed probably the most important one so far. However, a single currency was not yet in the mind of the authors of the Treaties of Rome; the aims and objectives of the original treaties were much more limited.

Another starting point might be 1989, when the European Council decided to initiate the realisation of EMU by the end of the century. However, it would be historically incorrect to discard the first steps towards European monetary integration, which had started in the mid-1960s. The early attempts at monetary integration were characterised by varying degrees of success, and progress alternated with setbacks. Nevertheless, the achievements of this period, and some of the lessons learned, were indispensable in shaping the process of monetary integration that finally took off in the 1990s.

Taking all this into account, the most appropriate starting point would therefore seem to be the year 1962 (see Box 1) and a European Commission document known as the *Marjolin Memorandum*. This memorandum initiated the first discussion on monetary integration at the Community level and prompted the first, albeit very limited, measures in the field of monetary cooperation.

I.I.I First steps towards European monetary integration

Europe's "founding fathers", who negotiated the Treaties of Rome in the 1950s, did not dwell on the idea of a common currency. To start with, the initial aims of the European Economic Community (EEC) were largely limited to realising a customs union and a common agricultural market, which was not perceived to require integration in the monetary field. Moreover, at the time, all the EEC countries were part of a reasonably well-functioning international monetary system (the Bretton Woods system). Within this system, exchange rates were fixed but adjustable and remained relatively stable until the mid-1960s, both within the EEC and globally.

---

[1] The Treaty establishing the European Economic Community (EEC) and the Treaty establishing the European Atomic Energy Community (Euratom). The Treaties entered into force on 1 January 1958. The two new Communities were added to the European Coal and Steel Community (ECSC), which had been established in 1952 for a period of 50 years.

Box I The road to the euro

1962	The European Commission makes its first proposal (*Marjolin Memorandum*) for economic and monetary union.
May 1964	A Committee of Governors of the central banks of the Member States of the European Economic Community (EEC) is formed to institutionalise the cooperation among EEC central banks.
1971	The Werner Report sets out a plan to realise an economic and monetary union in the Community by 1980.
April 1972	A system (the "snake") for the progressive narrowing of the margins of fluctuation between the currencies of the Member States of the European Economic Community is established.
April 1973	The European Monetary Cooperation Fund (EMCF) is set up to ensure the proper operation of the snake.
March 1979	The European Monetary System (EMS) is created.
February 1986	The Single European Act (SEA) is signed.
June 1988	The European Council mandates a committee of experts under the chairmanship of Jacques Delors (the "Delors Committee") to make proposals for the realisation of EMU.
May 1989	The "Delors Report" is submitted to the European Council.
June 1989	The European Council agrees on the realisation of EMU in three stages.
July 1990	Stage One of EMU begins.
December 1990	An Intergovernmental Conference to prepare for Stages Two and Three of EMU is launched.
February 1992	The Treaty on European Union (the "Maastricht Treaty") is signed.
October 1993	Frankfurt am Main is chosen as the seat of the EMI and of the ECB and a President of the EMI is nominated.
November 1993	The Treaty on European Union enters into force.
December 1993	Alexandre Lamfalussy is appointed as President of the EMI, to be established on 1 January 1994.
January 1994	Stage Two of EMU begins and the EMI is established.
December 1995	The Madrid European Council decides on the name of the single currency and sets out the scenario for its adoption and the cash changeover.
December 1996	The EMI presents specimen euro banknotes to the European Council.
June 1997	The European Council agrees on the Stability and Growth Pact.
May 1998	Belgium, Germany, Spain, France, Ireland, Italy, Luxembourg, the Netherlands, Austria, Portugal and Finland are considered to fulfil the necessary conditions for the adoption of the euro as their single currency; the Members of the Executive Board of the ECB are appointed.
June 1998	The ECB and the ESCB are established.
October 1998	The ECB announces the strategy and the operational framework for the single monetary policy it will conduct from 1 January 1999.
January 1999	Stage Three of EMU begins; the euro becomes the single currency of the euro area; conversion rates are fixed irrevocably for the former national currencies of the participating Member States; a single monetary policy is conducted for the euro area.

Box I   The road to the euro (cont'd)

January 2001	Greece becomes the 12th EU Member State to join the euro area.
January 2002	The euro cash changeover: euro banknotes and coins are introduced and become sole legal tender in the euro area by the end of February 2002.
May 2004	The NCBs of the ten new EU Member States join the ESCB.

The idea of a common currency for the EEC Member States was first launched in the European Commission's Memorandum of 24 October 1962 (the *Marjolin Memorandum*). In its Memorandum, the Commission called for the customs union to lead on to an economic union by the end of the 1960s with irrevocably fixed exchange rates between the Member States' currencies. However, since the Bretton Woods system was ensuring widespread exchange rate stability, the Member States considered that intra-EEC exchange rate stability could be secured without the need for new institutional arrangements at the Community level. Thus, no follow-up action was taken on the Memorandum, except that a Committee of Governors of the central banks of the Member States of the EEC (the Committee of Governors) was established in 1964. The Committee of Governors complemented the Monetary Committee provided for by Article 105(2) of the EEC Treaty.

Initially the Committee of Governors had a very limited mandate, but over the years it gradually gained in importance to become the focus of monetary cooperation among the Community central banks. In this capacity, the Committee developed and managed the framework for monetary cooperation that was subsequently established at the Community level. The Committee's work would also prove instrumental in the final move to EMU.[2]

By the end of the 1960s, the international environment had changed significantly. The Bretton Woods system was showing signs of increasing strain as a result of US balance of payments policy. The EEC Member States increasingly differed on economic policy priorities. Greater price and cost divergences between them led to several exchange rate and balance of payments crises, which in turn threatened to disrupt the customs union and the common agricultural market, which had been functioning quite successfully up to then.

In 1969 the European Commission submitted a plan (the *Barre Plan*) to create a distinct monetary identity in the Community.[3] On the basis of this plan, the Heads of State or Government, meeting in The Hague, called on the Council of Ministers to draw up a plan for the realisation in stages of an economic and monetary union. This work was done by a group of experts, chaired by Pierre Werner, the Prime Minister of Luxembourg. The resulting *Werner Report*[4], which was published in 1970, proposed to create economic and monetary union in several stages by 1980.

---

[2] For a more detailed discussion of this issue, see Andrews, D. (2003) and Baer, G. D. (1994).
[3] Communication from the Commission to the Council regarding the formulation of a plan by stages with a view to the creation of economic and monetary union, 12 February 1969.
[4] Report by the Working Group chaired by Pierre Werner on economic and monetary union, 8 October 1970.

In parallel to these developments, the first mechanisms for intra-Community monetary and financial assistance were established in 1970 and 1971.[5]

In March 1971 the Member States agreed to realise an economic and monetary union[6]. As part of the first stage, they established a Community system for the progressive narrowing of the fluctuation margins of the members' currencies. This system, which became known as the "snake"[7], was put into operation in April 1972. In 1973 the European Monetary Cooperation Fund (EMCF)[8] was set up as the nucleus of a future Community organisation of central banks. And in 1974, with a view to enhancing coordination of economic policies, the Council adopted a Decision on the attainment of a high degree of convergence in the Community[9] and a Directive on stability, growth and full employment[10].

Yet, by the mid-1970s the process of integration had lost momentum under the pressure of divergent policy responses to the economic shocks of the period. The "snake" became an exchange rate mechanism among the Deutsche Mark, the Benelux currencies and the Danish krone (for a while two non-Community currencies – the Swedish krona and Norwegian krone – were also part of the system). The other Community currencies remained outside the system for all or most of its existence.[11] The EMCF turned out to be an empty shell with limited "bookkeeping" tasks: because the legal basis of the EMCF brought it under the control of the Community institutions, the Member States and their central banks were reluctant to assign it policy functions.

---

[5] The Agreement of 9 February 1970 among the EEC central banks on the establishment of a short-term monetary support mechanism; and the Decision of the Council of Ministers of 22 March 1971 on the creation of a machinery for medium-term financial assistance among the EEC Member States.

[6] Resolution of the Council and of the Representatives of the Governments of the Member States of 22 March 1971 on the attainment by stages of economic and monetary union in the Community (OJ C 28, 27.3.1971, p. 1).

[7] Under the snake, the spot exchange rates of the participating currencies were to be kept within a band of 2.25%, compared with a theoretically possible spread of 4.5% resulting from each currency's fluctuation margin of ±2.25% around its central rate vis-à-vis the US dollar (snake in the tunnel). The respective maximum limits of fluctuation were to be defended by intervention in US dollars and Community currencies. On 19 March 1973 the fluctuation margins vis-à-vis the US dollar were suspended and the snake fluctuated freely.

[8] The EMCF was set up under Regulation (EEC) No 907/73 of the Council of 3 April 1973 establishing a European Monetary Cooperation Fund (OJ L 89, 5.4.1973, p. 2). Under Article 2 of this Regulation, the EMCF was required to promote i) the proper functioning of the progressive narrowing of the fluctuation margins of the Community currencies, ii) intervention on the exchange markets, and iii) settlements between central banks leading to a concerted policy on reserves. The EMCF was superseded by the EMI on 1 January 1994.

[9] Council Decision 74/120/EEC of 18 February 1974 on the attainment of a high degree of convergence of the economic policies of the Member States of the European Economic Community (OJ L 63, 5.3.1974, p. 16).

[10] Council Directive 74/121/EEC of 18 February 1974 on stability, growth and full employment in the Community (OJ L 63, 5.3.1974, p. 19).

[11] The pound sterling and the Irish pound participated in the system from April to June 1972 and the Italian lira from April 1972 to February 1973. The French franc, which had joined the system at the outset, was withdrawn in February 1974; it entered the snake again in July 1975 and left the mechanism definitively in November 1976.

1.1.2 The European Monetary System and the Single European Act

In March 1979 the process of monetary integration was relaunched with the creation of the European Monetary System (EMS). The EMS was established by a Resolution of the European Council[12], and its operating procedures were laid down in an Agreement between the participating central banks[13].

The EMS proved to be instrumental in furthering European monetary integration. Unlike the "snake", the EMS managed to keep most Community currencies in a single exchange rate system.[14] Some features of the EMS were similar to the "snake", for example the EMS was also built around a grid of fixed but adjustable central rates among the participating Community currencies. A new feature, however, was the introduction of the European Currency Unit (ECU), which was defined as a "basket" of fixed quantities of the currencies of the Member States.[15] The ECU was to serve as the numéraire[16] of the exchange rate mechanism (ERM), as a unit of account to denominate operations in the intervention and credit mechanisms and as a reserve asset and means of settlement among the participating central banks.

However, the EMS was not just an exchange rate mechanism. In line with its objective to promote internal and external monetary stability, the EMS also covered the adjustment of monetary and economic policies as tools for achieving exchange rate stability. Its participants were able to create a zone in which monetary stability increased and capital controls were gradually relaxed. The exchange rate constraint greatly helped those participating countries with relatively high rates of inflation to pursue disinflation policies, in particular through monetary policy. It thus fostered a downward convergence of inflation rates and brought about a high degree of exchange rate stability. This in turn helped to moderate cost increases in many countries and led to an improvement in overall economic performance. Moreover, reduced uncertainty about exchange rate developments and a perception that the parities of the participating currencies were not allowed to depart significantly from the economic fundamentals protected intra-European trade from excessive exchange rate volatility.

Although the EMS became the focal point of improved monetary policy coordination, its success in bringing about greater convergence of economic policies was rather limited. The lack of sufficient convergence in fiscal policy also remained a source of tension: some countries had persistently large budget

---

[12] Resolution of the European Council on the establishment of the European Monetary System (EMS) and related matters of 5 December 1978.

[13] Agreement of 13 March 1979 between the central banks of the Member States of the European Economic Community laying down the operating procedures for the European Monetary System.

[14] The main exception was the pound sterling which participated for less than a year.

[15] The value of the ECU vis-à-vis the US dollar was the weighted average of the US dollar exchange rates of the component currencies. Its value in each of the component currencies was determined by multiplying its US dollar value with the US dollar exchange rate of the respective component currency.

[16] The function of numéraire implied that the central rates of the participating currencies were expressed in terms of the ECU. The ECU central rates were then used to determine the bilateral ERM central rates around which the bilateral intervention rates were fixed.

deficits (leading to several exchange rate crises at the beginning of the 1990s), which put a disproportionate burden on monetary policy.

The European Council Resolution of 1978 stated that the ECU should be at the centre of the EMS; but, in practice, the ECU played only a limited role in the functioning of the system. In the financial markets, however, it gained some popularity as a means of portfolio diversification and as a hedge against currency risks. The expansion of financial market activity in ECU was driven by a growing volume of ECU-denominated debt instruments that were issued by Community bodies and the public-sector authorities of some member countries. However, in the absence of an anchor for the ECU, the further prospects of the ECU market remained limited.

A further impetus for economic and monetary union was provided by the adoption of the Single European Act (SEA), which was signed in February 1986 and entered into force on 1 July 1987. The main purpose of this Act was to introduce the Single Market as a further objective of the Community, to make the necessary decision-making changes to complete the Single Market and to reaffirm the need for the Community's monetary capacity for achieving economic and monetary union.

There was growing consensus among policy-makers that a market without internal borders would link the national economies much more closely together and increase significantly the degree of economic integration within the Community. This in turn would reduce the room for manoeuvre of national policies and thus oblige the Member States to step up convergence of their economic policies. If greater convergence did not occur, full freedom of capital movements and integrated financial markets was expected to put an undue burden on monetary policy. The integration process would therefore require more intensive and effective policy coordination for which the prevailing institutional framework was perceived to be insufficient.

In addition, the Single Market was not expected to be able to exploit its full potential without a single currency. A single currency would ensure greater price transparency for consumers and investors, eliminate exchange rate risks within the Single Market, reduce transaction costs and, as a result, significantly increase economic welfare in the Community.

Taking all these considerations into account, the then 12 Member States of the European Economic Community decided in 1988 to relaunch the EMU project. Where the Werner Plan of the early 1970s had failed, the second attempt at EMU would prove to be a success, finally turning the single currency dream into reality.

1.1.3 The Treaty on European Union

In June 1988 the European Council confirmed the objective of the progressive realisation of economic and monetary union and instructed a committee chaired by Jacques Delors, President of the European Commission, to propose "concrete stages" leading to EMU. The committee was composed of the governors of the

Community national central banks; Alexandre Lamfalussy, General Manager of the Bank for International Settlements (BIS); Niels Thygesen, Professor of Economics, Copenhagen; Miguel Boyer, President of the Banco Exterior de España; and Frans Andriessen, Member of the European Commission.

The resulting "Delors Report" of 17 April 1989[17] recommended that economic and monetary union be achieved in three *"discrete but evolutionary steps"*.

• Stage One was to focus on completing the internal market, reducing disparities between Member States' economic policies, removing all obstacles to financial integration and intensifying monetary cooperation.

• Stage Two would serve as a period of transition to the final stage, setting up the basic organs and organisational structure of EMU and strengthening economic convergence.

• In Stage Three exchange rates would be locked irrevocably and the various Community institutions and bodies would be assigned their full monetary and economic responsibilities.

Although Stage One was established within the existing institutional framework of the Community, changes to the institutional structure were needed for Stages Two and Three. It was necessary therefore to revise the Treaty establishing the European Economic Community. To this end, an Intergovernmental Conference (IGC) on EMU was convened, which opened in November 1990 in parallel with the IGC on European Political Union. At the European Council's invitation, the EMU IGC was prepared by the Council of Ministers, the European Commission, the Monetary Committee and the Committee of Governors, all within their respective fields of competence.

The outcome of the IGC negotiations was the Treaty on European Union (the EU Treaty, commonly known as the "Maastricht Treaty"), which was signed in Maastricht on 7 February 1992. The EU Treaty established the European Union and amended the founding treaties of the European Communities. The amendments to the EEC Treaty added, among others, a new chapter on economic and monetary policy. This new chapter laid down the foundations of EMU and set out a method and timetable for its realisation. Reflecting the Community's increasing powers and scope, the EEC was renamed the European Community. The Statute of the European System of Central Banks and of the European Central Bank (Statute of the ESCB) and the Statute of the European Monetary Institute (EMI Statute) were attached as Protocols to the EC Treaty. Denmark and the United Kingdom were given a special status that did not oblige them to participate in Stage Three of EMU (see Section 1.2.2).

The EU Treaty had been scheduled to enter into force on 1 January 1993. However, owing to delays in the ratification process in Denmark and Germany, it did not actually come into force until 1 November 1993.

---

[17] Committee for the study of economic and monetary union (1989), Report on economic and monetary union in the European Community, 1989.

1.1.4 The realisation of EMU and the changeover to the euro

Stage One of EMU

On the basis of the Delors Report, the European Council decided in June 1989 that the first stage of the realisation of economic and monetary union should begin on 1 July 1990. This was the date on which, in principle, all restrictions on the movement of capital between Member States were to be abolished. At this time, the Committee of Governors of the central banks of the Member States of the European Economic Community was given additional responsibilities, which were set out in a Council Decision of 12 March 1990[18]. They included holding consultations on, and promoting the coordination of, the monetary policies of the Member States, with the aim of achieving price stability. In view of the relatively short time available and the complexity of the tasks involved, the Committee of Governors initiated the preparatory work for Stage Three of EMU as soon as the Maastricht Treaty had been signed. The first step was to identify all the issues that should be examined at an early stage and establish a work programme by the end of 1993. Then it was necessary to define appropriate mandates for the existing sub-committees[19] and the new working groups which had been set up to look into specific issues[20].

Stage Two of EMU

The establishment of the EMI on 1 January 1994 marked the start of Stage Two of EMU. It was created as a transitory body to undertake the preparatory work for Stage Three of EMU, while the conduct of monetary and exchange rate policy in the European Union remained the preserve of national authorities. The Committee of Governors ceased to exist but was effectively reconstituted as the Council (governing body) of the EMI.

The two main tasks of the EMI were:

• to strengthen central bank cooperation and monetary policy coordination;

• to make the necessary preparations for establishing the ESCB, for the conduct of the single monetary policy and for creating a single currency in the third stage of EMU (see Box 2).

In December 1995 the Madrid European Council confirmed that Stage Three of EMU would start on 1 January 1999. It also named the single currency to be introduced at the start of Stage Three the "euro" and announced the sequence of events leading up to its introduction.[21] This scenario was mainly based on detailed proposals developed by the EMI,[22] which had also used the term "changeover to

---

[18] Council Decision 90/142/EEC of 12 March 1990 amending Council Decision 64/300/EEC on cooperation between the central banks of the Member States of the European Economic Community (OJ L 78, 24.3.1990, p. 25).

[19] The Monetary Policy Sub-Committee, the Foreign Exchange Policy Sub-Committee and the Banking Supervisory Sub-Committee.

[20] Working Groups on Accounting Issues, Banknotes, Information Systems, Payment Systems and Statistics; a Working Group of Legal Experts was set up in 1996.

[21] Madrid European Council (1995), "The scenario for the changeover to the single currency".

[22] EMI (1995), "The changeover to the single currency".

Box 2 **Overview of the preparatory work carried out by the EMI**

Under Article 117 of the EC Treaty, it was the task of the EMI, among other things, to specify the regulatory, organisational and logistical framework necessary for the ESCB to perform its tasks in the third stage of EMU. This framework was submitted to the ECB when it was established on 1 June 1998.

Within this mandate and in cooperation with the NCBs, the EMI:

• prepared a range of instruments and procedures for the conduct of the single monetary policy in the euro area and analysed potential monetary policy strategies;

• promoted harmonised methods for collecting, compiling and distributing money and banking, balance of payments and other financial statistics for the euro area;

• developed frameworks for conducting foreign exchange operations and for holding and managing the official foreign exchange reserves of the Member States participating in the euro area;

• promoted the efficiency of cross-border payment and securities settlement transactions in order to support the integration of the euro money market, in particular by developing the technical infrastructure for processing large-value, cross-border payments in euro (the TARGET system);

• prepared the technical and design specifications of the euro banknotes;

• drew up harmonised accounting rules and standards making it possible to construct a consolidated balance sheet of the ESCB for internal and external reporting purposes;

• put in place the necessary information and communications systems for the operational and policy functions to be undertaken within the ESCB;

• identified ways in which the ESCB could contribute to the policies conducted by the competent supervisory authorities to foster the stability of credit institutions and the financial system.

Furthermore, the EMI cooperated with Community institutions and bodies, in particular, the Commission and the Monetary Committee, in preparing for Stage Three of EMU. In particular, it:

• developed the scenario for the changeover to the single currency;

• developed a framework (ERM II) for monetary and exchange rate policy cooperation between the euro area and other EU countries;

• assisted in the preparation of Community legislation relating to the transition to Stage Three;

• monitored Member States' progress in fulfilling the conditions necessary for participation in EMU (economic and legal convergence) and kept track of technical preparations for the changeover to the euro;

• assisted the financial industry in developing structures and procedures for the integration of the financial markets within the euro area.

By June 1998 the EMI had completed an extensive body of conceptual, detailed design and implementation work. This preparatory work enabled the ECB to finalise its preparations in time for a smooth transition to Stage Three of EMU.

the euro" instead of "introduction of the euro"[23] to reflect the nature of the transition to the single currency. The EMI's changeover scenario recommended a transitional period of three years starting from 1 January 1999 to accommodate differences in the pace with which the various groups of economic agents (e.g. the financial sector, the non-financial corporate sector, the public sector, the general public) would be able to adapt to the single currency.

Also in December 1995, the EMI was given the task of carrying out preparatory work on the future monetary and exchange rate relationships between the euro and the currencies of the non-euro area EU countries. One year later, in December 1996, the EMI presented a report to the European Council, which subsequently formed the basis of a European Council Resolution on the principles and fundamental elements of the new exchange rate mechanism (ERM II)[24], which was adopted in June 1997.

In December 1996 the EMI presented to the European Council, and to the public, the design series that had won the euro banknote design competition and that would therefore feature on the banknotes to be put into circulation by the ESCB on 1 January 2002. The design of the euro coins which were to be issued by the EU Member States was endorsed by the European Council in 1997.

In June 1997 the European Council adopted the Stability and Growth Pact, which complements the Treaty provisions and aims to ensure budgetary discipline within EMU. The Pact consists of three instruments: a European Council Resolution[25] and two Council Regulations[26]. It was supplemented and the respective commitments enhanced by a Declaration of the Council in May 1998.

The Member States implemented policies to fulfil the economic "convergence criteria" (Article 121 of the EC Treaty) and revised extensively their national legislation to bring it into line with the requirements of legal convergence (Article 109 of the EC Treaty). The adaptations concerned in particular the legal and statutory provisions for their central banks with a view to their integration into the Eurosystem.

The final decisions on EMU were taken starting in May 1998. On 2 May 1998 the EU Council, meeting in the composition of the Heads of State or Government, decided unanimously that 11 Member States had fulfilled the conditions necessary to adopt the single currency on 1 January 1999. These

---

[23] European Commission (1995), "One Currency for Europe, Green Paper on Practical Arrangements for the Introduction of the Single Currency".

[24] Resolution of the European Council on the establishment of an exchange rate mechanism in the third stage of economic and monetary union, Amsterdam, 16 June 1997 (OJ C 236, 2.8.1997, p. 5).

[25] Resolution of the European Council on the Stability and Growth Pact, Amsterdam, 17 June 1997 (OJ C 236, 2.8.1997, p. 1).

[26] Council Regulation (EC) No 1466/97 of 7 July 1997 on the strengthening of the surveillance of budgetary positions and the surveillance and coordination of economic policies (OJ L 209, 2.8.1997, p. 1), and Council Regulation (EC) No 1467/97 of 7 July 1997 on speeding up and clarifying the implementation of the excessive deficit procedure (OJ L 209, 2.8.1997, p. 6).

countries (Belgium, Germany, Spain, France, Ireland, Italy, Luxembourg, the Netherlands, Austria, Portugal and Finland) would therefore participate in Stage Three of EMU.[27] Given their special status, Denmark and the United Kingdom "opted out" of Stage Three of EMU, and Greece and Sweden were not deemed to have met the conditions for adopting the single currency (see Section 1.2.2).

The Heads of State or Government also reached a political understanding on who to appoint as members of the future ECB's Executive Board. At the same time, the ministers of finance of the Member States adopting the single currency and the governors of the national central banks of these Member States agreed, together with the European Commission and the EMI, that the current ERM bilateral central rates of the currencies of the participating Member States would be used to determine the irrevocable conversion rates for the euro.[28]

On 25 May 1998 the President, Vice-President and the four other members of the ECB's Executive Board were formally appointed by common accord of the governments of the then 11 participating Member States at the level of the Heads of State or Government. In line with Article 50 of the Statute of the ESCB, their appointment was made on the basis of a recommendation from the ECOFIN Council and opinions from the European Parliament and the Council of the EMI (which acted instead of the Governing Council of the ECB not yet in place).

The six members of the Executive Board were appointed with effect from 1 June 1998 when the ECB was established. The EMI had completed its tasks and went into liquidation in line with Article 123(2) of the EC Treaty. The ECB, as liquidator of the EMI, inherited not only an extensive body of preparatory work but also the whole EMI infrastructure, including a body of staff which had been prepared to undertake its duties at the ECB. This greatly helped the ECB to make the Eurosystem operational within only seven months, i.e. in time for the start of Stage Three, and to complete the preparations for the euro cash changeover by 1 January 2002.

Stage Three of EMU
The third and final stage of EMU began on 1 January 1999. The conversion rates of the currencies of the 11 Member States initially participating in Monetary Union were irrevocably fixed (see Box 3) and the ECB took over responsibility for conducting the single monetary policy in the euro area.

In line with the legal framework established in secondary Community legislation by the EU Council, the euro replaced the national currencies immediately, making them non-decimal sub-divisions of the euro during the transitional period from 1 January 1999 to 31 December 2001. For the first three years, all agents were free to use either the euro or its national sub-divisions for denominating claims and liabilities and for cashless payments (principle of "no compulsion no prohibition"). However, Member States were entitled to oblige entities to use the

---

[27] Council Decision (98/317/EC) of 3 May 1998 in accordance with Article 109(4) of the Treaty (OJ L 139, 11.5.1998, p. 30).
[28] Joint Communiqué of 2 May 1998 on the determination of the irrevocable conversion rates for the euro.

	= 40.3399 Belgian francs
	= 1.95583 Deutsche Mark
	= 340.750 Greek drachmas
	= 166.386 Spanish pesetas
	= 6.55957 French francs
1 euro	= 0.787564 Irish pounds
	= 1,936.27 Italian lire
	= 40.3399 Luxembourg francs
	= 2.20371 Dutch guilders
	= 13.7603 Austrian schillings
	= 200.482 Portuguese escudos
	= 5.94573 Finnish markkas

Source: Council Regulation (EC) No 2866/98 of 31 December 1998 on the conversion rates between the euro and the currencies of the Member States adopting the euro (OJ L 359, 31.12.1998, p. 1), as amended by Regulation (EC) No 1478/2000 of 19 June 2000 (OJ L 167, 7.7.2000, p. 1).

euro for the redenomination of tradable outstanding debt instruments, for trading in regulated markets and the working of payment systems. This scope was used extensively by the Member States in the run-up to Stage Three of EMU. Furthermore, the EMI announced that the Eurosystem would conduct its monetary policy operations exclusively in euro and that the euro would be the single denominator for the functioning of the TARGET system (see Section 3.3.1).

Against this background, the financial sector made extensive preparations for operating in the integrated financial markets as from the start of Stage Three. The financial industry was itself interested in a rapid and comprehensive changeover of financial markets to the euro and no group of market participants wished to be left behind by its competitors. With the assistance of the EMI, financial market associations agreed on conventions for unifying market practices, and leading interest rate indicators (e.g. the EURIBOR and the EONIA) were developed.[29]

Thanks to these preparations, the financial markets were able to convert to the euro at once as from the start of Stage Three of EMU. Trading in financial markets was exclusively in euro and the bulk of outstanding tradable debt instruments was converted to euro. All large-value cross-border payment systems functioned in euro. Not only was the changeover of the financial market immediate, but it also went very smoothly.

Whereas the corporate sector gradually converted to the euro during the transitional period, individuals – in the absence of euro-denominated cash – did not at first use the euro much for transactions. That would all change of course with the introduction of euro banknotes and coins on 1 January 2002.[30]

---

[29] A further leading interest rate indicator, the EUREPO, was established in early 2002.
[30] See Scheller (1999), p. 243.

Box 4 Chronology of European integration

July 1952	European Coal and Steel Community (ECSC) is established by Belgium, Germany, France, Italy, Luxembourg and the Netherlands.
January 1958	The same six countries establish the European Economic Community (EEC) and the European Atomic Energy Community (Euratom).
January 1973	Denmark, Ireland and the United Kingdom join the three European Communities.
January 1981	Greece joins the three European Communities.
January 1986	Spain and Portugal join the three European Communities.
February 1986	The Single European Act is adopted.
November 1993	The Treaty on European Union (Maastricht Treaty), which was signed in February 1992, enters into force. It establishes the European Union with a three-pillar structure: i) the three European Communities; ii) the common foreign and security policy, and iii) justice and home affairs/police and judicial cooperation in criminal matters.
January 1995	Austria, Finland and Sweden join the European Union.
May 1999	The Treaty of Amsterdam, which was signed in June 1997, enters into force; it amends both the Treaty establishing the European Community and the Treaty on European Union.
February 2003	The Treaties are further amended by the Treaty of Nice, which was signed in 2001, to pave the way for an enlarged European Union.
2003	The Convention on the future of Europe draws up a draft Treaty establishing a Constitution for Europe.
May 2004	The Czech Republic, Estonia, Cyprus, Latvia, Lithuania, Hungary, Malta, Poland, Slovenia and Slovakia join the European Union, bringing the total number of Member States to 25.
June 2004	The EU Member States agree on a Treaty establishing a Constitution for Europe.

On 1 January 2001 Greece joined the euro area – bringing the number of participating countries to 12 – and the Bank of Greece became part of the Eurosystem. Under the procedure laid down in Article 122(2) of the EC Treaty, the EU Council had decided on 19 June 2000 that Greece fulfilled the conditions for adopting the euro.[31] The conversion rate between the euro and the Greek drachma had been pre-announced in a Council Regulation[32] on the same day.

The introduction of the euro was completed with the cash changeover on 1 January 2002: euro banknotes and coins were put into circulation and the residual function of the national currencies as non-decimal sub-divisions of the euro became obsolete. Cash denominated in the legacy currencies ceased to be legal tender by the end of February 2002 and, from that date, the euro banknotes and coins became the sole legal tender in the countries of the euro area.

EMU was created within the framework of the European Communities, which itself had increased significantly since its inception in 1952 (see Box 4). The

---

[31] Council Decision 2000/427/EC of 19 June 2000 in accordance with Article 122(2) of the Treaty on the adoption by Greece of the Single Currency in 2001 (OJ L 167, 7.7.2000, p. 20).
[32] Council Regulation (EC) No 1478/2000 of 19 June 2000 (OJ L 167, 7.7.2000, p. 1).

European Union now numbers 25 Member States, with the most recent addition of ten central and eastern European and Mediterranean countries on 1 May 2004. Although these new Member States will only join the euro area at a later stage, i.e. when they fulfil the necessary conditions for adopting the euro, they are committed to the objectives of EMU. Their respective NCBs became ex officio members of the ESCB on the same day and will prepare themselves for their eventual integration into the Eurosystem.

1.2 LEGAL BASIS AND CHARACTERISTICS OF EMU

Established by the EC Treaty, the ECB is embedded in the specific legal and institutional framework of the European Community. What distinguishes therefore the euro and the ECB from a national currency and a national central bank is their supranational status within a community of sovereign states. Unlike comparable central banks, such as the US Federal Reserve System or the Bank of Japan, which are the monetary authorities of their respective national states, the ECB is a central authority that conducts monetary policy for an economic area consisting of 12 otherwise largely autonomous states. Another specific feature of EMU is the fact that the euro area does not encompass all EU Member States since the realisation of EMU follows an approach of differentiated integration (see Section 1.2.2).

1.2.1 Legal basis

Monetary sovereignty has been transferred to the supranational level under the terms and conditions of the EC Treaty, as amended by the EU Treaty.

The present European Union is not a state. It rests on the European Communities and the policies and forms of cooperation established by the EU Treaty. The first pillar comprises the European Community and the European Atomic Energy Community (Euratom)[33], which both possess legal personality and are governed by separate treaties. These two Communities are of a supranational nature, acting within the limits of powers which have been delegated to them by the Member States. The second and third pillars of the EU are essentially intergovernmental arrangements on the common foreign and security policy (CFSP) and police and judicial cooperation in criminal matters.

In theory, it would have been possible to conclude a separate Treaty on EMU as a fourth pillar of the European Union; this approach was considered in the early stages of the IGC negotiations on EMU[34] but eventually rejected. Instead the legal foundations of EMU were enshrined in the EC Treaty, thus expanding the competence of the European Economic Community. Although Article 2 of the EU Treaty makes a brief reference to EMU as one of the Union's objectives, all the substantive, procedural and institutional provisions are laid down in the EC Treaty. As regards monetary policy, the Treaty provisions are further specified

---

[33] The third Community, the European Coal and Steel Community (ECSC), established in 1952, was dissolved in July 2002 when the ECSC Treaty, concluded for 50 years, expired.

[34] See Zilioli/Selmayr (2001), p. 12.

and substantiated in the Statute of the ESCB, which is annexed to the EC Treaty as a Protocol and thereby forms an integral part of primary Community law.

This means that EMU is governed by Community law and not by intergovernmental law. This approach has built on and further developed the existing institutional framework (avoiding the establishment of separate institutions) and greatly facilitated the setting-up of the ECB as an organisation which is independent vis-à-vis the Member States and the Community bodies.

The EC Treaty also provides for the possibility of secondary Community legislation on EMU matters with a view to dealing with all those aspects of EMU that are not laid down in an exhaustive manner in primary Community law, for example, aspects of the euro itself. The following Regulations form the core of the Community currency law:

• Council Regulation (EC) No 1103/97 of 17 June 1997 on certain provisions relating to the introduction of the euro[35], as amended by Regulation (EC) No. 2595/2000 of 27 November 2000[36];

• Council Regulation (EC) No 974/98 of 3 May 1998 on the introduction of the euro[37], as amended by Regulation (EC) No 2596/2000 of 27 November 2000[38];

• Council Regulation (EC) No 2866/98 of 31 December 1998 on the conversion rates between the euro and the currencies of the Member States adopting the euro[39], as amended by Regulation (EC) No 1478/2000 of 19 June 2000[40];

• Council Regulation (EC) No 1338/2001 of 28 June 2001 laying down measures necessary for the protection of the euro against counterfeiting[41], the provisions of which were extended to the Member States not participating in the euro area by Regulation (EC) No 1339/2001[42] of the same date.

In addition, the EC Treaty and the Statute of the ESCB provide for secondary Community legislation to complement some specific provisions of the Statute (see Section 2.5.4) and endow the ECB with its own regulatory powers (see Section 2.5.3).

The current EU and EC Treaties are scheduled to be superseded by the Treaty establishing a Constitution for Europe in November 2006. The Treaty was drawn up by the Convention on the future of Europe in 2003 and was eventually adopted by the IGC in June 2004. Subject to its ratification by all 25 EU Member States, the Constitution would simplify, streamline and clarify the legal and institutional framework of the European Union. However, it would not entail changes to the substance of the tasks, mandate, status and legal regime of the ECB and the ESCB.

[35] OJ L 162, 19.6.1997, p. 1.
[36] OJ L 300, 29.11.2000, p. 1.
[37] OJ L 139, 11.5.1998, p. 1.
[38] OJ L 300, 29.11.2000, p. 2.
[39] OJ L 359, 31.12.1998, p. 1.
[40] OJ L 167, 7.7.2000, p. 1.
[41] OJ L 181, 4.7.2001, p. 6.
[42] OJ L 181, 4.7.2001, p. 11.

1.2.2 Characteristics

Neither EMU nor the creation of the Single Market have been an end in themselves; they have been instrumental in furthering the fundamental objectives of the Community. Article 2 of the EC Treaty states that these fundamental objectives include *"a harmonious, balanced and sustainable development of economic activities, a high level of employment [...], sustainable and non-inflationary growth* [and] *a high degree of competitiveness and convergence of economic performance [...]"*. Under Article 4 of the EC Treaty, the guiding principles with constitutional status to achieve these fundamental objectives are *"stable prices, sound public finances and monetary conditions and a sustainable balance of payments"* and the *"principle of an open market economy with free competition"*. Within this overall policy framework, the EC Treaty assigns clear responsibilities to both monetary and economic policy.

The monetary and economic aspects of EMU

The monetary and economic aspects of EMU have been organised differently. Whereas monetary and exchange rate policies have been denationalised and centralised at the Community level, the responsibility for economic policy has remained with the Member States although national economic policies are to be conducted within a Community framework for cooperation in macroeconomic policies. The differences in organisation respect the principle of subsidiarity (Article 5 of the EC Treaty), i.e. the allocation of policy responsibilities to the Community level is only justified:

• if the Member States cannot sufficiently achieve the given objectives by themselves; or

• if the Community, by reason of the scale or effects of the proposed action, is better placed to achieve the objectives.

As explained below, centralisation at the Community level is justified for monetary and exchange rate policy because a single currency and national monetary and exchange rate policies are mutually exclusive. The situation is different for economic policies. To the extent that the Community framework ensures that national economic policies are actually in line with the aforementioned objectives of EMU, the conduct of such policies is best located at the national level. Thus, even a fully integrated economic zone like the euro area does not provide a compelling argument for a full transfer of economic policy responsibilities to the Community.

Monetary and exchange rate policy

The ECB, as the core of both the ESCB and the Eurosystem, has been assigned exclusive responsibility for the single monetary policy for the euro area (see Section 2.1). A single currency requires a single monetary policy with centralised decision-making. Since some monetary policy decisions need to be taken on a day-to-day basis, the decision-making framework must be permanent and institutionalised in a legal entity that is liable and politically accountable for its activities. Furthermore, given the mandate of monetary policy to maintain price stability, decision-making had to be entrusted to a body that was independent of both the Community institutions and the Member States (see Section 4.1).

Exchange rate policy has also been denationalised and centralised. As a single currency has a single exchange rate, there can only be one single exchange rate policy. Exchange rate policy decisions for the euro area are made jointly by the ECB and the ECOFIN Council, with the Council having the final say (see Section 3.2.1).

Economic policy

Unlike monetary and exchange rate policy, the responsibility for economic policy has largely remained with the Member States. Under Article 4(1) of the EC Treaty, the Community's economic policy is based on *"the close coordination of Member States' economic policies, on the internal market and on the definition of common objectives [...]"*. Article 98 of the EC Treaty states that *"Member States shall conduct their economic policies with a view to contributing to the achievement of the objectives of the Community [...] and in the context of the broad guidelines referred to in Article 99(2)"*. Article 99(1) of the EC Treaty requires the Member States *"to regard their economic policies as a matter of common concern"* and *"to coordinate them within the Council"*.

The Broad Economic Policy Guidelines (BEPGs) are the principal policy instrument for coordinating national economic policies.[43] They contain orientations for the general conduct of economic policy and make specific recommendations to each Member State and the Community. By outlining the necessary measures in different policy fields – public finances, structural reforms, taxation, labour market regulation or training and education – the BEPGs set the standard against which subsequent national and European policy decisions must be measured.

The BEPGs are adopted in the form of a recommendation and are therefore not legally binding or enforceable. Instead, they rely on persuasion and "peer pressure" to galvanise governments into appropriate policy action. However, their endorsement by the European Council[44] gives them political weight.

In addition, specific procedures, commonly called "processes", have been developed. The "Luxembourg process" is the coordination procedure for national employment policies. Its main policy instrument is the annual Employment Guidelines, which set out recommendations and priority areas of action, especially with regard to training and education and labour market reform, and the transposition of these orientations into national action plans.

The "Cardiff process" is a system of monitoring and peer review of structural reforms. The main instrument is the annual multilateral surveillance of the progress of economic reform. This exercise takes place on the basis of annual

---

[43] With respect to the independence and statutory mandate of the ECB, the BEPGs do not apply to monetary policy.

[44] The European Council's endorsement of the BEPG is the only formal action by this body in EMU matters. All other EMU matters which require action at the level of the Heads of State or Government involve either intergovernmental decisions or decisions of the EU Council meeting in the composition of the Heads of State or Government.

reports from the Member States and the European Commission and derives additional force from a more in-depth multilateral review of economic reforms by the Economic Policy Committee.

The "Cologne process" provides for macroeconomic dialogue among the social partners, national governments, the European Commission and the ECB. The main instrument of this process is an exchange of assessments of the economic situation and prospects of the EU. The macroeconomic dialogue forms part of the European Employment Pact and thus complements both the Luxembourg and Cardiff processes.

The "Lisbon Strategy" established a comprehensive reform agenda which aims, among other things, to enhance the functioning of the Single Market and overcome existing fragmentation and inefficiencies in areas as varied as securities markets, access to risk capital or air traffic control.

Unlike the BEPGs, the "excessive deficit procedure" for fiscal policies (Article 104 of the EC Treaty, complemented by the Stability and Growth Pact) is legally binding and enforceable (see Box 5). Budgetary discipline is supported by the prohibitions on granting central bank credit to the government sector (Article 101) and any form of privileged access for the public sector to financial institutions (Article 102). Under the "no bail out" clause, neither the Community nor any Member State is liable for or can assume the debts incurred by another Member State (Article 103). Thus high government debt cannot be "inflated" away, and a government that does not stick to the rules cannot rely on being eventually bailed out by other governments.

This asymmetry between the monetary and economic aspects of EMU implies that there is no "EU government" in the same way as there are national governments. However, this situation is not necessarily a flaw in the Community's economic policy framework. Allowing the Member States a large degree of autonomy in decision-making in important fields of economic policy provides vital room for manoeuvre and offers scope for the beneficial effects of healthy policy competition. At the same time, the rules and procedures of the economic policy framework ensure macroeconomic stability, provided that the policy-makers respect them.

Box 5 The Community framework for fiscal policies

The Treaty contains several provisions aimed at ensuring sound government finances in Stage Three of EMU, given that fiscal policy remains the responsibility of the national governments. One relates to the excessive deficit procedure, as defined in Article 104 and a protocol annexed to the Treaty. This procedure lays down the conditions that must prevail for a budgetary position to be judged sound. Article 104 decrees that "Member States shall avoid excessive government deficits". Compliance with this requirement is assessed on the basis of a reference value for the government deficit-to-GDP ratio of 3%, and a reference value for the government debt-to-GDP ratio of 60%. Under conditions defined in the Treaty and further specified in the Stability and Growth Pact (SGP), such as an annual fall of real GDP of at least 2%, deficit or debt ratios above the reference values may be tolerated, and will not be considered as implying the existence of an excessive deficit. Should the EU Council decide that an excessive deficit exists in a certain country, the excessive deficit procedure provides for further steps to be taken, including sanctions.

The SGP was adopted in 1997, and complements and further clarifies the implementation of the excessive deficit procedure. It consists of the Resolution of the European Council on the SGP, the "Council Regulation on the strengthening of the surveillance of budgetary positions and the surveillance and coordination of economic policies" and the "Council Regulation on speeding up and clarifying the implementation of the excessive deficit procedure". By agreeing to the SGP, Member States have committed themselves to pursuing the medium-term objective of budgetary positions "close to balance or in surplus". The idea is that having such positions would allow them to deal with the budgetary impact of normal cyclical fluctuations without breaching the 3% of GDP reference value.

In a framework of multilateral surveillance, euro area participants are obliged to submit stability programmes to the EU Council and the European Commission. The non-participating Member States have to submit convergence programmes. Both of these contain the information needed to assess the budgetary adjustments envisaged over the medium term to reach the close-to-balance or in-surplus position.

An essential complement to these ways of promoting stability-oriented fiscal policies is the Treaty's "no bail-out" clause. Article 103(1) of the Treaty states: *"The Community shall not be liable for or assume the commitments of central governments, regional, local or other public authorities, other bodies governed by public law, or public undertakings of any Member State [...]. A Member State shall not be liable for or assume the commitments of central governments, regional, local or other public authorities, other bodies governed by public law, or public undertakings of another Member State".* This clause ensures that the responsibility for repaying public debt remains national. It thus encourages prudent fiscal policies at the national level.

Further provisions contributing to fiscal discipline are the prohibitions of monetary financing of budget deficits and of any form of privileged access for the public sector to financial institutions. Article 101 of the Treaty forbids the ECB and the NCBs to provide monetary financing for public deficits using *"overdraft facilities or any other type of*

Box 5 The Community framework for fiscal policies (cont'd)

credit facility with the ECB or with the central banks of the Member States". Article 102 of the Treaty prohibits any measure that may establish privileged access to financial institutions for governments and Community institutions or bodies. In addition to increasing the incentives to pursue sound public finances and prudent fiscal policies, these provisions contribute to the credibility of the single monetary policy in the pursuit of price stability.

Excerpts from ECB (2004), *The monetary policy of the ECB*, p. 23.

Differentiated integration

EU membership does not automatically imply participation in the euro area. Besides the aforementioned special status of Denmark and the United Kingdom, participation in the euro area requires a Member State to fulfil the conditions necessary for the adoption of the single currency.

The conditions necessary for the adoption of the single currency are a high degree of sustainable convergence (**economic convergence**) and the compatibility of national legislation with the Treaty provisions on EMU (**legal convergence**) (see Box 6).

Under Article 121(1) of the EC Treaty, the achievement of a high degree of sustainable economic convergence is assessed by reference to the following criteria:

• a high degree of price stability;

• the sustainability of the government's financial position;

• the observance of the normal fluctuation margins provided for by the exchange rate mechanism of the European Monetary System for at least two years;

• the durability of convergence achieved by the Member State and of its participation in the exchange rate mechanism of the European Monetary System, as reflected in the long-term interest rate levels.

Before a Member State can join the euro area, it must prove that it has fulfilled these criteria in a lasting manner. This provision ensures that EMU remains in line with its fundamental objectives and guiding principles, in particular stable prices, sound public finances and monetary conditions, and a sustainable balance of payments.

The requirement of legal convergence obliges each Member State to adapt national legislation to ensure the independence of the respective NCB and to integrate it into the ESCB.

The European Commission and the ECB (in 1998, the EMI) independently assess both economic and legal convergence and report their findings to the EU Council (meeting in both the ECOFIN composition and the composition of the Heads of State or Government), which takes the final decision.

Box 6   Conditions necessary for the adoption of the euro

The conditions for the adoption of the euro are laid down in Article 121 of the EC Treaty and the Protocol annexed to the EC Treaty on the convergence criteria referred to in Article 121. The application of these provisions has been assessed in the convergence reports issued by the EMI and the ECB.

The conditions for the adoption of the euro are:

• achievement of a high degree of sustainable convergence ("economic convergence");

• compatibility of each Member State's national legislation with Articles 108 and 109 of the EC Treaty and the Statute of the ESCB ("legal convergence").

Economic convergence

Whether the Member State in question has achieved a high degree of sustainable convergence is assessed on the basis of four criteria: price stability, sound fiscal position, exchange rate stability and converging interest rates.

Price developments

The first indent of Article 121(1) of the EC Treaty requires *"the achievement of a high degree of price stability"*, and states that *"this will be apparent from a rate of inflation which is close to that of, at most, the three best performing Member States in terms of price stability"*.

Article 1 of the Protocol states that *"the criterion on price stability [...] shall mean that a Member State has a price performance that is sustainable and an average rate of inflation, observed over a period of one year before the examination, that does not exceed by more than 1½ percentage points that of, at most, the three best performing Member States in terms of price stability. Inflation shall be measured by means of the consumer price index on a comparable basis, taking into account differences in national definitions"*.

Fiscal developments

The second indent of Article 121(1) of the EC Treaty requires *"the sustainability of the government financial position"*, and states that *"this will be apparent from having achieved a government budgetary position without a deficit that is excessive as determined in accordance with Article 104(6)"*.

Article 2 of the Protocol states that this criterion *"[...] shall mean that at the time of the examination the Member State is not the subject of a Council decision under Article 104(6) of this Treaty that an excessive deficit exists"*.

Box 6   Conditions necessary for the adoption of the euro (cont'd)

Under Article 104(2) of the EC Treaty, Member States "*shall avoid excessive government deficits*". The Commission examines compliance with budgetary discipline, in particular on the basis of the following criteria:

"*(a) whether the ratio of the planned or actual government deficit to gross domestic product exceeds a reference value* [defined in the Protocol on the excessive deficit procedure as 3% of GDP], *unless:*

• *either the ratio has declined substantially and continuously and reached a level that comes close to the reference value,*

• *or, alternatively, the excess over the reference value is only exceptional and temporary and the ratio remains close to the reference value;*

(b)   whether the ratio of government debt to gross domestic product exceeds a reference value [defined in the Protocol on the excessive deficit procedure as 60% of GDP], *unless the ratio is sufficiently diminishing and approaching the reference value at a satisfactory pace*".

Exchange rate developments

The third indent of Article 121(1) of the EC Treaty requires "*the observance of the normal fluctuation margins provided for by the exchange-rate mechanism of the European Monetary System, for at least two years, without devaluing against the currency of any other Member State*".

Article 3 of the Protocol states that "*the criterion on participation in the exchange-rate mechanism of the European Monetary System […] shall mean that a Member State has respected the normal fluctuation margins provided for by the exchange-rate mechanism of the European Monetary System without severe tensions for at least the last two years before the examination. In particular, the Member State shall not have devalued its currency's bilateral central rate against any other Member State's currency on its own initiative for the same period*".

As regards the application of these provisions, the EMI and the ECB have pointed out in the convergence reports of 1998, 2000 and 2002 that, when the Treaty was conceived, the normal fluctuation margins were ±2.25% around bilateral central rates, whereas a ±6% band was a derogation from the rule. In August 1993, the decision was taken to widen the fluctuation margins to ±15%, and the interpretation of the criterion, in particular the concept of "normal fluctuation margins", became less straightforward. Account would therefore need to be taken of how each exchange rate had developed within the European Monetary System (EMS) since 1993 in forming an ex post judgement. Emphasis is therefore placed on exchange rates being close to the respective ERM/ERM II central rates.

Long-term interest rate developments

The fourth indent of Article 121(1) of the EC Treaty requires "*the durability of convergence achieved by the Member State and of its participation in the exchange-rate mechanism of the European Monetary System being reflected in the long-term interest-rate levels*".

Box 6 Conditions necessary for the adoption of the euro (cont'd)

Article 4 of the Protocol states that *"the criterion on the convergence of interest rates [...] shall mean that, observed over a period of one year before the examination, a Member State has had an average nominal long-term interest rate that does not exceed by more than 2 percentage points that of, at most, the three best performing Member States in terms of price stability. Interest rates shall be measured on the basis of long-term government bonds or comparable securities, taking into account differences in national definitions"*.

Legal convergence

All Member States' national legislation, including the statutes of their NCBs, must be compatible with Articles 108 and 109 of the EC Treaty and with the Statute of the ESCB. The term "compatible" indicates that the Treaty does not require "harmonisation" of the statutes of the NCBs, either among themselves or with that of the ESCB. Instead it means that national legislation should be adjusted to eliminate inconsistencies with the Treaty and the Statute of the ESCB, in particular provisions that would infringe on the independence of the respective NCB and its role as an integral part of the ESCB.

Incompatibilities have been removed by the time the Member State adopts the euro. A Member State's obligation to adjust its legislation exists despite the supremacy of the Treaty and the Statute of the ESCB over national legislation. It ensures that national legislation is a priori consistent with Community law.

For the purpose of identifying the areas in which adaptation is necessary the ECB examines:

- the independence of the NCB (legal, institutional and functional independence and security of tenure of the members of the decision-making bodies);

- the legal integration of the NCB into the ESCB (including statutory objectives, tasks, instruments, organisation and financial provisions);

- other legislation which has a bearing on the full participation of the Member State in Stage Three of EMU (including provisions on the issue of banknotes and coins, holding and management of foreign reserves and exchange rate policy).

Other factors

Article 121(1) of the EC Treaty also requires the Commission and EMI (now the ECB) to take account of several other factors, namely *"the development of the ecu, the results of the integration of markets, the situation and development of the balances of payments on current account and an examination of the development of unit labour costs and other price indices"*. The development of the ECU was a factor considered in 1998 during the move to Stage Three of EMU. However, now that the euro has superseded the ECU this factor will no longer play a role in assessments of convergence.

Box 6 **Conditions necessary for the adoption of the euro (cont'd)**

Procedures

The ECB (in 1998, the EMI) and the European Commission assess whether each EU Member State has fulfilled the above conditions. Both bodies act individually and independently. Their first convergence reports were issued in 1998 at the time of the move to Stage Three of EMU. The situation of Member States with a derogation is assessed at least once every two years or at the request of a Member State with a derogation.

The procedural steps for the move to Stage Three of EMU in 1998 were carried out in line with Article 121 of the EC Treaty:

• Reports by the EMI and the European Commission;

• Recommendations from both the Commission and the ECOFIN Council;

• Consultation of the European Parliament;

• Decision of the EU Council, meeting in the composition of the Heads of State or Government.

For the review and abrogation of a derogation, Article 122 of the EC Treaty requires the following procedural steps:

• Reports by the ECB and the European Commission;

• Proposal from the Commission;

• Consultation of the European Parliament;

• Discussion in the EU Council, meeting in the composition of the Heads of State or Government;

• Decision by the ECOFIN Council.

EU Member States with a derogation

Under Article 122 of the EC Treaty, an EU Member State that does not fulfil the conditions necessary for the adoption of the euro is deemed to have a **derogation**. This means that the Member State concerned does not participate in the single currency area. It retains its monetary sovereignty with its own currency and existing powers in the field of monetary policy and is not bound by the rules concerning economic policy that only apply to Member States participating in Stage Three of EMU. However, the Member States with a derogation remain committed to the objective of the introduction of a single currency (Article 4(2) of the EC Treaty) and are under the obligation to achieve economic and legal convergence as a precondition for the eventual adoption of the single currency. Likewise, Article 108 on central bank independence also applies to these Member States.

A derogation is temporary. The EU Council reviews the situation once every two years on the basis of reports from the ECB and the European Commission. If the Council (meeting in both the ECOFIN composition and the composition of Heads of State or Government) concludes that a Member State fulfils the criteria of economic and legal convergence, its derogation is abrogated and it must adopt the euro as its currency.

At present, Sweden and the ten countries that joined the European Union on 1 May 2004 are Member States with a derogation. Sweden has not yet fulfilled the requirement of legal convergence. The ten new Member States must still prove in the years ahead that they fulfil the conditions necessary for the adoption of the euro as their currency.

EU Member States with a special status

Under Protocols annexed to the EC Treaty[45], Denmark and the United Kingdom have been exempted from participation in Stage Three of EMU. This means that Denmark and the United Kingdom had the right to choose whether or not to participate in Stage Three of EMU before it started on 1 January 1999. Both countries exercised this right (Denmark in December 1992 and the United Kingdom in October 1997) and notified the EU Council of their intention not to move to Stage Three.

As regards the scope of the exemptions, the Protocol on Denmark states that the exemption shall have the same effect as a derogation. The Protocol on the United Kingdom goes much further. It exempts it from further Treaty provisions. In particular, it waives the application of Article 4(2) of the EC Treaty under which both the Community and the Member States remain committed to the objective of the introduction of a single currency and Article 108 on central bank independence.

The exemptions granted to Denmark and the United Kingdom are permanent. However, both Member States have retained the right to "opt in" at a later stage, provided that they then fulfil the conditions necessary for the adoption of the euro.

---

[45] Protocol on certain provisions relating to Denmark; and Protocol on certain provisions relating to the United Kingdom of Great Britain and Northern Ireland.

Governing Council meeting at
the ECB on 22 July 2004.
Credit: ECB/Martin Joppen.

2 CENTRAL BANKING IN EMU: LEGAL, INSTITUTIONAL AND ORGANISATIONAL ASPECTS

Having adopted the euro as their single currency, the EU Member States that are part of the euro area have relinquished their monetary sovereignty. The ECB, as the core of the newly established central banking system called the European System of Central Banks (ESCB), has taken on responsibility for the monetary policy in the euro area.

2.1 THE ECB, THE ESCB AND THE EUROSYSTEM

Under the EC Treaty, the ESCB is entrusted with carrying out central banking functions for the euro. However, as the ESCB has no legal personality of its own, and because of differentiated levels of integration in EMU, the real actors are the ECB and the NCBs of the euro area countries. They exercise the core functions of the ESCB under the name "Eurosystem".

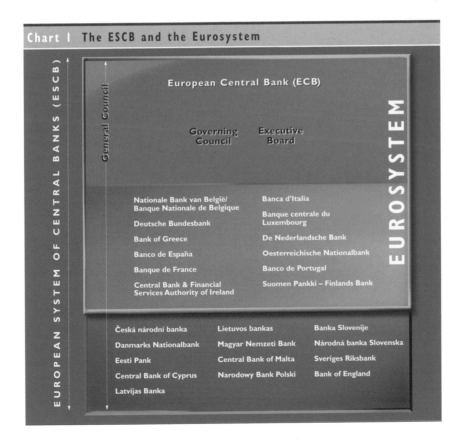

Chart 1   The ESCB and the Eurosystem

2.1.1 ESCB and Eurosystem as the organic link between the ECB and the NCBs

The ESCB is made up of the ECB and the NCBs of the 25 EU Member States. Its "organic law" is the Protocol on the Statute of the European System of Central Banks and of the European Central Bank (Statute of the ESCB), which is annexed to the EC Treaty.

Unlike the ECB and the NCBs, the ESCB has no legal personality, no capacity to act and no decision-making bodies of its own. Instead, the components of the ESCB – the ECB and the NCBs – are the legal persons and actors. They do have the capacity to act but when they perform tasks assigned to the ESCB they act in line with its objectives, the rules of the Treaty and the Statute and the decisions taken by the decision-making bodies of the ECB. Thus, the term ESCB denotes an institutional framework that establishes an "organic link" between the ECB and the NCBs. It ensures that i) decision-making is centralised, and ii) the tasks that the EC Treaty has assigned to the ESCB are performed jointly and consistently in line with the allocation of powers and the objectives of the system.

The ESCB includes the NCBs of all EU Member States, even those which have not adopted the euro (see Section 1.2.2) because of their special status (Denmark and the United Kingdom) or because of a derogation (Sweden and the ten new EU Member States). As the non-participating Member States have maintained their monetary sovereignty, their respective central banks are not involved in carrying out the System's core functions. Therefore, to help the public to understand the complex structure of the European central banking system more easily, the Governing Council of the ECB decided in November 1998 to adopt the term "Eurosystem". This term refers to the composition – the ECB and the NCBs of the Member States that have adopted the euro – in which the ESCB performs its basic tasks.

There are three main political and economic reasons why a system was established to carry out central bank functions for the euro, and not a single central bank:

1. The establishment of a single central bank for the whole euro area (possibly concentrating central bank business in one single place) would not have been acceptable on political grounds.

2. The Eurosystem approach builds on the experience of the NCBs, preserves their institutional set-up, infrastructure and operational capabilities and expertise; moreover, NCBs continue to perform some non-Eurosystem-related tasks.

3. Given the large geographic area of the euro area, it was deemed appropriate to give credit institutions an access point to central banking in each participating Member State. Given the large number of nations and cultures in the euro area, domestic institutions (rather than a supranational one) were considered best placed to serve as points of access to the Eurosystem.

The construction of the Eurosystem builds on established central bank structures and respects the cultural and national diversity of the euro area. At the same time, the fact that the NCBs are autonomous entities fosters cross-fertilisation and, where appropriate, emulation as regards best practices and thus creates a potential for improving the efficiency of operational management within the Eurosystem.

2.1.2 The ECB as a specialised organisation of Community law

The EC Treaty has established the ECB as a specialised, independent organisation for conducting monetary policy and performing related functions. To this end, the ECB has been given a legal personality of its own, with its own decision-making bodies and powers. Its organisation as a central bank responds to the specific nature of monetary policy, i.e. a public policy function that is implemented mainly by financial market operations.

Legal personality
The ECB has legal personality under Article 107(2) of the EC Treaty and enjoys the most extensive legal capacity accorded to legal persons under the respective national law of each Member State under Article 9.1 of the Statute of the ESCB. It may therefore acquire or dispose of movable and immovable property and be party to legal proceedings. In addition, the ECB enjoys those privileges and immunities that are necessary for the performance of its tasks, under the conditions laid down in the Protocol on the privileges and immunities of the European Communities of 8 April 1965[1].

As a legal person under public international law, the ECB is in a position to, among other things, conclude international agreements in matters relating to its field of competence and participate in the work of international organisations such as the International Monetary Fund (IMF), the Bank for International Settlements (BIS) and the Organisation for Economic Co-operation and Development (OECD).

Institutional status
Although performing a policy function under the EC Treaty the ECB is not a Community institution in the proper meaning of the term. It is not referred to in Article 7 of the EC Treaty which establishes the five institutions of the Community: the European Parliament, the Council, the European Commission, the Court of Justice and the Court of Auditors. These institutions are entrusted with the broad mandate of carrying out the tasks of the Community within the limits of the powers conferred upon them by the Treaty.

Instead, the legal basis of the ESCB and the ECB is provided for in a separate article (Article 8 of the Treaty). This underpins the specific status of the ECB within the overall context of the European Community, sets it apart from the other institutions and their auxiliary bodies and limits its activities to a clearly defined special task.

---

[1] Article 23 of the Protocol states that the Protocol applies to the European Central Bank, to the members of its organs and to its staff, without prejudice to the provisions of the Statute of the ESCB.

As an organisation created by the EC Treaty, the ECB enjoys genuine powers. These powers have not been delegated by the Community institutions; they are genuine powers given to the ECB by the EC Treaty. This feature distinguishes the ECB from the various decentralised agencies of the Community, which possess their own legal personality but have competences delegated to them by the Community institutions.[2]

2.1.3 The euro area NCBs as an integral part of the Eurosystem

Each NCB of the Eurosystem has legal personality within the national law of its respective country. However, all euro area NCBs are integral parts of the Eurosystem by virtue of Article 105 of the EC Treaty and Article 14.3 of the Statute of the ESCB. Under Article 12.1 of the Statute, they carry out those Eurosystem tasks which have been delegated to them by the ECB in line with the principle of decentralisation (see Section 2.4) and act in accordance with the guidelines and instructions of the ECB (Article 14.3 of the Statute). At the same time, the Governors of the Eurosystem NCBs are, alongside the members of the Executive Board, ex officio members of the Governing Council of the ECB (Article 10 of the Statute of the ESCB). As "shareholders" of the ECB, the Eurosystem NCBs endow the ECB with capital and foreign reserve assets and participate in its financial results (Articles 28, 30 and 33 of the Statute).

To integrate the NCBs into the Eurosystem, the relevant national legislation has been brought into line with Community law: national laws and statutes have to ensure, in particular, that the NCBs and their decision-making bodies are independent of the authorities of the respective EU Member States (see Section 4.1). Independence is a requirement because of the NCBs' and their Governors' involvement in the functioning of the Eurosystem.

The functional integration of the NCBs into the Eurosystem does not infringe upon their existing institutional, financial and administrative autonomy. Under the Statute of the ESCB, the NCBs may perform non-Eurosystem functions on their own responsibility, provided that these functions do not interfere with the objectives and tasks of the Eurosystem. Non-Eurosystem functions vary according to countries and mainly consist of various types of financial and administrative services to the governments of the respective countries. Most NCBs are also involved in supervising financial institutions in their respective countries (see Section 3.7).

2.1.4 The NCBs of the non-participating EU Member States

The NCBs of the non-participating EU Member States are also members of the ESCB but have a special status. They are responsible for their respective national monetary policies and are thus excluded from taking part in the core activities of the Eurosystem, in particular the conduct of the single monetary policy. Their

---

[2] For example, the European Environment Agency (EEA), the Office for Harmonisation in the Internal Market (OHIM) and the European Agency for the Evaluation of Medicinal Products (EMEA).

Governors are not members of the ECB's Governing Council and do not take part in the decision-making process for the Eurosystem's core activities. Likewise, these NCBs are not involved in implementing the single monetary policy and related functions.

The non-participating NCBs are nevertheless committed to the principles of price stability-oriented monetary policy. Furthermore, being members of the ESCB implies that they need to work closely with the Eurosystem in several fields: for instance, they provide support for the collection of statistics (see Section 3.5). In addition, the European Exchange Rate Mechanism II (ERM II) provides a framework for monetary and exchange rate policy cooperation with the Eurosystem (see Section 3.2.1). The institutional forum for such cooperation is the General Council of the ECB (see Section 2.5.1).

2.2 OBJECTIVES

In line with Article 105(1) of the Treaty, the primary objective of the ESCB is to maintain price stability. Without prejudice to this objective, it shall support the general economic policies in the Community with a view to contributing to the achievement of the objectives of the Community (which include a high level of employment and sustainable and non-inflationary growth). Furthermore, the ESCB shall act in line with the principle of an open market economy with free competition.

Since Article 105(1) of the Treaty does not apply to the EU Member States which have not adopted the euro the term "ESCB" must be read as "Eurosystem".

2.2.1 The primary objective of price stability

The primary objective of the Eurosystem to maintain price stability is the key provision of the monetary policy chapter of the Treaty. It reflects modern economic thinking about the role, scope and limits of monetary policy and underlies the institutional and organisational set-up of central banking in EMU.

The objective of maintaining price stability has been assigned by the EC Treaty for good reasons. First, decades of practical experience and a large number of economic studies suggest that monetary policy will contribute most to improving economic prospects and raising the living standards of citizens by maintaining price stability in a lasting way (see Box 7).

Second, the theoretical foundations of monetary policy as well as experience drawn from the past demonstrate that monetary policy can ultimately only influence the price level in the economy (see Section 3.1.1). Thus, price stability is the only feasible objective for the single monetary policy over the medium term. By contrast, apart from the positive impact of price stability, monetary policy has no scope for exerting any lasting influence on real variables.

Box 7   The benefits of price stability

The objective of price stability refers to the general level of prices in the economy and implies avoiding both prolonged inflation and deflation. There are several ways in which price stability contributes to achieving high levels of economic activity and employment.

1. Price stability makes it easier for people to recognise changes in relative prices since such changes are not obscured by fluctuations in the overall price level. This enables firms and consumers to make better-informed decisions on consumption and investment. This in turn allows the market to allocate resources more efficiently. By helping the market to guide resources to where they can be used most productively, price stability raises the productive potential of the economy.

2. If investors can be sure that prices will remain stable in the future, they will not demand an "inflation risk premium" to compensate them for the risks associated with holding nominal assets over the longer term. By reducing such risk premia in the real interest rate, monetary policy can contribute to the allocative efficiency of the capital market and thus increases the incentives to invest. This in turn fosters economic welfare.

3. The credible maintenance of price stability also makes it less likely that individuals and firms will divert resources from productive uses to hedge against inflation. For example, in a high inflation environment there is an incentive to stockpile real goods since they retain their value better than money or some financial assets in such circumstances. However, stockpiling goods is not an efficient investment decision, and therefore hinders economic growth.

4. Tax and welfare systems can create perverse incentives that distort economic behaviour. In most cases, these distortions are exacerbated by inflation or deflation. Price stability eliminates the real economic costs entailed when inflation exacerbates the distortionary impact of tax and social security systems.

5. Maintaining price stability prevents the considerable and arbitrary redistribution of wealth and income that arises in both inflationary and deflationary environments. An environment of stable prices therefore helps to maintain social cohesion and stability. Several cases in the twentieth century have shown that high rates of inflation or deflation tend to create social and political instability.

Source: ECB (2004), *The monetary policy of the ECB*, p. 42.

Although the EC Treaty clearly establishes maintaining price stability as the primary objective of the ECB, it does not define what "price stability" actually means. With this in mind, in October 1998, the ECB announced a quantitative definition of price stability. This definition is part of the ECB's monetary policy strategy (see Section 3.1.2).

2.2.2 The support of general economic policies

By fulfilling its clearly defined mandate to maintain price stability in the euro area, the ECB supports the general economic policies in the Community *"with a view to contributing to the achievement of the objectives of the Community as laid down in Article 2"*. Indeed, as shown above, the best contribution which the ECB can make to promoting, among other things, *"sustainable and non-inflationary growth"* and a *"high level of employment"*, as referred to in Article 2 of the EC Treaty, is to pursue a monetary policy aimed at price stability. In this way, a stability-oriented monetary policy creates a stable environment for other policies to be carried out as effectively as possible.

By contrast, monetary policy has very limited scope to exert a lasting influence on real variables through other channels; in the long run, real income is essentially determined by supply-side factors (e.g. technology, population growth, the flexibility of markets and the efficiency of the institutional framework of the economy). It is therefore the task of fiscal and structural policies – but also of those involved in the wage-bargaining process – to enhance the growth potential of the economy.

Accordingly, the mandate to support the general economic policies in the euro area does not give the ECB direct responsibility for any additional objectives other than price stability. Instead, the Treaty requires the ECB to take account of the other Community objectives in pursuing its primary objective. In particular, given that monetary policy can affect real activity in the shorter term, the ECB typically should avoid generating excessive fluctuations in output and employment on condition that this does not jeopardise its pursuit of its primary objective.

Likewise, the mandate to support the general economic policies in the Community does not require the ECB to coordinate its policy ex ante with the economic policies in the Community. It is, however, part of the rationale behind the dialogue between the ECB and the economic policy-makers at the Community level (see Section 4.3).

2.2.3 The principle of an open market economy

The EC Treaty also binds the Eurosystem to the principle of an open market economy with free competition. The Eurosystem complies with this principle in several ways. By maintaining price stability, the ECB contributes to the proper operation of the price mechanism, which is an essential feature of a well-functioning market economy and which favours an efficient allocation of resources. The monetary policy instruments of the Eurosystem are based on market mechanisms, and credit institutions are given equal access to the Eurosystem facilities.

2.3 ASSIGNMENT OF TASKS BY THE TREATY

The Treaty entrusts the ESCB with the task of performing the central bank function for the Community. Given the fact that some EU Member States do not participate in EMU, the terms "ESCB" and "Community" are to be read as "Eurosystem" and "euro area" respectively.

2.3.1 Basic tasks of the Eurosystem

Article 105(2) of the EC Treaty and Article 3.1 of the Statute of the ESCB confer upon the Eurosystem the sole competence for the following basic tasks:

• to define and implement the monetary policy of the euro area;
• to conduct foreign exchange operations;
• to hold and manage the official foreign reserves of the euro area Member States;
• to promote the smooth operation of payment systems.

Other related tasks include:

• the issue of euro banknotes as the only such notes to have the status of legal tender in the euro area (Article 106(1) of the EC Treaty and Article 16 of the Statute);

• the collection of the statistical information necessary for the tasks of the Eurosystem (Article 5 of the Statute).

The Eurosystem's capacity to formulate and implement the **monetary policy** of the euro area is ensured by its full control over base money. Under Article 106 of the Treaty, the ECB and the NCBs are the only institutions that are entitled to actually issue legal tender banknotes in the euro area; the euro area Member States' right to mint coins is restricted to low denominations and the volume of coins issued is subject to approval by the ECB. Given the dependency of the banking system on base money, the Eurosystem is thus in a position to exert a dominant influence on money market conditions and money market interest rates (see Section 3.1).

The conduct of **foreign exchange operations** is an important corollary function of the conduct of monetary policy. Assigning this task to the Eurosystem not only exploits the operational capabilities of central banks but also ensures that foreign exchange operations remain consistent with the aims of monetary policy. Foreign exchange operations influence exchange rates and domestic liquidity conditions, which are relevant variables for monetary policy. They have to be compatible with the framework which the Treaty has established for the exchange rate policy of the euro area. In this field, the ECB shares responsibility with the EU Council as the ultimate decision-maker (see Section 3.2.1).

The task of holding and managing the **official foreign reserves** of the euro area is the logical complement to the Eurosystem's function of conducting foreign exchange operations. It is complemented by the ECB's power under Article 31 of the Statute to control the use of NCBs' foreign exchange holdings as well as Member States' residual working balances in foreign currencies (see Section 3.2.2).

Assigning to the Eurosystem the task of promoting the **smooth operation of payment systems** (see Section 3.3) acknowledges the importance of sound and efficient systems not only for the conduct of monetary policy but also for the economy as a whole.

For the performance of these Eurosystem tasks, the Statute of the ESCB assigns to the ECB and the euro area NCBs a wide range of functional and operational competences under Articles 17 to 24 of the Statute. In addition, the ECB:

• enjoys regulatory powers and the right to impose enforceable sanctions in case of non-compliance with ECB Regulations and Decisions under Article 110 of the Treaty and Article 34 of the Statute (see Section 2.5.3);

• monitors compliance by the NCBs with the prohibition of monetary financing and privileged access to financial institutions for the public sector (see Section 2.5.5).

2.3.2 Other tasks

In addition to its core functions, the Eurosystem has to contribute to *"the smooth conduct of policies pursued by the competent authorities relating to the prudential supervision of credit institutions and the stability of the financial system"* (Article 105(5) of the EC Treaty). As these functions fall primarily within the responsibility of the Member States, the Eurosystem's role is limited to making a *contribution* only. Although the scope of the Eurosystem's contribution is not specified precisely, the Treaty thereby acknowledges the legitimate interest of the ECB and the NCBs to be involved in Community arrangements for prudential supervision and financial stability (see Section 3.7).

Another major assignment is the ECB's task of advising the appropriate Community institutions and bodies and national authorities in its fields of competence (Article 105(4) of the EC Treaty and Article 4 of the Statute) and its right to initiate secondary Community legislation in the cases specified in the Treaty (see Section 2.5.4).

Finally, under Article 123(2) of the Treaty and Article 44 of the Statute, the ECB must also carry out those functions of the EMI which still need to be performed because not all EU Member States have yet adopted the euro (see Section 2.5.6).

2.4 CENTRALISED DECISION-MAKING AND OPERATIONAL DECENTRALISATION

Under Article 8 of the Statute of the ESCB, the ECB's decision-making bodies govern the Eurosystem. Within their respective responsibilities, these bodies take all the necessary decisions to enable the ESCB and Eurosystem to carry out their respective tasks.

Centralised decision-making through the ECB's decision-making bodies is not limited to the formulation of policies, such as changes in the key ECB interest rates. It extends to the implementation of policies through the ECB and the NCBs.

Except for the statutory tasks that have been exclusively assigned to the ECB in its capacity as the core and leader of the Eurosystem (see Section 2.5), the Statute of the ESCB does not indicate to what extent ECB policies are to be implemented through activities of the ECB or the NCBs. For the bulk of the Eurosystem's activities, the actual intra-system division of labour has been guided by the principle of decentralisation, i.e. *"the ECB shall have recourse to the NCBs, to the extent deemed possible and appropriate, to carry out operations which form part of the tasks of the Eurosystem"* (Article 12.1 of the Statute of the ESCB).

The principle of decentralisation should not be confused with the "principle of subsidiarity", as set out in Article 5 of the EC Treaty. Subsidiarity means that the need for centralisation must be proven conclusively before action at the Community level can be taken. In Stage Three of EMU, however, monetary policy has been made an area in which action is taken exclusively at the Community level. Therefore centralisation does not have to be justified; instead, it is for the ECB to evaluate the extent to which decentralisation is possible and appropriate.

The operational set-up of the Eurosystem takes full account of the principle of decentralisation. As shown in Chapter 3, the NCBs perform almost all operational tasks of the Eurosystem. In particular, the NCBs conduct the monetary policy operations and, as agents of the ECB, most external operations, provide payment and securities settlement facilities, and ensure the procurement, issue and post-issue handling of euro banknotes. They also collect statistics for the ECB, collaborate with the ECB on translation and the production of publications and contribute to economic analysis and research which is conducted within the framework of organised networks.

By contrast, as also shown in Chapter 3, the ECB itself carries out few operations. The ECB manages its own funds, oversees cross-border large-value payment and clearing systems and acts as a settlement agent for some of them. Other operational activities of the ECB include external operations, although in practice the bulk of them are executed by the NCBs. However, this limited scope of the ECB's own operational activities does not mean that it is largely disconnected from the operational side of the Eurosystem. Instead, the ECB ensures in various ways that the operations of the Eurosystem are performed consistently by the euro area NCBs (see Section 2.5.2).

The high degree of operational decentralisation within the Eurosystem is also mirrored in the distribution of staff among the ECB and the NCBs. The 12 euro area NCBs have a combined total of more than 50,000 employees; the ECB currently has fewer than 1,300 staff members. Even if one takes into account that around 50% of NCB staff are estimated to be involved in non-Eurosystem activities[3], the ECB's share in the total central bank staff working for the Eurosystem does not exceed 5%.

2.5 THE ECB'S ROLE IN THE EUROSYSTEM

Under Article 9.2 of the Statute of the ESCB, the ECB ensures that the tasks of the Eurosystem are carried out either by its own activities or through the NCBs.

In line with this statutory role, the ECB exercises several specific functions. In particular, it:

• is the decision-making centre of the ESCB and the Eurosystem;

• ensures consistent implementation of ECB policies;

• exercises regulatory powers and the right to impose sanctions;

• initiates Community legislation and advises the Community institutions and EU Member States on draft legislation;

• monitors compliance with the provisions of Articles 101 and 102 of the Treaty;

• carries out those tasks of the former EMI which still need to be performed in Stage Three of EMU because not all EU countries participate in EMU.

2.5.1 Decision-making centre of the ESCB and the Eurosystem

The Eurosystem and the ESCB are governed by the two main decision-making bodies of the ECB: the **Governing Council** and the **Executive Board** (Article 9.3 of the Statute). A third decision-making body, the **General Council**, will exist as long as some EU Member States have not adopted the euro (Article 45 of the Statute). The functioning of these decision-making bodies is governed by the Treaty, the Statute of the ESCB and the relevant Rules of Procedure.

The decision-making bodies of the ECB have a double function: i) to govern the ECB itself, and ii) to govern the Eurosystem and the ESCB. This section focuses on the latter function; Chapter 6 looks at how the decision-making bodies govern the ECB.

The ECB's decision-making bodies are specifically tailored to the requirements of monetary policy decision-making in a single currency area. The two-layer approach with the Governing Council and the Executive Board, both of which are

---

[3] Since these activities are conditioned by local factors, they vary substantially from one NCB to another. Together with geography and population variations, this accounts for the large differences in the staff numbers of different NCBs, ranging from less than 200 in Luxembourg to more than 10,000 in France and Germany.

endowed with genuine decision-making powers within their respective fields of competence, ensures the ECB's capacity to respond promptly to market developments.

Governing Council

The Governing Council is the main decision-making body of the ECB and is entitled to take the most important and strategically significant decisions for the Eurosystem.

Composition

The Governing Council comprises the six members of the Executive Board and the governors of the NCBs of the Member States that have adopted the euro (currently 12 governors).[4] Membership in the Governing Council is personal and inalienable, i.e. it cannot be delegated to a third person. However, there are two exceptions (Article 10 of the Statute of the ESCB):

i.   in the case of financial matters (see below), a governor who is unable to participate may appoint an alternate to cast his/her vote (Article 10.3 of the Statute);

ii. if a member of the Governing Council is prevented from voting for a prolonged period (i.e. one month) he/she may appoint an alternate as a member of the Governing Council (Article 3.3 of the Rules of Procedure in conjunction with Article 10.2 of the Statute). This clause has been used a few times to date to cover the prolonged illness of a Governor or when a Governor relinquished office before the successor was appointed.

The members of the Executive Board participate in the decision-making of the Governing Council with the same rights and responsibility as the NCB governors, thus underlining the supranational nature of the ECB. The Executive Board's involvement also ensures that Governing Council decisions take account of the expertise of those who are responsible for the implementation of the ECB's policies.

Under Article 113(1) of the EC Treaty, the President of the ECOFIN Council and a member of the European Commission (usually the Commissioner responsible for Economic and Monetary Affairs) may also participate in meetings of the Governing Council, but they do not have the right to vote. The President of the ECOFIN Council may submit a motion for deliberation to the Governing Council. Following an informal agreement between the ECOFIN Council and the ECB, the President of the Eurogroup (see Section 4.3.2) assumes the statutory responsibilities of the President of the ECOFIN Council. This ensures that when a non-euro area Member State holds the rotating Council Presidency the ECOFIN Council is still represented by the minister of a euro area member country at meetings of the Governing Council.

---

[4] Box 2.1 lists all the members of the Governing Council since the ECB was established on 1 June 1998.

Under Article 3.2 of the Rules of Procedure of the ECB, all governors may be accompanied by one person from their NCB at meetings of the Governing Council. The accompanying persons are in general members of the decision-making bodies of the NCBs or senior officials.

Competences

In line with Article 12.1 of the Statute of the ESCB, the Governing Council is responsible for all decisions except for those explicitly reserved to the Executive Board. With regard to the objectives and tasks entrusted to the Eurosystem, it is in particular responsible for formulating the monetary policy of the euro area. In this context, the Governing Council defines the ECB's monetary policy strategy and the operational framework, takes the necessary decisions (for instance on the key ECB interest rates) and adopts the guidelines to be followed by the Eurosystem NCBs for the execution of monetary policy operations.

Other competences include:

• issuing guidelines for all other operations of the NCBs as well as for the transactions of euro area countries in their foreign exchange working balances;

• adopting the regulations which the ECB may enact in application of the Treaty or by delegation from the EU Council (see Section 2.5.3);

• authorising the issue of euro banknotes and the volume of issue of euro coins for the euro area (see Section 3.4);

• establishing the rules to standardise the accounting and reporting of NCB operations (see Section 2.5.2);

• initiating Community legislation and fulfilling the advisory function of the ECB (see Section 2.5.4) and deciding on the international representation of the Eurosystem (see Chapter 5);

• deciding on the allocation of financial resources to the ECB and the appropriation of its financial results, and adopting the rules governing the allocation of monetary income among the euro area NCBs (see Section 3.8);

• adopting the Annual Report and Annual Accounts of the ECB.

In addition, the Governing Council is the supreme decision-making body for the administration of the ECB itself. It adopts the Rules of Procedure of the ECB, determines the conditions of employment of the members of the Executive Board and the ECB staff and sets the ECB's budget (see Chapter 6).

General voting rules

The Governing Council acts as a collegiate body in line with the *one member, one vote* principle. This means that except for decisions on certain financial matters (see below), the votes are not weighted. Thus, the vote of the governor of the NCB of the biggest euro area country counts as much as that of the NCB governor of the smallest country, with each member having in principle one vote. The principle reflects the fact that all the members, including the NCB governors, are appointed in their personal capacity and not as representatives of their countries or their NCBs. Instead, they have to act in the interest of, and with due regard to the situation in, the euro area as a whole.

For the time being, each of the current 18 members has the right to vote. This will only change when the euro area has more than 15 member countries and the regime of rotating voting rights becomes effective (see below). It is also important to note that the Executive Board members do not have the right to vote when the Governing Council is deciding on their terms and conditions of employment (Article 11.3 of the Statute).

The Governing Council normally acts by a simple majority of the votes cast by the members who are present in person. In the event of a tie, the President has the deciding vote. These rules ensure that decisions cannot be blocked by a minority of Governing Council members and that the ECB preserves its capacity to act at any point in time.

In two specific cases, a two-thirds majority of the votes cast is required:

i.   if the Governing Council finds that non-Eurosystem functions performed by an NCB interfere with the respective objectives and tasks of the Eurosystem;

ii. if the Governing Council decides on the use of operational methods of monetary control other than those specified in the Statute of the ESCB.

Unanimity is required to recommend an amendment to the Statute of the ESCB through the simplified amendment procedure (Article 41 of the Statute) or the enabling clause (Article 10.6 of the Statute).

All the aforementioned cases refer to fundamental measures where the wish for a broad or full consensus prevails over the risk of these measures being blocked by an opposing minority of Governing Council members.

Fast and simple decision-making is also supported by the rules on the quorum which prescribe the presence of two-thirds of the members of the Governing Council, i.e. currently 12 members. If the quorum is not met the President may convene an extraordinary meeting at which decisions may be taken without regard to the quorum.

New voting modalities for an enlarged euro area

When the euro area has more than 15 member countries, and thus the number of NCB governors in the Governing Council exceeds 15, the number of NCB governors holding a voting right will be restricted to 15.

To maintain the Governing Council's capacity for efficient and timely decision-making within an enlarged euro area, Article 10.2 of the Statute of the ESCB was amended by the EU Council in line with the "enabling clause" of Article 10.6 of the Statute.[5] The adjustment of voting modalities in the Governing Council took effect from 1 May 2004 following ratification of the EU Council Decision by the EU Member States in line with their constitutional requirements.

The new wording of Article 10.2 of the Statute states that all members of the Governing Council will continue to attend meetings and participate in the deliberations in a personal and independent capacity. The six members of the Executive Board will maintain permanent voting rights, whereas the NCB governors will exercise voting rights on the basis of a pre-established rotation system. To ensure that the governors with voting rights are from countries which, taken together, are always representative of the euro area economy as a whole, they will exercise voting rights with different frequencies which are pre-established according to objective criteria.

For the governors having a voting right at any given time, the "one member, one vote" principle will continue to apply. NCB governors will be allocated to different groups according to a ranking of the size of their respective countries' economies. The country ranking is based on a composite indicator consisting of two components:

i.   the share of the country in the aggregate gross domestic product (GDP) at market prices;

ii. the share of the country in the total assets of the aggregated balance sheet of the monetary financial institutions (TABS-MFI).

The weights of the two components are $5/6$ for GDP and $1/6$ for TABS-MFI.

Table 1	The two-group rotation system (first stage) – voting frequencies of governors in each group						
		Number of governors in the Governing Council					
		16	17	18	19	20	21	22 and more
1st group	No. of voting rights/ No. of governors	5/5	5/5	5/5	4/5	4/5	4/5	*Second stage: rotation system with three groups (see Table 2)*
	Voting frequency	*100%*	*100%*	*100%*	*80%*	*80%*	*80%*	
2nd group	No. of voting rights/ No. of governors	10/11	10/12	10/13	11/14	11/15	11/16	
	Voting frequency	*91%*	*83%*	*77%*	*79%*	*73%*	*69%*	
Σ **voting rights**		**15**	**15**	**15**	**15**	**15**	**15**	**15**

---

[5] Decision 2003/223/EC of the Council, meeting in the composition of the Heads of State or Government, of 21 March 2003 on an amendment to Article 10.2 of the Statute of the European System of Central Banks and the European Central Bank (OJ L 83, 1.4.2003, p. 66).

The rotation system will start operating with two groups once there are more than 15 euro area member countries. The first group will be composed of five governors from the euro area countries which occupy the highest positions in the cuntry ranking; this group will share four voting rights. The second group will be composed of the remaining governors and will share 11 voting rights.

Table 2	The three-group rotation system (second stage) – voting frequencies of governors in each group							
		Number of governors in the Governing Council						
		16-21	**22**	**23**	**24**	**25**	**26**	**27**
1st group	No. of voting rights/ No. of governors		4/5	4/5	4/5	4/5	4/5	4/5
	Voting frequency		*80%*	*80%*	*80%*	*80%*	*80%*	*80%*
2nd group	No. of voting rights/ No. of governors	*First stage: rotation system with two groups (see Table 1)*	8/11	8/12	8/12	8/13	8/13	8/14
	Voting frequency		*73%*	*67%*	*67%*	*62%*	*62%*	*57%*
3rd group	No. of voting rights/ No. of governors		3/6	3/6	3/7	3/7	3/8	3/8
	Voting frequency		*50%*	*50%*	*43%*	*43%*	*38%*	*38%*
Σ **voting rights**		**15**	**15**	**15**	**15**	**15**	**15**	**15**

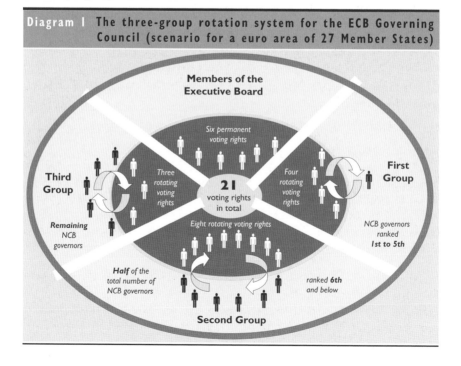

Diagram 1   The three-group rotation system for the ECB Governing Council (scenario for a euro area of 27 Member States)

When there are at least 22 euro area member countries, the rotation system will be based on three groups. The first group will be composed of five governors from the euro area countries which occupy the highest positions in the country ranking and will share four voting rights. The second group will be composed of half of all the NCB governors and will share eight voting rights. The third group will be composed of the remaining governors and will share three voting rights.

The size of the groups and the NCB governors' voting frequencies will be adjusted over time to accommodate any sequencing of euro area enlargement up to 27 member countries. At an appropriate stage, the Governing Council will decide on the exact implementing provisions by a two-thirds majority of all its members.

Voting on financial matters

For decisions on some financial matters set out in the Statute of the ESCB, the votes in the Governing Council are weighted according to the NCBs' shares in the subscribed capital of the ECB. In line with Article 46.3 of the Statute, the term "subscribed capital of the ECB" is to be read as the capital of the ECB subscribed by the euro area NCBs, i.e. excluding the shares subscribed by the non-euro area NCBs. The votes of the Executive Board members are zero-weighted. As already mentioned above, in the case of weighted voting, governors who are unable to participate may appoint an alternate to cast their vote.

Under Article 10.3 of the Statute, financial matters requiring weighted voting are: the paying-up and increases in the ECB's capital (Article 28), revisions of the ECB's key for capital subscription (Article 29), transfers of foreign reserve assets to the ECB (Article 30), the allocation of NCBs' monetary income (Articles 32 and 51) and the allocation of the ECB's net profits and losses (Article 33).

As a rule, the Governing Council decides by simple majority of the weighted votes, i.e. a decision is adopted if the votes cast in its favour represent more than 50% of the subscribed capital of the ECB. For some decisions (such as increases in the capital of the ECB in line with Article 28.3 of the Statute and derogations from the rules for the allocation of monetary income in line with Article 32.3 of the Statute), a qualified majority of two-thirds and at least half of the shareholders is required.

Date and place of meetings and confidentiality of the proceedings

The Governing Council meets, as a rule, twice a month. It conducts an in-depth assessment of monetary and economic developments and takes related decisions specifically at its first meeting in the month. The first meeting of the month is usually followed by a press conference in which the President and the Vice-President report on the outcome of the deliberations. The second meeting usually focuses on issues related to other tasks and responsibilities of the ECB and the Eurosystem.

Meetings of the Governing Council are in general held at the premises of the ECB in Frankfurt. However, since 2000, two meetings per year are held outside Frankfurt in member countries of the euro area and hosted by the respective central bank. Occasionally, meetings are held by teleconference. Furthermore, decisions may be taken by written procedure.

Box 8 Members of the Governing Council (1 June 1998 to 1 July 2004)

President of the ECB

Willem F. Duisenberg	1 June 1998 to 31 October 2003
Jean-Claude Trichet	since 1 November 2003

Vice-President of the ECB

Christian Noyer	1 June 1998 to 31 May 2002
Lucas D. Papademos	since 1 June 2002

Other Executive Board members

Sirkka Hämäläinen	1 June 1998 to 31 May 2003
Eugenio Domingo Solans	1 June 1998 to 31 May 2004
Otmar Issing	since 1 June 1998
Tommaso Padoa-Schioppa	since 1 June 1998
Gertrude Tumpel-Gugerell	since 1 June 2003
José Manuel González-Páramo	since 1 June 2004

Euro area NCB governors

Nationale Bank van België/Banque Nationale de Belgique

Alfons Verplaetse	1 June 1998 to 28 February 1999
Guy Quaden	since 1 March 1999

Deutsche Bundesbank

Hans Tietmeyer	1 June 1998 to 31 August 1999
Ernst Welteke	1 September 1999 to 16 April 2004
Axel Weber	since 30 April 2004

Bank of Greece

Lucas D. Papademos	1 January 2001 to 31 May 2002
Nicholas C. Garganas	since 1 June 2002

Banco de España

Luis Ángel Rojo	1 June 1998 to 11 July 2000
Jaime Caruana	since 12 July 2000

Banque de France

Jean-Claude Trichet	1 June 1998 to 31 October 2003
Christian Noyer	since 1 November 2003

Central Bank & Financial Services Authority of Ireland

Maurice O'Connell	1 June 1998 to 10 March 2002
John Hurley	since 11 March 2002

Banca d'Italia

Antonio Fazio	since 1 June 1998

Banque centrale du Luxembourg

Yves Mersch	since 1 June 1998

De Nederlandsche Bank
Nout Wellink   since 1 June 1998

Oesterreichische Nationalbank
Klaus Liebscher   since 1 June 1998

Banco de Portugal
António José Fernandes de Sousa   1 June 1998 to 22 February 2000
Vítor Constâncio   since 23 February 2000

Suomen Pankki – Finlands Bank
Matti Vanhala   1 June 1998 to 15 March 2004
Erkki Liikanen   from 12 July 2004
(Ad interim, Matti Louekoski, Deputy Governor)

In line with Article 10.4 of the Statute, the proceedings of the meetings are confidential. While this provision does not allow the ECB to release the minutes of the meetings it does not prevent it from informing the public of all relevant aspects of the deliberations in the Governing Council (see Section 4.2.3).

Executive Board

The Executive Board is the operational decision-making body of the ECB. It is responsible for all the decisions that have to be taken on a day-to-day basis. Given the nature of monetary policy, the ECB is required to react and adapt to rapidly changing conditions in the money and capital markets, to address specific cases and to deal with matters of urgency. This function can only be performed by a body whose members are involved permanently and exclusively in the implementation of the ECB's policies.

Composition
The Executive Board has six members – the President, the Vice-President and four other members – who are all persons of recognised standing and professional experience in monetary and banking matters. Appointments are made by common accord of the governments of the euro area countries at the level of Heads of State or Government, on a recommendation from the EU Council, after consulting the European Parliament and the Governing Council of the ECB. Prior to the establishment of the ECB, the EMI Council was consulted in May 1998 on the six nominees for the ECB's first Executive Board.

The members of the Executive Board are appointed on a full-time basis. Their terms and condition of employment (e.g. salaries, pensions and other social security benefits) are the subject of contracts with the ECB and are fixed by the Governing Council (without the votes from the members of the Executive Board). In these matters, the Governing Council acts on proposals from a Committee comprising three members appointed by the Governing Council and three members appointed by the Council. The three appointees of the Governing

Council are current or former NCB governors, while those of the EU Council are chosen from among the members of the ECOFIN Council.

Responsibilities

The main responsibilities of the Executive Board are:

- to prepare Governing Council meetings;

- to implement the monetary policy of the euro area in line with the guidelines and decisions laid down by the Governing Council and, in so doing, to give the necessary instructions to the euro area NCBs;

- to manage the current business of the ECB;

- to exercise certain powers delegated to it by the Governing Council, including some of a regulatory nature.

Preparing the meetings of the Governing Council involves drawing up the agendas of the meetings, preparing the necessary documents for the Governing Council's deliberation and making proposals for the decisions to be taken. Thus, in practice, albeit not formally, the Executive Board has the right of initiative for decisions by the Governing Council.

Implementing the monetary policy is an exclusive competence assigned to the Executive Board by the EC Treaty; the Governing Council may not therefore perform this function. Responsibility for implementing monetary policy is substantiated in the Executive Board's power to adopt ECB instructions addressed to euro area NCBs; assigning this function to the Board ensures the ECB's capacity to react and adapt to rapidly changing conditions in the money and capital markets, and to deal with specific and urgent cases.

By delegation from the Governing Council, the Executive Board adopts and publishes the monthly reports (Article 15.1 of the Statute of the ESCB), the weekly consolidated financial statements (Article 15.2) and the consolidated balance sheets (Article 26.3) from among the statutorily prescribed reports of the ECB.[6] It also assumes delegated powers in relation to the management of the ECB's foreign reserve holdings. Finally, the Executive Board is also responsible for imposing sanctions on third parties for failure to comply with the regulations of the ECB (see Section 2.5.3).

In terms of managing the current business of the ECB, the Executive Board is also responsible for organising the internal structure of the ECB and establishing the rules for selecting, appointing and promoting the staff of the ECB (see Section 6.2).

---

[6] The Annual Reports are adopted by the Governing Council and the Convergence Reports are adopted by the General Council.

Procedures

Like the Governing Council, the Executive Board acts as a collegiate body. Article 11.5 of the Statute of the ESCB states that *"each member of the Executive Board present in person shall have the right to vote and shall have, for that purpose, one vote"*. The principle of collegiate responsibility means that decisions are subject to collective deliberation and that all members bear collective responsibility for them.

The Executive Board currently meets at least once a week. It normally acts by a simple majority of the votes cast by the members who are present in person. In the event of a tie, the President has the casting vote.

Specific responsibilities of the ECB President

As member of the Executive Board, the President of the ECB is a first among equals and bound by the decisions of the Executive Board. Nevertheless, the Statute of the ESCB gives the President a prominent role by reserving certain important functions exclusively for him (or, in his absence, the Vice-President): the chair of all three decision-making bodies of the ECB, the casting vote in the Governing Council and on the Executive Board, the external representation of the ECB (for instance at the international level), the presentation of the ECB's Annual Report to the European Parliament and the EU Council and the possibility to attend sessions of the ECOFIN Council and the Eurogroup. Under the ECB's Rules of Procedure, decisions on the individual responsibilities of the members of the Executive Board with respect to the current business of the ECB cannot be taken against the vote of the President.

General Council

The General Council ensures an institutional link between the Eurosystem and the NCBs of the non-euro area Member States. Its existence, composition and responsibilities are a consequence of the different levels of integration in EMU (see Section 1.2.2). As such, the General Council will be dissolved when all EU Member States have adopted the euro as their currency.

The status of the General Council as a decision-making body of the ESCB underlines the importance which the authors of the Treaty attached to preserving links and cooperation with the NCBs of EU Member States that have not yet adopted the euro.

Composition

The General Council comprises the President and Vice-President of the ECB and the governors of all EU NCBs; so it currently has 27 members. The other four members of the Executive Board may attend meetings but do not have a right to vote. As with the Governing Council, the President of the EU Council and a member of the European Commission may also participate in General Council meetings, but they do not possess voting rights either.

Responsibilities

The General Council performs the tasks taken over from the EMI which, given that not all Member States have adopted the euro, still have to be performed by the ECB in Stage Three of EMU. Therefore, it is primarily responsible for giving advice on the necessary preparations for joining the Eurosystem. In this context, the General Council also adopts the convergence reports which are required by the Treaty (see Section 1.2.2).

The General Council also monitors the functioning of ERM II (see Section 3.2.1). In this context, it assesses the sustainability of the bilateral exchange rate between each participating non-euro area currency and the euro and serves as a forum for monetary and exchange rate policy coordination and for administering the intervention and financing mechanism of ERM II.

Furthermore, the General Council:

• monitors whether the EU NCBs and the ECB comply with the provisions of Articles 101 (overdraft and credit facilities) and 102 (ban on privileged access to financial institutions) of the EC Treaty (see Section 2.5.5);

• contributes to activities such as the ECB's advisory functions and the collection of statistical information (see Sections 2.5.4 and 3.5);

• is consulted on changes to the rules on accounting and financial reporting, the determination of the ECB's key for capital subscription and the conditions of employment of ECB staff.

The ECB President is required to inform the General Council of the decisions taken by the Governing Council to ensure that the governors of the non-euro area NCBs receive direct information about the Governing Council deliberations.

Procedures

The General Council has adopted its own Rules of Procedure and is chaired by the President of the ECB or, in his absence, the Vice-President. It normally meets four times a year in Frankfurt am Main; meetings may also be held by teleconference.

2.5.2 Consistent implementation of policy decisions

To ensure that ECB policies are implemented consistently and the system remains integral, the ECB issues guidelines and instructions for the decentralised execution of Eurosystem operations. It also hosts and supports the ESCB committees, which have been established as a forum for intra-system cooperation. The ECB is also the "hub" of several common operational systems that ensure the real-time exchange of information between the ECB and the NCBs and thus enable the ECB to monitor all decentralised operations and ensure compliance with guidelines and instructions.

Intra-Eurosystem legal acts

There are three intra-Eurosystem legal acts, namely:

• ECB guidelines;
• ECB instructions;
• internal decisions.

ECB guidelines and ECB instructions are special types of legally binding and judicially enforceable instruments. They are enacted to ensure that decentralised operations are carried out consistently by the NCBs in line with the internal division of competences.

As ECB guidelines and instructions are part of Community law, they prevail over pre-existing and subsequent national legislation within their scope of applicability (principle of supremacy).[7] It is up to the Governing Council to ensure compliance with ECB guidelines and instructions. The Executive Board supports the Governing Council in this task with regular compliance reports.

The ECB is also competent to adopt internal decisions on organisational, administrative or financial matters of the Eurosystem. These internal decisions are also legally binding for all members of the Eurosystem.

The formal requirements for the adoption of ECB guidelines, instructions and internal decisions are not specified in either the Treaty or the Statute; they are laid down in the ECB's Rules of Procedure, and follow the general principles of Community law.

Given that the legal effect of these instruments is intra-Eurosystem only, there are no obligations under Community law to publish ECB guidelines, instructions and internal decisions. However, in the interests of transparency, the ECB generally publishes guidelines and internal decisions that are of interest to market operators and the general public. The few legal acts that are not published tend to be those referring to detailed technical and operational issues, especially where changes are likely to be frequent for operational reasons.

ECB guidelines

ECB guidelines set the general framework and main rules for the NCBs' decentralised execution of Eurosystem operations and the collection of statistics.

As ECB guidelines are internal to the Eurosystem and only addressed to the euro area NCBs, they do not affect – directly or individually – the legal rights of the NCBs' counterparties. To become effective, their provisions need to be substantiated by the NCBs into the respective relationships with their counterparties.

---

[7] However, so far there have been no cases of conflict between an ECB guideline and a national law; the ECB's policy has always been to ensure that its guidelines are compatible with national law.

Given the differences in the financial market structures and legal systems of the euro area countries, ECB guidelines have been designed to allow some leeway for this substantiation, insofar as this is compatible with the requirements of a single monetary policy in the euro area. Depending on the legal arrangements of individual NCBs, these relationships are governed either by means of contracts concluded between the NCBs and their counterparties, or by regulatory acts addressed to the counterparties. However, although the formal substantiation of provisions may vary from country to country, this does not affect the substance.

In line with the ECB's Rules of Procedure, guidelines are adopted by the Governing Council and then notified to the euro area NCBs. With a view to facilitating amendments to the guidelines, the Governing Council may decide to delegate its power to adopt guidelines to the Executive Board, provided that it specifies the limits and scope of the delegated competences.

ECB instructions

ECB instructions are adopted by the Executive Board. They are designed to ensure implementation of monetary policy decisions and guidelines by giving specific and detailed instructions to the NCBs of the euro area. One prominent example is the instructions that are given by the Executive Board for the execution of open market operations (see Section 3.1.3).

Internal decisions

Internal decisions address internal organisational or administrative matters. These decisions are "atypical" in that there are no explicit addressees, but they are legally binding on the members of the Eurosystem.

Examples of such decisions (all of which have been published in the Official Journal of the European Union) are the ECB decisions concerning:

• public access to documentation and the archives of the ECB;
• the NCBs' percentage shares in the key for the capital of the ECB;
• the paying-up of the ECB's capital;
• the issue of euro banknotes; and
• the distribution of monetary income among the NCBs.

ESCB committees

The ESCB committees were established by the Governing Council, under Article 9 of the ECB's Rules of Procedure, to assist the work of the ECB's decision-making bodies. The ESCB committees provide expertise in their fields of competence and facilitate the decision-making process and implementation of decisions.

ESCB committees are usually chaired by senior ECB members of staff and report to the Governing Council via the Executive Board. Participation in the ESCB committees is usually restricted to staff members of the Eurosystem central banks. However, representatives of the non-participating NCBs take part in meetings when an ESCB committee is dealing with matters that fall within the field of competence of the General Council. If appropriate, representatives of other competent bodies may also be invited to attend ESCB committee meetings, such as national supervisory authorities in the case of the Banking Supervision Committee.

At present there are 12 ESCB committees. Besides the Banking Supervision Committee (BSC), the functions of which will be described in Section 3.7 in connection with the ESCB's statutory tasks in the field of the prudential supervision of credit institutions and the stability of the financial system, these are as follows:

- The **Accounting and Monetary Income Committee (AMICO)** advises on all intra-Eurosystem issues relating to accounting, financial reporting and the allocation of monetary income.

- The **Banknote Committee (BANCO)** promotes intra-Eurosystem cooperation in the production, issue and post-issue handling of euro banknotes.

- The **External Communications Committee (ECCO)** assists the ECB in its communication policy, particularly on issues related to multilingual publications.

- The **Information Technology Committee (ITC)** assists in the development, implementation and maintenance of IT networks and communications infrastructure which support the joint operational systems.

- The **Internal Auditors Committee (IAC)** develops common standards for auditing Eurosystem operations and audits joint projects and operational systems at the Eurosystem/ESCB level.

- The **International Relations Committee (IRC)** assists the ECB in performing its statutory tasks relating to international cooperation and acts as a forum for exchanging views on matters of common interest in this field.

- The **Legal Committee (LEGCO)** provides advice on all legal issues relating to the ECB's statutory tasks.

- The **Market Operations Committee (MOC)** assists the Eurosystem in carrying out monetary policy operations and foreign exchange transactions, and in managing the ECB's foreign reserves and the operation of ERM II.

- The **Monetary Policy Committee (MPC)** advises mainly on strategic and longer-term issues relating to the formulation of the monetary and exchange rate policy and is responsible for the regular Eurosystem staff projections of macroeconomic developments in the euro area (see Section 3.1.2).

- The **Payment and Settlement Systems Committee (PSSC)** advises on the operation and maintenance of TARGET, general payment systems policy and oversight issues, and issues of interest for central banks in the field of securities clearing and settlement.

- The **Statistics Committee (STC)** advises on the design and the compilation of statistical information collected by the ECB and NCBs.

Common operational systems

The ECB and the NCBs have established a number of common operational systems to make it easier to carry out decentralised operations. These systems provide the "logistical support" for the Eurosystem's functional integrity.

The common operational systems encompass information systems, applications and procedures. They are organised according to a "hub-and-spoke" approach, with the hub located at the ECB. The system owners are the competent ESCB committees, while the systems are managed by the competent business area of the ECB.

Eurosystem operations use the following common operational systems:

- Systems for tender operations and bilateral market intervention, which ensure the secure and speedy transmission of instructions for carrying out decentralised monetary policy operations.

- The system for the exchange of non-statistical data, which serves as the communication channel for the NCBs' and the ECB's daily balance sheet data, reported to the ECB's liquidity management function and used for the daily money market analysis.

- The common front office system, used for recording and processing of transactions carried out by NCBs with the ECB's foreign reserve assets, and by the ECB with its own funds, and for monitoring positions, limits, risks and performance.

- The Currency Information System, which monitors the NCBs' banknote stocks to identify potential shortages and surplus stocks of euro banknotes at the Eurosystem's different access points. This system makes it possible to correct imbalances by transporting surplus stocks of banknotes from one country to compensate for potential shortages in another.

Other common operational systems include the NCBs of the non-euro area Member States:

- The TARGET system (see Section 3.3).

- CebaMail, which is a closed electronic mail system for the secure exchange of information among the EU NCBs.

- The Teleconference System, which is a closed and secure system for holding teleconferences among the ESCB members at governor and expert levels.

- The Counterfeit Monitoring System, which enables centralised information about the details of counterfeit euro banknotes in the EU to be shared securely with all authorised parties.

- The Exchange of Statistical Data System, which ensures the secure and speedy transmission of statistical data in common format within the ESCB.

- The MFI Statistics and Monetary Database, which is the centralised register of the monetary financial institutions that make up the reporting population for money and banking statistics. Among them are the credit institutions, which are subject to minimum reserve requirements. The database also lists the assets which are eligible to be used as collateral in the Eurosystem's intraday credit and monetary policy operations.

Intra-Eurosystem reporting

Given the high degree of operational decentralisation, extensive intra-Eurosystem reporting is required to provide the decision-making bodies of the ECB with all the information and data necessary for the centralised implementation of ECB policies and thus to preserve the Eurosystem's functional integrity.

The Eurosystem's operations are reflected almost exclusively in the balance sheets of the NCBs and give rise to large intra-Eurosystem balances. These arise primarily from cross-border transactions via the TARGET system (see Section 3.3.1) that give rise to bilateral claims and liabilities between NCBs in their local accounts, but are also due to the arrangements for periodically allocating the euro banknotes in circulation among the Eurosystem central banks (see Section 3.4). However, in a single currency area, only the aggregated and consolidated results of these operations are significant for analytical and operational purposes. In this context, it is important that operations carried out by the NCBs are accounted for and reported according to a harmonised method, and that intra-Eurosystem balances are duly consolidated.

The Governing Council has adopted rules on the basis of Article 26.4 of the Statute for accounting and financial reporting in the Eurosystem[8]. Under these rules, the accounts of the ECB and the NCBs are prepared on a historical cost basis, modified to include market valuation of marketable securities, gold and all other on-balance-sheet and off-balance-sheet assets and liabilities denominated in foreign currency.

Given the large exposure that the Eurosystem bears in foreign exchange holdings, particular attention is paid to the issue of prudence. A prudent approach is applied particularly to the different treatments of unrealised gains and unrealised losses for the purpose of recognising income. Thus, realised financial gains and all (realised and unrealised) financial losses are recorded in the profit and loss account; unrealised financial gains are credited to a revaluation account. The mutual claims and liabilities of the Eurosystem central banks are offset against each other so that the consolidated financial statements reflect only the Eurosystem's position vis-à-vis third parties.

---

[8] Guideline ECB/2002/10 of 5 December 2002 on the legal framework for accounting and financial reporting in the European System of Central Banks (OJ L 58, 3.3.2003, p. 1).

The NCBs send balance sheet data daily to the ECB. The ECB uses these reports, in particular, for the daily money market analysis, which is necessary for the conduct of its monetary policy. They are also the basis for the Eurosystem's weekly consolidated financial statement, and the consolidated annual balance sheet.

The decentralised operational set-up of the Eurosystem also requires a large amount of non-financial reporting. A prominent example is reports that allow the ECB to check NCB compliance with its guidelines and instructions. Another example is the NCBs' regular reports on the flows of banknotes within the euro area, which are aimed at identifying potential shortages and surplus stocks of euro banknotes at the different access points of the Eurosystem.

2.5.3 The ECB's regulatory powers

In pursuing the tasks assigned to the Eurosystem, the ECB may also adopt legal acts that have a direct effect on third parties other than the NCBs of the Eurosystem (Article 110(1) of the EC Treaty and Article 34.1 of the Statute of the ESCB). These instruments are **ECB Regulations** and **ECB Decisions**.

The regulatory powers of the ECB enable it to fulfil its mandate autonomously without relying on legal acts by the Community institutions or the Member States. However, in line with the principle of limited powers, the ECB may only exercise its regulatory powers to the extent that this is *necessary* to carry out the tasks of the Eurosystem.

Undertakings that fail to comply with their obligations under ECB Regulations and Decisions are liable to fines or periodic penalty payments which may be imposed by the ECB under Article 110(3) of the Treaty and Article 34.3 of the Statute. The ECB exercises this power within the limits and under the conditions laid down in complementary legislation.[9]

All measures taken by the ECB that are intended to have binding legal effect are open to review or interpretation by the European Court of Justice.

ECB Regulations

As with the regulations adopted by the legislative bodies of the European Community, ECB Regulations have general application, are binding in their entirety and are directly applicable in all euro area countries. *General application* means that they are applicable to an unlimited number of entities and cases. *Directly applicable* means that ECB Regulations do not need to be transposed into national law. As *binding* legal acts, they impose direct obligations on third parties.

ECB Regulations are adopted by the Governing Council of the ECB and signed on its behalf by the President. The Governing Council may decide to delegate its

---

[9] Council Regulation (EC) No 2532/98 of 23 November 1998 concerning the powers of the European Central Bank to impose sanctions (OJ L 318, 27.11.1998, p. 4).

authority to adopt ECB Regulations to the Executive Board of the ECB, but in doing so it must specify the limits and scope of the powers delegated.

In order to be binding and enter into force, ECB Regulations must be published in the Official Journal of the European Union in all official Community languages.

To date, the ECB has adopted Regulations on the application of minimum reserves[10], on data to be reported for the consolidated balance sheet of the monetary financial institutions sector[11] and for statistics on interest rates paid and charged by them[12], and on the ECB's powers to impose sanctions[13].

ECB Decisions

ECB Decisions are binding in their entirety on the addressees and take effect on notification to them. They may be addressed to any legal or natural person, including the euro area member countries.

ECB Decisions may be adopted by the Governing Council or by the Executive Board in their respective spheres of competence. Decisions adopted by the Executive Board may be appealed by the party concerned to the Governing Council.

ECB Decisions are addressed to the euro area member countries when the ECB approves the volume of coin issuance in line with Article 106(2) of the EC Treaty. Decisions addressed to other parties generally concern sanctions imposed by the ECB for failure to comply with its Regulations, for instance, infringements on the minimum reserve requirements.

All ECB Decisions are issued in the language(s) of the addressees. The ECB may decide to publish its Decisions in the Official Journal, in which case they are published in all official Community languages.

2.5.4 The ECB's advisory activities

As part of its advisory activities, the ECB may adopt recommendations and opinions within its field of competence. ECB recommendations and opinions are non-binding legal acts. They are issued in the language(s) of the addressee. If they are of general relevance the ECB may decide to publish them in the Official Journal, in which case they are published in all official Community languages.

---

[10] Regulation (EC) No 1745/2003 of the ECB of 12 September 2003 on the application of minimum reserves (ECB/2003/9), OJ L 250, 2.10.2003, p. 10.
[11] Regulation (EC) No 2423/2001 of the ECB of 22 November 2001 concerning the consolidated balance sheet of the monetary financial institutions sector (ECB/2001/13), OJ L 333, 17.12.2001, p. 1, as last amended by Regulation (EC) No 1746/2003 of the ECB of 18 September 2003 (ECB/2003/10), OJ L 250, 2.10.2003, p. 17.
[12] Regulation (EC) No 63/2002 of the ECB of 20 December 2001 concerning statistics on interest rates applied by monetary financial institutions to deposits and loans vis-à-vis households and non-financial corporations (ECB/2001/18), OJ L 10, 12.1.2002, p. 24.
[13] Regulation (EC) No 2157/1999 of the ECB of 23 September 1999 on the powers of the European Central Bank to impose sanctions (ECB/1999/4), OJ L 264, 12.10.1999, p. 21.

ECB recommendations

There are two types of ECB recommendations:

- ECB recommendations within the meaning of the Community legal terminology are the instruments by which the ECB may initiate Community legislation in its field of competence;

- ECB recommendations in the more traditional sense of the term are the instruments by which the ECB provides the impetus for action to be taken.

Initiating Community legislation

The ECB shares with the European Commission the right to initiate the adoption of secondary Community legislation complementary to, or amending, the Statute of the ESCB. The Commission may submit proposals in all the areas where the ECB may make recommendations, but so far it has in general not exercised this right. The party that does not exercise its right of initiative is to be consulted by the EU Council before the legislation is adopted, i.e. the Commission is consulted when the ECB recommends legislation and vice versa.

Complementary legislation

Article 107(6) of the EC Treaty and Article 42 of the Statute of the ESCB specify the areas in which the EC Treaty requires complementary legislation to the Statute. These areas mainly concern the limits and conditions under which the ECB may require credit institutions to hold minimum reserves with the euro area NCBs (see Section 3.1.3), collect statistics (see Section 3.5), exercise its regulatory powers (see Section 2.5.3), increase its capital (see Section 3.8) or make further calls on foreign reserve assets (see Section 3.2.2). The EU Council adopted such complementary legislation – mainly on the basis of ECB recommendations[14] – at the start of Stage Three of EMU in line with Article 123 of the EC Treaty.

Amendments to the Statute of the ESCB

In addition to the normal procedure for Treaty changes (Article 48 of the EU Treaty), the EC Treaty sets out two special procedures for amending the Statute of the ESCB:

i.   the **simplified amendment procedure** as laid down in Article 107(5) of the EC Treaty and Article 41 of the Statute;

---

[14] See Recommendation (ECB/1998/8) for a Council Regulation (EC) concerning the application of minimum reserves by the European Central Bank (OJ C 246, 6.8.1998, p. 6); Recommendation (ECB/1998/9) for a Council Regulation (EC) concerning the powers of the European Central Bank to impose sanctions (OJ C 246, 6.8.1998, p. 9); Recommendation (ECB/1998/10) for a Council Regulation (EC) concerning the collection of statistical information by the European Central Bank (OJ C 246, 6.8.1998, p. 12); Recommendation (ECB/1998/11) for a Council Regulation (EC) concerning the limits and conditions for capital increases of the European Central Bank (OJ C 411, 31.12.1998, p. 10); Recommendation (ECB/1999/1) for a Council Regulation (EC) concerning further calls of foreign reserve assets by the European Central Bank (OJ C 269, 23.9.1999, p. 9).

ii.   the **enabling clause** of Article 10.6 of the Statute, which was introduced by the Treaty of Nice in February 2003.

The **simplified amendment procedure** applies to several areas of activities, for example, statistics, accounting, open market and credit operations, minimum reserves, clearing and payment systems, external operations and the allocation of monetary income. It enables the EU Council to adjust, with the assent of the European Parliament, technical provisions of the Statute as and when necessary without recourse to the normal procedure for Treaty amendments, i.e. an IGC and ratification by the EU Member States. So far, however, the simplified amendment procedure has not been used.

The **enabling clause** in Article 10.6 of the Statute allows the voting modalities in the Governing Council to be amended by an EU Council decision. But given the far-reaching implications of such amendments, the EU Council adopts these decisions in the composition of the Heads of State or Government. The enabling clause was actually activated in 2003. On the basis of a recommendation from the ECB, the EU Council amended Article 10.2 of the Statute. The amendment entered into force on 1 May 2004 (see Section 2.5.1).

Other recommendations

ECB recommendations, in the traditional sense of the term, may serve as instruments by which the ECB provides the impetus for action (not only of a legal nature) to be taken by Community institutions or Member States. For example, the ECB recommends the appointment of external auditors of the Eurosystem NCBs to the EU Council in line with Article 27.1 of the Statute of the ESCB. ECB recommendations to Member States concern primarily cooperation with national authorities on statistical matters, for example, the ECB recommendation to the statistical authorities (other than the NCBs) of some Member States on the ECB's statistical reporting requirements in the field of balance of payments and international investment position statistics[15]. Another example is the ECB recommendation to the euro area member countries on the abrogation of provisions limiting the amount of coins denominated in a national currency unit that can be used in any single payment[16].

ECB opinions

ECB opinions are delivered:

• whenever the ECB is consulted by the Community institutions or by the Member States in line with the Treaty or the Statute; or

• on the ECB's own initiative, i.e. whenever the ECB deems it appropriate, on matters falling within its field of competence.

[15] Recommendation (ECB/2003/8) of 2 May 2003 on the statistical reporting requirements of the European Central Bank in the field of balance of payments and international investment position statistics, and the international reserves template (OJ C 126, 28.5.2003, p. 7).

[16] Recommendation (ECB/2001/17) of 6 December 2001 regarding the abrogation of participating Member States' provisions limiting the amount of coins denominated in a national currency unit that can be used in any single payment (OJ C 356, 14.12.2001, p. 9).

The Community legislative bodies are required to consult the ECB on any proposed Community act that falls within its field of competence. Likewise, within the limits and under the conditions laid down in a Council Decision[17], EU Member States must consult the ECB on draft legislative provisions that fall within its field of competence. Subject areas include currency matters, means of payment, NCBs, the collection, compilation and distribution of monetary, financial, banking, payment system and balance of payments statistics, and rules applicable to financial institutions insofar as they materially influence the stability of financial institutions and markets. In addition, the authorities of the non-euro area Member States must consult the ECB on any draft legislative provisions on the instruments of monetary policy. However, the United Kingdom has been exempted from the obligation to consult the ECB by a Protocol annexed to the Treaty[18] *"if and so long as the United Kingdom does not move to the third stage* [of EMU]*"*.

Finally, Article 48 of the EU Treaty states that the ECB must also be consulted *"in the case of institutional changes in the monetary area"*. The ECB was consulted on the basis of this provision during the negotiations on the Treaty of Nice[19] and the draft Treaty establishing a Constitution for Europe[20]. The ECB welcomed the draft Constitution as simplifying, streamlining and clarifying the legal and institutional framework of the European Union. Despite this generally positive assessment, the ECB's opinion identified some articles in the draft Constitution which would benefit from further clarification and adjustment. Furthermore, the ECB intervened formally in the negotiations of the IGC. In a letter to the President of the EU Council dated 26 November 2003, the ECB's President conveyed serious concerns from the Governing Council on a proposal from the Council Presidency, according to which basic provisions governing the ECB's decision-making bodies could have been amended in a simplified procedure without ratification by the Member States. Subsequent to the ECB's intervention, the proposal was withdrawn.[21]

The ECB may also submit opinions on its own initiative to Community institutions or national authorities on matters within its field of competence. These matters are not limited to draft legislation but extend to all issues relevant for the ECB.

The ECB's advisory role ensures that it is involved in all Community and national legal acts within its field of competence and gives its advice as an independent Community organisation vested with its own exclusive competences. As the list of opinions published on the ECB's website shows, they cover a wide range of topics.

---

[17] Council Decision 98/415/EC of 29 June 1998 on the consultation of the European Central Bank by national authorities regarding draft legislative provisions (OJ L 189, 3.7.1998, p. 42).
[18] Protocol on certain provisions relating to the United Kingdom of Great Britain and Northern Ireland.
[19] Opinion on the amendments of Article 10.2 of the Protocol on the Statute of the European System of Central Banks and of the European Central Bank (OJ C 362, 16.12.2000, p. 13).
[20] Opinion on the draft Treaty establishing a Constitution for Europe (OJ C 229, 25.9.2002, p. 7).
[21] See ECB (2004), Annual Report 2003, Section 4.1.

2.5.5 Monitoring compliance with the prohibition of monetary financing and privileged access

Under Article 237(d) of the EC Treaty, the ECB is entrusted with the task of monitoring compliance with the provisions of Articles 101 and 102 of the Treaty and Council Regulations (EC) Nos 3603/93[22] and 3604/93[23]. Article 101 of the Treaty prohibits the ECB and the NCBs from providing overdraft facilities or any other type of credit facility to governments and Community institutions or bodies, and from purchasing debt instruments directly from them; an exception to this is the UK government's "ways and means" facility with the Bank of England[24]. Article 102 prohibits any measure, not based on prudential considerations, that establishes privileged access for governments and Community institutions or bodies to financial institutions.

Within the ECB, the General Council performs the task of monitoring compliance with these provisions since they apply to the central banks of all EU Member States. The European Commission monitors Member States' compliance.

The ECB also monitors the EU central banks' secondary market purchases of debt instruments issued by both the domestic public sector and the public sector of other EU Member States. According to Council Regulation (EC) No 3603/93, the acquisition of public sector debt instruments in the secondary market must not be used to circumvent the objective of Article 101 of the Treaty, thereby becoming a way of indirectly financing the public sector.

2.5.6 Performance of tasks taken over from the EMI

Since some EU Member States do not participate in Stage Three of EMU (see Section 1.2.2), some tasks of the EMI still need to be performed. Following the liquidation of the EMI, Article 123(2) of the EC Treaty and Article 44 of the Statute of the ESCB entrusted these transitional tasks to the ECB.

The two basic tasks taken over by the ECB from the EMI are:

• to foster cooperation between the Eurosystem and the non-euro area NCBs;

• to make the preparations required for the integration of new Member States' NCBs into the ESCB and for the eventual accession of non-euro area NCBs to the Eurosystem.

---

[22] Council Regulation (EC) No 3603/93 of 13 December 1993 specifying definitions for the application of the prohibitions referred to in Articles 104 and 104b(1) of the Treaty (OJ L 332, 31.12.1993, p. 1).
[23] Council Regulation (EC) No 3604/93 of 13 December 1993 specifying definitions for the application of the prohibition of privileged access referred to in Article 104a of the Treaty (OJ L 332, 31.12.1993, p. 4).
[24] Paragraph 11 of the Protocol on certain provisions relating to the United Kingdom of Great Britain and Northern Ireland.

The accession of ten new Member States to the European Union on 1 May 2004 and the prospect of further EU enlargement give a new dimension to the tasks taken over from the EMI. Although new Member States will only adopt the euro at a later stage, i.e. when they fulfil the necessary conditions, their NCBs have become ex officio members of the ESCB. As regards the recent EU enlargement, the ECB had been preparing the integration into the ESCB of the ten new NCBs for the past few years and, looking ahead, it is now considering the implications of these countries' eventual integration into the Eurosystem.

Also under Article 123(2) of the EC Treaty and in line with Article 9 of Council Regulation (EC) No 332/2002[25], the ECB administers the borrowing and lending operations of the European Community under the medium-term financial assistance mechanism[26]. The mechanism is based on Article 119 of the Treaty, which gives, among other things, assistance to non-euro area Member States in case of serious balance of payments difficulties. The proceeds of such operations may only be transferred to the central banks of the beneficiary Member States. Currently, the mechanism is not used.

[25] Council Regulation (EC) No 332/2002 of 18 February 2002 establishing a facility providing medium-term financial assistance for Member States' balances of payments (OJ L 53, 23.2.2002, p. 1).
[26] Decision ECB/2003/14 of 7 November 2003 concerning the administration of the borrowing- and-lending operations concluded by the European Community under the medium-term financial assistance facility (OJ L 297, 15.11.2003, p. 35).

Illuminated euro symbol in
front of the Eurotower.
Credit: ECB/Claudio Hils.

3 ECB POLICIES AND EUROSYSTEM ACTIVITIES

3.1 THE CONDUCT OF MONETARY POLICY

A detailed description of the ECB's monetary policy including theoretical foundations and practical implementation is given in *The monetary policy of the ECB*, published by the ECB in January 2004. The present publication limits itself to the presentation of basic considerations on this policy function.

3.1.1 Theoretical foundations

The capacity of monetary policy to ensure price stability over the medium term is based on the banking system's dependence on money issued by the central bank (known as "base money") to:

i.   meet the demand for currency in circulation;

ii.   clear interbank balances;

iii.   meet the requirements for the minimum reserves that may have to be deposited with the central bank.

Given its monopoly over the creation of base money, the Eurosystem is in a position to exert a dominant influence on money market conditions and money market interest rates. Changes in money market rates induced by the central bank set in motion a number of mechanisms and actions by economic agents, ultimately influencing developments in economic variables such as output or prices (see Box 9). This process, which is known as the "monetary policy transmission mechanism" and described in detail in the ECB's publication *The monetary policy of the ECB* is complex. Since it involves a number of different mechanisms and actions by economic agents at various stages, monetary policy action usually takes a considerable time to affect price developments. Furthermore, the size and strength of the different effects can vary according to the state of the economy, which makes the precise impact difficult to estimate.

However, it is a widely accepted proposition in the economic profession that, in the long run, i.e. after all adjustments in the economy have worked through, a change in the quantity of money in the economy (all other things being equal) will be reflected in a change in the general level of prices and will not induce permanent changes in real variables such as real output or unemployment. Related to this is the assertion that inflation is ultimately a monetary phenomenon. Indeed, prolonged periods of high inflation are typically associated with high monetary growth. While other factors (such as variations in aggregate demand, technological changes or commodity price shocks) can influence price developments over shorter horizons, over time their effects can be offset by some degree of adjustment of the money stock. In this sense, the longer-term trends of prices or inflation can be controlled by central banks.

Box 9   The transmission mechanism of monetary policy

The starting point of the transmission process of monetary policy is the changes in money market rates which the central bank can trigger through its control over money market conditions. Changes in money market rates in turn affect other interest rates, albeit to varying degrees. For example, changes in money market rates have an impact on the interest rates set by banks on short-term loans and deposits. In addition, expectations of future official interest rate changes affect longer-term market interest rates, since these reflect expectations of the future evolution of short-term interest rates. However, the impact of money market rate changes on interest rates at very long maturities (e.g. 10-year government bond yields, long-term bank lending rates) is less direct. Those rates depend to a large extent on market expectations for long-term growth and inflation trends in the economy. In other words, changes in the central bank's official rates do not normally affect these longer-term rates unless they were to lead to a change in market expectations concerning long-term economic trends.

Because of the impact it has on financing conditions in the economy – but also because of its impact on expectations – monetary policy can affect other financial variables such as asset prices (e.g. stock market prices) and exchange rates.

Changes in interest rates and financial asset prices in turn affect the saving, spending and investment decisions of households and firms. For example, all other things being equal, higher interest rates tend to make it less attractive for households or companies to take out loans in order to finance their consumption or investment. Higher interest rates also make it more attractive for households to save their current income rather than spend it, since the return on their savings is increased. Furthermore, changes in official interest rates may also affect the supply of credit. For example, following an increase in interest rates, the risk that some borrowers cannot safely pay back their loans may increase to a level such that banks will not grant a loan to these borrowers. As a consequence, such borrowers, households or firms, would be forced to postpone their consumption or investment plans.

Finally, movements in asset prices may affect consumption and investment via income and wealth effects. For example, as equity prices rise, share-owning households become wealthier and may choose to increase their consumption. Conversely, when equity prices fall, households may well reduce consumption. An additional way in which asset prices can impact on aggregate demand is via the value of collateral that allows borrowers to get more loans and/or to reduce the risk premia demanded by lenders/banks. Lending decisions are often influenced to a large extent by the amount of collateral. If the value of collateral falls then loans will become more expensive and may even be difficult to obtain at all, with the result that spending will fall.

As a consequence of changes in consumption and investment, the level of domestic demand for goods and services relative to domestic supply will change. When demand exceeds supply – all other things being equal – upward pressures on prices emerge. Moreover, changes in aggregate demand may translate into tighter or looser conditions in labour and intermediate product markets, and these in turn can affect wage and price-setting in the respective market.

Box 9   The transmission mechanism of monetary policy (cont'd)

Changes in the exchange rate will normally affect inflation in three ways: First, exchange rate movements may directly affect the domestic price of imported goods. If the exchange rate appreciates, the price of imported goods tends to fall, thus helping to reduce inflation directly, insofar as these products are directly used in consumption. Second, if these imports are used as inputs into the production process, lower prices for inputs might, over time, feed through into lower prices for final goods. Third, exchange rate developments may also have an effect via their impact on the competitiveness of domestically produced goods on international markets. If an appreciation in the exchange rate makes domestically produced goods less competitive on the world market, this tends to constrain external demand and thus reduce overall demand pressure in the economy. All other things being equal, an appreciation of the exchange rate would tend to reduce inflationary pressures. The importance of these exchange rate effects will depend on how open the economy is to international trade. The exchange rate channel of monetary policy transmission is less important for a large, relatively closed currency area like the euro area than for a small open economy. Clearly, financial asset prices depend on many other factors in addition to monetary policy, and changes in the exchange rate are also often dominated by these factors.

Other channels through which monetary policy can influence price developments mainly work by influencing the private sector's longer-term expectations. If a central bank enjoys a high degree of credibility in pursuing its objective, monetary policy can exert a powerful direct influence on price developments by guiding economic agents' expectations of future inflation and thereby influencing their wage and price-setting behaviour. The credibility of a central bank to maintain price stability in a lasting manner is crucial in this respect. Only if economic agents believe in the central bank's ability and commitment to maintain price stability will inflation expectations remain firmly anchored to price stability. This in turn will influence wage and price-setting in the economy given that, in an environment of price stability, wage and price-setters will not have to adjust their prices upwards for fear of higher inflation in the future. In this respect, credibility facilitates the task of monetary policy.

Source: ECB (2004), *The monetary policy of the ECB,* pp. 44-47.

The transmission mechanism of monetary policy is thus a complex web of economic interactions, and central banks are confronted with long, variable and uncertain lags in the conduct of monetary policy. The ECB may even face more uncertainty than many other central banks since it is responsible for a multinational currency area that was only established in 1999. Moreover, institutional and behavioural changes following the introduction of the single currency may have changed the relationships between different economic variables. As more information and research results have become available over time, a more detailed understanding of monetary policy transmission in the euro area has developed. Nevertheless, further progress is needed.

3.1.2 The ECB's monetary policy strategy

The first element of the ECB's monetary policy strategy is a quantitative definition of price stability. In addition, the strategy provides for a framework which ensures that the Governing Council of the ECB assesses all the relevant information and analysis needed to take monetary policy decisions in a forward-looking manner.

Taking a quantitative approach to price stability

Although the EC Treaty clearly establishes maintaining price stability as the primary objective of the ECB, it does not define what "price stability" actually means.

With this in mind, in October 1998 the Governing Council of the ECB announced a quantitative definition of price stability. There were three main reasons for choosing a quantitative approach:

1. The definition helps to make monetary policy more **transparent**.

2. A quantitative definition provides a **yardstick** against which the public can hold the ECB accountable. As deviations of price developments from price stability can be easily identified, the ECB must account for sustained deviations from this definition and explain how price stability will be re-established within an acceptable period of time.

3. The definition is intended to **guide** expectations of future price developments and thus build up credibility and increase the effectiveness of the ECB's monetary policy. The ECB's overriding commitment to maintain price stability should give both financial markets and the public good reason to expect that medium-term inflation will lie within the range deemed compatible with price stability. Stabilising longer-term inflation expectations in this way should help to prevent firms, trade unions and individual agents involved in the wage and price-setting process from incorporating higher rates of inflation into their decisions which, in turn, would make it more difficult to maintain price stability.

The ECB's definition of price stability

In October 1998 the Governing Council of the ECB defined price stability as *"a year-on-year increase in the Harmonised Index of Consumer Prices (HICP) for the euro area of below 2%"* and added that price stability *"was to be maintained over the medium term"*. The Governing Council confirmed this definition in May 2003 following a thorough evaluation of the ECB's monetary policy strategy. On that occasion, the Governing Council clarified that *"in the pursuit of price stability, it aims to maintain inflation rates below but close to 2% over the medium term"*.

The reference to *"the HICP for the euro area"* indicates two things: first that the goal of the ECB's monetary policy is price stability in the euro area as a whole, and second that it reflects the public's usual focus on consumer prices. The HICP is the index that most closely approximates the changes over time in the price of a representative basket of consumer goods and services purchased by euro area households.

The phrase *"below 2%"* sets a clear upper boundary for the rate of measured HICP inflation that is consistent with price stability over the medium term. At the same time, aiming for low positive inflation rates *"close to 2%"* provides *"an adequate margin to avoid the risks of deflation"*[1] (see Box 10). In addition, it takes into account the possible presence of a measurement bias in the HICP and the implications of inflation differentials of a structural nature within the euro area.

Finally, the term *"over the medium term"* reflects the consensus that monetary policy cannot fine-tune developments in prices or inflation over short horizons of a few weeks or months. Changes in monetary policy only affect prices with a time lag, and the magnitude of the eventual impact is uncertain. This implies that monetary policy cannot offset all unanticipated shocks to the price level in a short period of time. Some short-term volatility in inflation is therefore inevitable.

The main principles of the ECB's monetary policy strategy

The ECB influences conditions in the money market, and thus the level of short-term interest rates, in such a way that price stability is best maintained over the medium term through the effects on the price level via the monetary policy transmission process. It does this in line with its monetary policy strategy to ensure that a consistent and systematic approach is taken to monetary policy decisions over time. Such consistency helps to stabilise inflation expectations and bolster the ECB's credibility.

Given the lags in the transmission process, monetary policy changes made today will only affect the price level after a number of months or even years. This means that central banks need to ascertain what policy stance is needed today to maintain price stability in the future. In this sense, monetary policy must also be forward-looking.

Furthermore, as the transmission lags make it impossible in the short run for monetary policy to offset unanticipated shocks to the price level (for example, those caused by changes in international commodity prices), some short-term volatility in inflation rates is unavoidable. In addition, owing to the complexity of the transmission process, there is always a large element of uncertainty surrounding the effects of monetary policy. For these reasons, a medium-term orientation of monetary policy is important: it is consistent with the ECB's statement that *"price stability is to be maintained over the medium term"* and avoids excessive activism and the introduction of unnecessary (and possibly self-sustaining) volatility into the real economy.

Finally, the ECB is faced with considerable uncertainty about the reliability of economic indicators, the structure of the euro area economy and the transmission mechanism of the single monetary policy, in particular during the first few years of EMU. However, all central banks face a large degree of uncertainty – this is certainly not unique to the ECB – and so a successful monetary policy must therefore be broadly based, taking into account all the relevant information and not relying on a single model of the economy.

---

[1] See ECB (2004), *The monetary policy of the ECB*, p. 51.

Box 10   Why maintain a low positive rate of inflation?

Avoiding deflation is important because it entails similar costs to the economy as inflation. Furthermore, once deflation occurs it may become entrenched as nominal interest rates cannot fall below zero.

• Maintaining a low positive rate of inflation reduces the probability that nominal interest rates will approach their lower boundary at zero. If nominal interest rates hit zero, there is likely to be increased uncertainty about the effectiveness of monetary policy. And if this event were to coincide with a strong decline in demand, such a situation could complicate the central bank's ability to restore price stability by using its interest rate instrument. Examples of this are rare and even if it were to occur, a number of effective monetary policy actions are still possible at zero nominal interest rates. Various plausible solutions for escaping from a liquidity trap have been proposed. Despite this, prevention is better than cure and a safety margin for inflation rates above zero helps to avoid the need to test the effectiveness of these alternative policies in practice.

In order to calibrate the safety margin for inflation rates, the ECB took account of studies which have tried to assess the likelihood of nominal interest rates hitting the zero lower boundary for various levels of inflation objective. Results in this area differ to some extent, as they depend on a number of specific assumptions. But the available studies indicate that the likelihood decreases dramatically when the central bank aims at an inflation rate above 1%.

• The second reason for aiming at low positive inflation is that inflation statistics may be subject to a positive measurement error. This error would imply that zero inflation means de facto a declining price level. In the specific case of the HICP, the precise estimation of such a measurement bias continues to be surrounded by uncertainty. But taking into account the continuous improvements implemented by Eurostat in the index, the bias is likely to be small and to decline further in the future.

• The third reason for aiming at low positive inflation is linked to the possible presence of sustained inflation differentials within the euro area. In principle, inflation differentials across the regions are a normal feature of any monetary union. They are an integral part of the adjustment mechanism resulting from divergent economic developments across regions forming the area in which monetary union has been established. However, the single monetary policy can only influence the price level of the area as a whole; it cannot address inflation differentials, in the same way that monetary policy in a single country cannot reduce inflation differentials across regions or cities.

Inflation differentials due to transitory factors are of little economic concern. Of greater concern are the structural inflation differentials resulting from incomplete real convergence between regions, for example, initial differences in income levels and an ongoing catch-up process in standards of living. Their emergence could potentially create economic problems in countries or regions with below-average inflation, particularly if downward nominal rigidities impede the necessary adjustment of relative prices and thus hamper the efficient allocation of resources.

Box 10   Why maintain a low positive rate of inflation? (cont'd)

It has been argued that the ECB's monetary policy should target a medium-term inflation rate for the euro area that is high enough to prevent regions with structurally lower inflation rates from having to meet the costs of possible downward nominal rigidities or entering periods of protracted deflation. Available studies agree that a rate of inflation below but close to 2% for the euro area provides a sufficient margin in this respect.

The two-pillar approach of the ECB's monetary policy strategy

The Governing Council of the ECB agreed on the main elements of its monetary policy strategy in October 1998. The strategy was confirmed and further clarified in May 2003 after an extensive review of all relevant aspects.

In addition to the definition of price stability, the ECB uses two analytical perspectives (referred to as the two "pillars") as the basis for its approach to organising, evaluating and cross-checking the information relevant for assessing the risks to price stability:

• The first perspective is aimed at assessing the short to medium-term determinants of price developments, with a focus on real activity and financial conditions in the economy (**economic analysis**).

• The second perspective (**monetary analysis**) mainly serves as a means to cross-check, from a medium to long-term perspective, the indications from the economic analysis.

The two-pillar approach (see Box 11) ensures that appropriate attention is paid to different perspectives to be able to make an overall judgement of the risks to price stability. The diversified approach to the interpretation of economic conditions reduces the risk of policy error caused by over-reliance on a single indicator, forecast or model.

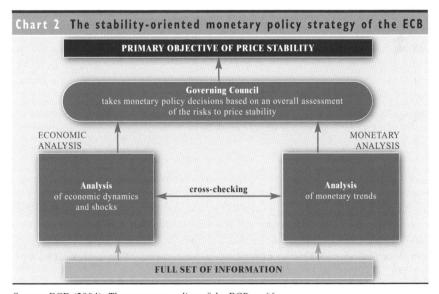

Chart 2   The stability-oriented monetary policy strategy of the ECB

PRIMARY OBJECTIVE OF PRICE STABILITY

Governing Council
takes monetary policy decisions based on an overall assessment
of the risks to price stability

ECONOMIC ANALYSIS

MONETARY ANALYSIS

Analysis of economic dynamics and shocks

cross-checking

Analysis of monetary trends

FULL SET OF INFORMATION

Source: ECB (2004), *The monetary policy of the ECB*, p. 66.

Box II   The two pillars of the ECB's monetary policy strategy

The two pillars of the ECB's monetary policy strategy are **economic analysis** and **monetary analysis**.

Economic analysis

The economic analysis focuses on the assessment of current economic and financial developments and the implied short to medium-term risks to price stability. It analyses all factors which are helpful in assessing the dynamics of real activity and the likely development of prices in terms of the interplay between supply and demand in the goods, services and labour markets. The economic analysis also pays due attention to the need to identify the nature of shocks hitting the economy, their effects on cost and pricing behaviour and the short to medium-term prospects for their propagation. To take appropriate decisions, the Governing Council needs to have a comprehensive understanding of the prevailing economic situation and be aware of the specific nature and magnitude of economic disturbances which threaten price stability.

The ECB regularly reviews developments in overall output, demand and labour market conditions, a broad range of price and cost indicators, fiscal policy, and the balance of payments for the euro area. Developments in financial market indicators and asset prices are also closely monitored. Movements in asset prices may affect price developments via income and wealth effects. For example, as equity prices rise, share-owning households become wealthier and may choose to spend more on consumption. This adds to consumer demand and may fuel domestic inflationary pressures. Conversely, should equity prices fall, households may reduce consumption.

Asset prices and financial yields can also be used to derive information about expectations in the financial markets, including expected future price developments. For example, when buying and selling bonds, financial market participants implicitly express expectations about future developments in interest rates and prices. Using a variety of techniques, the ECB can analyse financial prices to extract the markets' implicit expectations for future developments.

Developments in the exchange rate are also carefully assessed for their implications for price stability. Exchange rate movements have a direct effect on price developments through their impact on import prices. Changes in the exchange rate may also alter the price competitiveness of domestically produced goods on international markets, thereby influencing demand conditions and potentially the outlook for prices. If such exchange rate effects alter the expectations and behaviour of wage and price-setters, the potential for second-round effects may exist.

The Eurosystem's staff macroeconomic projections, which are prepared twice a year by the staff of the ECB and the NCBs, play an important role in the economic analysis. The Governing Council evaluates them together with many other pieces of information and forms of analysis organised within the two-pillar framework; but it does not assume responsibility for the projections. The published projections are the result of a scenario based on a set of technical assumptions, including the assumption of unchanged short-term interest rates. In view of this, the projections represent a scenario that is unlikely to materialise since monetary policy will always act to address any threats to price stability.

Box 11   The two pillars of the ECB's monetary policy strategy (cont'd)

Therefore, the macroeconomic projections of inflation prepared by Eurosystem staff should under no circumstances be seen as questioning the commitment of the Governing Council to maintaining price stability over the medium term. Wage and price-setters, as well as firms and households, should rely on the ECB's quantitative definition of price stability as the "best prediction" of medium-term price developments.

Monetary analysis

The ECB's monetary analysis relies on the fact that monetary growth and inflation are closely related in the medium to long run. Assigning money a prominent role therefore underpins the medium-term orientation of the ECB's monetary policy strategy. Indeed, by taking policy decisions not only on the basis of the short to medium-term indications stemming from the economic analysis, but also on the basis of money and liquidity considerations, the ECB is able to see beyond the transient impact of the various shocks and avoids any temptation to take an overly activist course.

To signal its commitment to monetary analysis and provide a benchmark for the assessment of monetary developments, the ECB has announced a reference value for the growth of the broad monetary aggregate M3. This reference value refers to the rate of M3 growth that is deemed to be compatible with price stability over the medium term. In December 1998 the Governing Council set this reference value at $4\frac{1}{2}\%$ per annum and confirmed it in subsequent reviews. The reference value is based on the definition of price stability and on the medium term assumptions of potential real GDP growth of $2\text{-}2\frac{1}{2}\%$ and a decline in the velocity of circulation of money of between $\frac{1}{2}\%$ and 1%.

The reference value is not a monetary target but a benchmark for analysing the information content of monetary developments in the euro area. Owing to the medium to long-term nature of the monetary perspective, there is no direct link between short-term monetary developments and monetary policy decisions. Monetary policy does not therefore react in a mechanical way to deviations of M3 growth from the reference value.

The ECB's monetary analysis is not limited to the assessment of M3 growth in relation to its reference value. Many other monetary and financial variables are closely analysed on a regular basis. For example, developments in the components of M3 (e.g. cash in circulation, time deposits) are studied because they can offer an insight into the overall changes in M3. In this respect, narrower aggregates such as M1 may contain some information about real activity. Similarly, changes in credit extended to the private sector can be informative about financial conditions and, through the monetary financial institutions (MFI) balance sheet, can provide additional information about money. Such analysis helps to provide both a better insight into the behaviour of M3 in relation to the reference value and a broad picture of the liquidity conditions in the economy and their consequences in terms of risks to price stability.

3.1.3 Monetary policy operations

In accordance with its monetary policy strategy, the ECB steers short-term money market rates by signalling its monetary policy stance and by managing the liquidity situation in the money market. As well as steering interest rates by managing liquidity, the ECB can also signal its monetary policy stance to the money market by changing the conditions under which the Eurosystem is willing to enter into transactions with the money market.

In the operations of the Eurosystem, the ECB also aims to ensure an orderly functioning of the money market and to help banks meet their liquidity needs in a smooth and well-organised manner. This is achieved by providing regular refinancing to the banks and facilities that allow them to deal with end-of-day balances and to cushion transitory liquidity fluctuations.

Table 3 Eurosystem monetary policy operations

Monetary policy operations	Types of transactions		Maturity	Frequency	Procedure
	Provision of liquidity	Absorption of liquidity			
Open market operations					
Main refinancing operations	Reverse transactions	-	One week	Weekly	Standard tenders
Longer-term refinancing operations	Reverse transactions	-	Three months	Monthly	Standard tenders
Fine-tuning operations	Reverse transactions Foreign exchange swaps	Reverse transactions Collection of fixed-term deposits Foreign exchange swaps	Non-standardised	Non-regular	Quick tenders Bilateral procedures
	Outright purchases	Outright sales	-	Non-regular	Bilateral procedures
Structural operations	Reverse transactions	Issuance of debt certificates	Standardised/ non-standardised	Regular and non-regular	Standard tenders
	Outright purchases	Outright sales	-	Non-regular	Bilateral procedures
Standing facilities					
Marginal lending facility	Reverse transactions	-	Overnight	Access at the discretion of counterparties	
Deposit facility	-	Deposits	Overnight	Access at the discretion of counterparties	

The operational framework of the Eurosystem is based on provisions laid down in the Statute of the ESCB. It has been designed in compliance with Article 105 of the EC Treaty, according to which the Eurosystem "[...] *shall act in accordance with the principle of an open market economy with free competition, favouring an efficient allocation of resources* [...]" and in line with the following principles:

• operational efficiency, which enables monetary policy decisions to feed through as precisely and as quickly as possible to short-term money market rates;

• equal treatment of financial institutions, irrespective of their size and where they are located in the euro area;

• the decentralised execution of the Eurosystem's monetary policy operations through the NCBs;

• simplicity, transparency, continuity, safety and cost efficiency.

Simplicity and transparency ensure that the intentions behind monetary policy operations are correctly understood. The principle of continuity aims at avoiding frequent major changes in instruments and procedures, so that central banks and their counterparties can draw on experience when participating in monetary policy operations. The principle of safety requires that the Eurosystem's financial and operational risks be kept to a minimum. In particular, all lending to credit institutions must be collateralised as required by Article 18 of the Statute of the ESCB. Cost efficiency means keeping down the operational costs to both the Eurosystem and its counterparties.

Box 12 Open market operations and standing facilities

The Eurosystem's open market operations can be divided into the following four categories according to their aim, regularity and the procedures followed:

- main refinancing operations;
- longer-term refinancing operations;
- fine-tuning operations;
- structural operations.

Main refinancing operations

The main refinancing operations are the most important open market operations and represent the key monetary policy instrument of the Eurosystem. They provide the bulk of liquidity to the banking system and play a pivotal role in steering interest rates, managing the liquidity situation in the market and signalling the stance of monetary policy.

Main refinancing operations are conducted on a weekly basis and have a maturity of one week[2]. They are executed through standard tenders, a type of tender conducted in accordance with a pre-announced schedule and executed within a period of 24 hours from the announcement of the tender to the communication of the results. All counterparties fulfilling general eligibility criteria may participate in these operations. In principle, all credit institutions located in the euro area are potentially eligible counterparties of the Eurosystem.

Longer-term refinancing operations

In addition to the weekly main refinancing operations, the Eurosystem also executes monthly longer-term refinancing operations with a three-month maturity.

[2] In March 2004 the maturity was shortened from two weeks to one week.

Box 12 Open market operations and standing facilities (cont'd)

These operations are aimed at providing longer-term liquidity to the banking system. This prevents all the liquidity in the money market from having to be rolled over every week. Like the main refinancing operations, longer-term refinancing operations are conducted as standard tenders in a decentralised manner, and all counterparties fulfilling general eligibility criteria may participate.

Fine-tuning operations

The Eurosystem may also carry out open market operations on an ad hoc basis, i.e. fine-tuning operations. Fine-tuning operations can be liquidity-absorbing or liquidity-providing. They are aimed at managing the liquidity situation and steering interest rates in the money market, in particular to smooth the effects on interest rates of unexpected liquidity fluctuations in the money market.

In view of their purpose, fine-tuning operations are normally executed through "quick" tenders. These take one hour from their announcement to the communication of the allotment results. For operational reasons, only a limited number of selected counterparties may participate in fine-tuning operations. Fine-tuning operations can also be executed through bilateral procedures, where the Eurosystem conducts a transaction with one or a few counterparties without a tender.

Fine-tuning operations are normally executed in a decentralised manner by the NCBs, but the Governing Council can decide, under exceptional circumstances, to have bilateral fine-tuning operations executed by the ECB.

Structural operations

The operational framework also provides the Eurosystem with the possibility of conducting structural operations. Such operations are designed to adjust the structural liquidity position of the Eurosystem vis-à-vis the banking system, i.e. the amount of liquidity in the market over the longer term. They could be conducted using reverse transactions, outright operations or the issuance of debt certificates. So far, the Eurosystem has had no need to conduct operations to adjust the structural liquidity position of the banking system.

Standing facilities

The marginal lending facility provides overnight loans from the central bank against collateral at a predetermined interest rate. The interest rate on these overnight loans is normally substantially higher than the corresponding market rate. As a result, credit institutions only use the marginal lending facility to obtain funds as a last resort. Since access to the marginal lending facility is only limited by the amount of collateral available, the interest rate on the facility normally provides a ceiling for the overnight rate in the money market.

The deposit facility, by contrast, allows banks to make overnight deposits with the central bank at a predetermined interest rate. The interest rate on these overnight deposits is normally substantially lower than the corresponding market rate. Therefore, counterparties only make overnight deposits with the Eurosystem if they cannot use their funds in any other way. Just

Box 12 Open market operations and standing facilities (cont'd)

as the interest rate on the marginal lending facility provides a ceiling, the interest rate on the deposit facility normally provides a floor for the overnight rate in the money market.

The incentive for banks to use the standing facilities is significantly reduced by the rates applied to them. Thus, the average daily use of the standing facilities is in general limited. It mostly remains below €1 billion, demonstrating that they serve only to provide and absorb liquidity in exceptional circumstances.

Open market operations (see Box 12) are the most important group of monetary policy operations. They are generally executed by the NCBs on the initiative of the ECB, usually in the money market, i.e. the market in which the maturity of transactions is generally less than one year. Open market operations play an important role in steering interest rates, signalling the stance of monetary policy and managing the liquidity situation in the money market.

The **standing facilities** (see Box 12) – the marginal lending facility and the deposit facility – are available to the Eurosystem's counterparties on their own initiative. By setting the rates on the standing facilities, the ECB determines the corridor within which the overnight money market rate can fluctuate.

The operational framework is supplemented by the system of **minimum reserves** to be held by credit institutions with the NCBs (see Box 13). The key functions of the minimum reserve system are to help stabilise money market interest rates and to enlarge the structural liquidity shortage of the banking system, increasing the demand for central bank refinancing.

Box 13 Minimum reserve requirements

The ECB requires credit institutions to hold deposits on accounts with the NCBs: these are called "minimum" or "required" reserves. The amount of required reserves to be held by each institution is determined by its reserve base multiplied by a reserve ratio.

The reserve base of an institution is defined in relation to the short-term liabilities on its balance sheet. Liabilities vis-à-vis other credit institutions included in the list of institutions subject to the Eurosystem's minimum reserve system and liabilities vis-à-vis the ECB and the NCBs are not included in the reserve base.

The first key function of the minimum reserve system is to stabilise money market interest rates. This function is performed by the averaging provision. This provision means that credit institutions' compliance with reserve requirements is judged on the basis of the average of the daily balances on their reserve accounts over a reserve maintenance period of around one month. Credit institutions can thus smooth out daily liquidity fluctuations (e.g. those arising from fluctuations in the demand for banknotes), since transitory reserve imbalances can be offset by opposite reserve imbalances within the same maintenance period.

The averaging provision also implies that institutions can profit from lending in the market and run a reserve deficit whenever the shortest money market rates are above those expected to prevail for the remainder of the maintenance period. In the opposite scenario, they can borrow in the market and run a reserve surplus. This mechanism stabilises the overnight interest rate during the maintenance period and makes it unnecessary for the central bank to intervene frequently in the money market.

A second important function performed by the minimum reserve system is the enlargement of the structural liquidity shortage of the banking system. The need for credit institutions to hold reserves with the NCBs helps to increase the demand for central bank refinancing which, in turn, makes it easier for the ECB to steer money market rates via regular liquidity-providing operations.

The minimum reserve system was designed in such a way as to neither put a burden on the banking system in the euro area nor hinder the efficient allocation of resources. To achieve these objectives, credit institutions' holdings of required reserves are remunerated at very close to short-term money market interest rates. The remuneration rate corresponds to the average, over the maintenance period, of the marginal rate (weighted according to the number of calendar days) in the main refinancing operations.

3.2 EXTERNAL OPERATIONS

As far as the external operations of the Eurosystem are concerned, Article 23 of the Statute of the ESCB entitles the ECB and the NCBs:

• to establish relations with central banks and financial institutions in other countries and, where appropriate, with international organisations;

- to acquire and sell spot and forward all types of foreign exchange assets and precious metals;

- to manage the foreign assets they hold;

- to conduct all types of banking transactions in relations with third countries and international organisations, including borrowing and lending operations.

3.2.1 Foreign exchange operations

The most important type of foreign exchange operation of the Eurosystem is intervention on foreign exchange markets. Intervention operations are effected solely through the foreign reserves held by the ECB. They may be conducted in the currencies of countries outside the European Union, e.g. the US dollar or the Japanese yen, within the euro area's exchange rate policy. They may also occur in the framework of the intra-Community exchange rate mechanism II (ERM II).

In line with Article 105(2) of the EC Treaty and Article 3 of the Statute of the ESCB, the foreign-exchange operations of the Eurosystem have to be *"consistent with the provisions of Article 111 of the Treaty"*. Article 111 defines the institutional framework for the exchange rate policy of the euro area.

The institutional framework for the euro area's exchange rate policy

Under Article 105(2) of the EC Treaty and Article 3 of the Statute of the ESCB, the Eurosystem's foreign exchange operations have to be consistent with Article 111 of the EC Treaty.

- Under Article 111(1), the EU Council, acting unanimously, may conclude formal agreements on an exchange rate system for the euro vis-à-vis currencies outside the EU.

- Article 111(2) states that, in the absence of such an exchange rate system, the EU Council, acting by qualified majority, may formulate general orientations for exchange rate policy.

However, both these institutional measures must respect the primary objective of maintaining price stability and may only be initiated on a recommendation from the ECB or the European Commission, after consulting the ECB. In the case of a formal exchange rate system for the euro, the EU Council must take note of the ECB's opinion *"in an endeavour to reach a consensus consistent with the objective of price stability"* (Article 111(1) of the Treaty).

So far, neither of the above procedures has been initiated. At its meeting in Luxembourg on 13 December 1997, the European Council stressed that the exchange rate of the euro should be seen as the outcome of both economic developments and economic policies, rather than as an independent objective. In this vein, it stated that general orientations for the exchange rate policy of the euro area would only be drawn up under exceptional circumstances; for example in the case of a clear misalignment. Such orientations should always respect the independence of the ESCB and be consistent with the primary objective of the ESCB to maintain price stability

Intervention in non-EU currencies

In the absence of both institutional arrangements and an exchange rate target of the ECB, intervention on the foreign exchange market vis-à-vis non-EU currencies only occurred twice in the first five years of Monetary Union, in the autumn of 2000. Having declined continuously since late 1998, the euro exchange rate had become increasingly out of line with the fundamentals of the euro area and risked generating significant misalignments. This in turn could have had an adverse impact on the world economy and price stability in the euro area. Thus, on 22 September 2000, the ECB, together with the monetary authorities of the United States, Japan, the United Kingdom and Canada, initiated concerted intervention in the foreign exchange markets; the ECB intervened again in early November 2000.

The exchange rate mechanism II

A new exchange rate mechanism, ERM II, entered into force at the start of Stage Three of EMU. It replaced the European Monetary System, which had played an instrumental role in the move towards EMU (see Section 1.1.2) but had to be adjusted to the new environment created by EMU.

Like its predecessor, ERM II is an intergovernmental arrangement which is based on two legal documents:

• Resolution of the European Council on the establishment of an exchange-rate mechanism in the third stage of economic and monetary union, Amsterdam, 16 June 1997;[3]

• Agreement of 1 September 1998 between the European Central Bank and the national central banks of the Member States outside the euro area laying down the operating procedures for an exchange rate mechanism in stage three of Economic and Monetary Union[4], as amended by the Agreement of 14 September 2000[5].

The purpose of ERM II is to link the currencies of the Member States outside the euro area to the euro. The link is established by mutually agreed, fixed but adjustable central rates vis-à-vis the euro and a standard fluctuation band of ±15%. Narrower fluctuation margins may be mutually agreed if appropriate in the light of progress towards convergence.

[3] OJ C 236, 2.8.1997, p. 5.
[4] OJ C 345, 13.11.1998, p. 6.
[5] OJ C 362, 16.12.2000, p. 11.

Participation in ERM II is optional for the Member States outside the euro area. However, as stated in the above-mentioned Resolution of the European Council, a Member State with a derogation *"can be expected to join"* ERM II. Article 124 of the EC Treaty requires each non-euro area Member State to *"treat its exchange rate policy as a matter of common interest"* and to take account of the *"experience acquired in cooperation within the framework of the EMS"*. In line with Articles 122 and 123, membership in ERM II for at least two years without severe tensions is one of the criteria for assessing whether a Member State has fulfilled the conditions for adopting the euro as its currency. ERM II therefore fosters convergence and helps the Member States outside the euro area in their efforts to adopt the euro. It also helps to protect the Member States inside and outside the euro area from unwarranted pressures in the foreign exchange markets.

Decisions on central rates and fluctuation margins are taken by mutual agreement of the finance ministers of the euro area countries, the ECB and the finance ministers and the central bank governors of the participating non-euro area Member States. The procedure provides for a multilateral discussion (normally at a meeting) which also involves the Commission and the Economic and Financial Committee (see Section 4.3.4).

Intervention in ERM II

Central bank intervention should a currency approach the margins of the fluctuation band is in principle automatic and unlimited. However, the intervention and financing obligations incurred by the ECB are without prejudice to the primary objective of maintaining price stability. Under the terms of both the above Resolution and Agreement, the ECB and the participating non-euro area NCBs could suspend automatic intervention and their financing if this were to conflict with their primary objective of price stability. In the same vein, all parties to the Agreement *"have the right to initiate a confidential procedure aimed at reconsidering central rates"*.

The Danish krone has been a member of ERM II from the outset, with a fluctuation margin of ±2.25% around its central rate vis-à-vis the euro. The Greek drachma participated in ERM II before Greece joined the euro area in 2001 (see Section 1.1.4). No intervention has so far been necessary to preserve stability in the system.

The number of participants increased recently when the currencies of three new EU Member States (Estonia, Lithuania and Slovenia) entered ERM II on 27 June 2004. The fluctuation margin is ±15% vis-à-vis the euro. ERM II membership is likely to expand significantly in the next few years as some further or all other of the ten countries which became EU Member States on 1 May 2004 join the system.

3.2.2 Management of foreign exchange reserves

Both the ECB and the NCBs hold and manage foreign reserves: the ECB holds and manages the foreign reserves that are transferred to it for the purposes set out in the Statute of the ESCB; those foreign reserves remaining with the NCBs are held and managed by them.

The ECB's foreign reserves

The ECB's foreign reserves are mainly held and managed to serve as a means of intervention by the ECB, should the need arise.

The size of the ECB's foreign reserves

Article 30.1 of the Statute of the ESCB provided for an initial transfer of foreign reserve assets from the NCBs to the ECB of up to €50 billion[6]. In January 1999 at the start of Stage Three of EMU the euro area NCBs transferred foreign reserve assets to the ECB worth €39.46 billion. This transfer was the maximum amount allowed under the Statute of the ESCB, adjusted downwards by deducting the shares in the ECB capital of the NCBs of the countries not participating in the euro area from the outset. When Greece joined the euro area on 1 January 2001, the Bank of Greece transferred additional reserve assets equivalent to €1.28 billion. The total amount of foreign reserve assets transferred by the NCBs to the ECB in proportion to their capital shares, for which they received in exchange interest-bearing euro-denominated claims, was equivalent to €40.74 billion. 15% of these transfers were made in gold and the remaining 85% in US dollars and Japanese yen.

Since then the ECB's foreign reserves have fluctuated markedly as a result of transactions and exchange rate movements. At the end of 2003, they stood at €38.3 billion. This net reduction in the value of the ECB's foreign reserves mainly reflected the ECB's intervention sales in the autumn of 2000 (see Section 3.2.1) and the recent depreciation of the US dollar compared with its level at the start of Stage Three of EMU. This decrease was partially offset by the higher market value of the ECB's gold holdings.

Furthermore, Article 30.4 of the Statute of the ESCB entitles the ECB to make further calls of foreign reserve assets beyond the amount of the ceiling on the initial transfer. Such calls are subject to secondary Community legislation. To this end, on a recommendation from the ECB, the EU Council adopted a Regulation[7] allowing the ECB to make further calls up to the amount of €50 billion. The ECB would only make these calls to replenish depleted reserves and not to increase its reserve

---

[6] When further countries join the EU, this initial limit increases automatically in proportion to the share of their NCBs in the subscribed capital of the ECB (Article 49.3 of the Statute). When the ten central and eastern European and Mediterranean countries joined the EU on 1 May 2004, the limit increased to around €55.6 billion. This automatic increase means that proportional transfers of foreign reserve assets can be made by the NCBs of all prospective euro area member countries without the ECB being obliged to retransfer foreign reserves to current euro area NCBs.

[7] Council Regulation (EC) No 1010/2000 concerning further calls of foreign reserve assets by the European Central Bank (OJ L 115, 16.5.2000, p. 2).

holdings. If deemed necessary, additional transfers of foreign reserve assets to the ECB may also take place on the basis of further secondary Community legislation.

Management of the ECB's foreign exchange holdings

The aim of the ECB's foreign reserve management is to ensure that, at any point in time, the ECB has an amount of liquid resources sufficient for any foreign exchange intervention. This implies that liquidity and security are the basic requirements for the investment of the foreign reserves. Subject to these constraints, the ECB's foreign reserves are managed in such a way as to maximise their value.

The ECB's foreign reserves are managed by the NCBs in line with the strategic and tactical investment framework that is determined centrally by the decision-making bodies of the ECB. This framework includes the currency distribution, the trade-off between interest rate risk and return, and the credit risk and liquidity requirements.

The Governing Council has defined the currency distribution of the foreign reserves of the ECB on the basis of prospective operational needs and may change it if deemed appropriate. There is, however, no active management of the currency composition of reserves for investment purposes, which avoids any interference with the single monetary and exchange rate policy of the ECB.

The ECB's investment decisions are conveyed to the NCBs in the form of investment benchmarks and limits to be implemented. When implementing these investment decisions, NCBs act on behalf of the ECB on a disclosed agency basis. This is so that the ECB's counterparties in the international financial markets can distinguish between the operations carried out by the NCBs on behalf of the ECB and those carried out by the NCBs to manage their own reserves. The ECB receives online information on the deals carried out by all NCBs on its behalf through a portfolio management system operating over the ESCB's own secure communications network.

The ECB has defined four key parameters for the investment of its foreign reserves:

i.   a two-level investment benchmark (i.e. a strategic and a tactical benchmark) for each currency;

ii.   permitted deviations from these benchmarks in terms of interest rate risk;

iii. a list of eligible instruments and operations;

iv.   limits for credit risk exposure.

Details of these parameters are not published to avoid any unwarranted impact on financial markets.

As regards the investment benchmarks, the strategic benchmark for each currency, established by the Governing Council, reflects the long-term policy requirements and risk and return preferences of the ECB. The tactical benchmark, established by the Executive Board, which must be kept within pre-set bands around the strategic benchmark, reflects the short to medium-term risk and return preferences of the ECB within the prevailing market conditions.

Concerning the daily management of foreign reserves, the NCBs have a margin of discretion within the deviation bands and limits defined by the ECB. The purpose of this is to make the management of the ECB's foreign reserves as efficient as possible.

The counterparties and intermediaries used in operations involving foreign reserve assets are selected by the ECB on recommendations from the NCBs. In making its selection, the ECB follows a uniform approach based on two sets of criteria:

• an assessment of the creditworthiness of the counterparties;

• efficiency considerations, in particular the research service provided, price competitiveness and counterparties' ability to handle large volumes in all market conditions.

The transactions conducted with the ECB's counterparties are documented under standard market agreements. The ECB has also developed a proprietary master netting agreement, which has been accepted by its counterparties.

From time to time, the ECB modifies the list of instruments eligible for use in its foreign reserve management. The choice of instruments aims to achieve an increasing degree of sophistication while meeting the requirements for high levels of security and liquidity.

The ECB's gold holdings

The ECB's gold reserves (approximately 750 tonnes of gold) are not actively managed. The ECB is party to the Central Bank Gold Agreement, which was concluded in September 1999 by 15 central banks, including those belonging to the Eurosystem. The Agreement was renewed in March 2004 for a further period of five years (see Box 14).

The NCBs' foreign reserves

The foreign reserves that have not been transferred to the ECB continue to be held and managed by the NCBs. At the end of 2003, the foreign reserves held by NCBs amounted to €332 billion, which is roughly the same value as at the start of 1999.

Since intervention on the foreign exchange markets is effected through the reserves held by the ECB, the foreign reserves of the NCBs no longer serve foreign exchange policy purposes. As explained above, however, they may be subject to further calls on reserves by the ECB.

European Central Bank
Banca d'Italia
Banco de España
Banco de Portugal
Bank of Greece
Banque centrale du Luxembourg
Banque de France
Banque Nationale de Belgique
Central Bank & Financial Services Authority of Ireland
De Nederlandsche Bank
Deutsche Bundesbank
Oesterreichische Nationalbank
Suomen Pankki – Finlands Bank
Schweizerische Nationalbank
Sveriges Riksbank

In the interest of clarifying their intentions with respect to their gold holdings, the undersigned institutions make the following statement:

1. Gold will remain an important element of global monetary reserves.

2. The gold sales already decided and to be decided by the undersigned institutions will be achieved through a concerted programme of sales over a period of five years, starting on 27 September 2004, just after the end of the previous agreement. Annual sales will not exceed 500 tonnes and total sales over this period will not exceed 2,500 tonnes.

3. Over this period, the signatories to this agreement have agreed that the total amount of their gold leasings and the total amount of their use of gold futures and options will not exceed the amounts prevailing at the date of the signature of the previous agreement.

This agreement will be reviewed after five years.

Source: ECB Press Release of 8 March 2004.

Article 31 of the Statute of the ESCB states that foreign exchange operations carried out by the NCBs with their foreign reserves are subject to prior approval by the ECB. This requirement ensures consistency with the single monetary and exchange rate policy of the ECB. It applies to transactions that may affect exchange rates or domestic liquidity conditions and exceed the limits established by ECB guidelines. NCBs' investment operations in foreign financial markets are not subject to prior authorisation since they do not affect the single monetary and exchange rate policy of the ECB. Transactions carried out by NCBs – either by themselves or on behalf of national governments – in fulfilment of their obligations towards international organisations, such as the BIS and the IMF, are also exempt from this requirement.

By analogy with euro area NCBs and in line with Article 31.3 of the Statute, EU Member States' transactions with their foreign currency working balances are also subject to control by the ECB.[8]

Banking services to official foreign customers

The central banks of the Eurosystem offer banking services to official foreign customers (non-Eurosystem central banks, monetary authorities, third countries and international institutions). However, the extent of this activity and the conditions under which such services are offered have hitherto varied among central banks. As regards reserve management services to official foreign customers, a common Eurosystem framework is scheduled to be implemented in the second half of 2004. The new framework will offer a range of services that will allow these customers to manage their euro-denominated reserve assets under harmonised conditions through any of the Eurosystem central banks that have opted to provide this range of services.

3.3 PAYMENT AND CLEARING SYSTEMS

The Eurosystem's task to *promote the smooth operation of payment systems* is substantiated in Article 22 of the Statute which entitles the ECB and the NCBs to provide facilities to ensure efficient and sound clearing and payment systems within the Community and other countries. To the same end, the ECB may issue regulations.[9]

Efficient and sound payment systems and securities clearing and settlement systems are indispensable for the effectiveness of monetary policy. The Eurosystem uses payment systems to settle its monetary policy and intraday credit operations. Since these operations have to be collateralised, the ability of the Eurosystem's counterparties to provide collateral rests on a sound and efficient infrastructure of securities clearing and settlement systems. The smooth working of both payment systems and securities settlement systems is also crucial for the functioning of the euro money market and, more generally, for other national and international financial markets (such as foreign exchange, securities and derivatives markets).

There are two basic kinds of financial risk associated with payment systems and securities clearing and settlement systems:

• the risk that a party within the system may be unable to meet its obligations either when such obligations fall due or at any time in the future (credit risk);

---

[8] Guideline ECB/2003/12 of 23 October 2003 for participating Member States' transactions with their foreign exchange working balances pursuant to Article 31.3 of the Statute of the European System of Central Banks and of the European Central Bank (OJ L 283, 31.10.2003, p. 81).

[9] So far, the ECB has not had need for recourse to the regulatory powers provided for by Article 22 of the Statute of the ESCB. For a more detailed discussion of the scope of the ECB's regulatory powers under Article 22 of the Statute, see the Article entitled "The role of the Eurosystem in payment and clearing systems" in the April 2002 issue of the ECB's *Monthly Bulletin*.

- the risk that a party within the system may have insufficient funds or securities to meet its obligations as and when expected, although it may be able to do so later (liquidity risk).

Both categories of financial risk might lead to a situation where the failure of one participant in an interbank funds transfer or securities clearing and settlement system to meet its obligations results in a domino effect in which other participants become unable to meet their obligations when due. Such a scenario could lead to widespread disturbances in the financial markets as a whole (systemic risk) which could also affect the broader economy.

In the case of securities clearing and settlement systems, there is also the risk of the loss or unavailability of securities held in custody caused by the insolvency or negligence of the custodian bank, or by any other adverse situation in which it finds itself (custody risk). This too has an impact on the ability of a participant to deliver securities when needed.

Besides being secure, payment and securities clearing and settlement systems should also be efficient and practical, both for their users and for the economy as a whole. However, there is always a trade-off between minimising costs and meeting other objectives, such as safety. Minimum safety and efficiency standards and recommendations are therefore warranted to guide stakeholders in payment and securities clearing and settlement systems in making their choices, which, in turn, fosters competition between payment systems and among securities clearing and settlement systems, and helps to avoid regulatory arbitrage.

In line with these considerations and the mandate given by the EC Treaty and the Statute of the ESCB, the policy objectives of the Eurosystem are geared towards ensuring safe and efficient systems. To this end, the Eurosystem:

- provides payment and securities settlement facilities;
- oversees the systems with a view to ensuring their efficiency and security.

3.3.1 Provision of payment and securities settlement facilities

In line with its statutory task to promote the smooth functioning of payment systems, the Eurosystem provides a wide range of payment and securities settlement facilities, the most important of which is the TARGET system.

TARGET (Trans-European Automated Real-time Gross settlement Express Transfer system)

The Eurosystem has developed TARGET to process large-value payments in euro in real time throughout the euro area. TARGET provides a level playing field for market participants and a tool through which the monetary policy-related transactions between the NCBs of the Eurosystem and credit institutions can be carried out in a timely and secure manner. It is the only payment system carrying out cross-border payments in euro which is directly accessible to all monetary policy counterparties. It thus enables the euro money market to function as a single market and makes a single monetary policy possible.

The current system

TARGET began live operation on 4 January 1999 and has a decentralised structure. It comprises and interlinks 15 national RTGS systems and the ECB payment mechanism (EPM). The 15 national RTGS systems are the systems of the 12 euro area countries and those of Denmark, Sweden and the United Kingdom. Given that these non-euro area NCBs had to prepare their TARGET connections prior to Stage Three of EMU, they have been connected to TARGET on a contractual basis. TARGET is also open to the new member countries but they have chosen to join TARGET when they adopt the euro, with the exception of Poland which intends to join in February 2005.

The ECB Guideline on TARGET[10] lays down the rules governing the operation of the system, including its national components. It also contains provisions on a number of minimum common features (e.g. access criteria, currency unit, pricing rules, time of operation, payment rules, irrevocability, finality and intraday credit) with which each national RTGS system participating in TARGET must comply. A multilateral agreement that mirrors the TARGET Guideline has been concluded between the Eurosystem and the three non-euro area NCBs.

TARGET must be used for all payments directly resulting from or made in connection with:

i.   the Eurosystem's monetary policy operations;

ii.   the settlement of the euro leg of foreign exchange operations involving the Eurosystem;

iii. the settlement operations of large-value systems handling euro transfers.

For other payments, such as interbank and commercial payments in euro, market participants are free to use TARGET or another payment system.

In 2003 there were 3,351 participants in TARGET with 43,450 branches being accessible worldwide. In the same year, 87% of the total turnover of large value payments in euro was executed via TARGET.[11]

TARGET2

The current structure of TARGET was decided on in 1994 and was based on the principles of minimum harmonisation and interconnection of existing infrastructures. This was the best way of ensuring that the system would be operational from the very start of Stage Three of EMU. However, in view of

---

[10] Guideline ECB/2001/3 of 26 April 2001 on a Trans-European Automated Real-time Gross settlement Express Transfer system (TARGET) (OJ L 140, 24.5.2001, p. 72), as last amended by Guideline ECB/2003/6 of 4 April 2003 (OJ L 113, 7.5.2003, p. 74).
[11] See ECB (2004), Annual Report 2003, Chapter 2.

increasing financial integration within the euro area and the fact that the business needs of TARGET users are becoming even more similar, preparations for a new enhanced system (TARGET2) started in October 2002. These preparations are aimed at TARGET2 starting operations on 2 January 2007.

Settlement agent for private systems

The Eurosystem also acts as settlement agent for payment systems that it does not operate itself. For example, the ECB is the settlement agent for the EURO1 system operated by the Euro Banking Association (EBA), and some NCBs settle for privately operated retail payment systems and securities settlement systems. The function performed by the ECB and some NCBs as settlement agents ensures that these payment systems settle in central bank money to minimise the risk of failures with critical systemic consequences for the financial system.

The Continuous Linked Settlement system

The Continuous Linked Settlement (CLS) system has been operating since 2002 to settle foreign exchange transactions between member banks on a payment versus payment basis in the books of the CLS Bank, which is based in New York. The US Federal Reserve is the main overseer of the system. The ECB provides account facilities for the CLS system and is the overseer for the euro which is the second most important currency in the CLS system.

Retail payment systems

The Eurosystem's involvement in retail payment systems is diverse. Several euro area NCBs, for example the Banca d'Italia, the Nationale Bank van België/Banque Nationale de Belgique and the Deutsche Bundesbank, have a long tradition of operating in retail payment systems. They offer neutral and open networks in which banks can participate, irrespective of the size of their business. The degree of Eurosystem involvement in retail payment systems will largely depend on the efforts of the banking sector to provide an efficient retail payments infrastructure for the euro in the future.

The correspondent central banking model

In the absence of adequate market facilities for the cross-border mobilisation of assets throughout the euro area, the Eurosystem has set up a correspondent central banking model (CCBM) for its own operations. This system ensures that all payment system participants and monetary counterparties are able to provide collateral for Eurosystem credit operations, irrespective of where the collateral is located. To this end, each NCB acts as a custodian for the other NCBs. The CCBM was developed as an interim solution, until such time as the market developed alternatives, and was not intended to compete with market initiatives to provide cross-border services for market operations.

Central securities depository activities

Eurosystem NCBs have traditionally played an operational role in the settlement of securities. Although various tasks have now been transferred to private entities, some of the NCBs still act as a central securities depository (CSD) or registrar for some government and other securities.

3.3.2 Oversight of payment and securities settlement systems

Payment systems oversight sets standards for the security of payment systems and ensures that they are applied correctly. Based on a combination of moral suasion and regulatory pressure, the main purpose of oversight is to protect the functioning of the payment systems. Oversight is therefore different from banking supervision. Banking supervision involves monitoring individual banks or financial institutions with a view to ensuring their financial stability and, primarily, to protect depositors and bank customers.

Since 1999 payment systems oversight has been a shared responsibility between the ECB and the euro area NCBs. The ECB is the overseer of European wide large-value payment systems (including TARGET) whereas the NCBs oversee the respective domestic systems.

Oversight is performed in line with the safety and efficiency standards which have been set by the ECB for payment systems operating in euro. In February 2001 the ECB took over the "Core Principles for Systemically Important Payment Systems"[12], which had been drawn up in January 2001 by the G10 Committee on Payment and Settlement Systems (CPSS).[13] These now form part of the set of standards that the ECB and the Eurosystem NCBs use for monitoring large-value euro payment systems.

As far as the oversight of securities clearing and settlement systems is concerned, the powers of the Eurosystem are less explicit and exclusive. However, since 2001, the ESCB and the Committee of European Securities Regulators (CESR) cooperate closely on securities clearing and settlement systems. A joint working group, composed of a representative of each central bank of the ESCB and from each securities regulator from the CESR, has developed European standards for clearing and settlement, based on the recommendations of the CPSS and the International Organization of Securities Commissions (IOSCO). These ESCB-CESR standards aim at increasing the safety, soundness and efficiency of securities clearing and settlement systems in the European Union and also take into account the need to remove the barriers to efficient cross-border clearing and settlement processes within this area.

---

[12] CPSS Publications No 43, *Core Principles for Systemically Important Payment Systems*, published by the BIS in January 2001.
[13] The CPSS is a standing committee which was established by the G10 central bank governors and which is hosted by the BIS (see Section 5.4).

The Eurosystem also encourages the market to think about future challenges and devise possible solutions. The Eurosystem provides a forum for discussion with market participants – through bilateral or multilateral meetings, presentations, speeches and publications – with a view to paving the way for further enhancements to payment systems and new infrastructure developments. In the field of securities settlement systems, the ECB closely monitors the consolidation process, pursuing a policy line that fosters efficiency, particularly in cross-border transfers of securities throughout the euro area.

3.4 EURO BANKNOTES AND COINS

Under Article 106 of the EC Treaty and Article 16 of the Statute of the ESCB, the Governing Council of the ECB has the exclusive right to authorise the issue of banknotes within the euro area. The ECB and the NCBs are the only institutions that are entitled to actually issue legal tender banknotes in the euro area. Under Article 106(2) of the Treaty, the issuing rights of the euro area countries have been limited to coins, *"subject to approval by the ECB of the volume of the issue"*.

Issuing modalities for euro banknotes

Between 1999 and 2002, in the absence of euro-denominated banknotes, national banknotes in the legacy currencies were the only legal tender banknotes in the euro area. They were issued by the NCBs under the authorisation granted by the Governing Council of the ECB, but in contrast to the subsequent regime for euro banknotes, each NCB issued its national banknotes for its own account and benefit.

Since 1 January 2002, the NCBs and the ECB have issued euro banknotes on a joint basis. Unlike the national banknotes in the legacy currencies, euro banknotes do not show which central bank issued them. Eurosystem NCBs are required to accept euro banknotes put into circulation by other Eurosystem members and these banknotes are not repatriated. However, although they may be considered to represent an obligation of the Eurosystem as a whole, it is necessary for the central banks to act as the legal issuers because the Eurosystem has no legal personality.

The ECB issues 8% of the total value of banknotes issued by the Eurosystem. Given that the solidarity scheme involves all members of the Eurosystem, the ECB acts as one of the legal issuers and therefore shows these banknotes in its balance sheet. In practice, the ECB's banknotes are put into circulation by the NCBs, thereby incurring matching liabilities vis-à-vis the ECB. These liabilities carry interest at the main refinancing rate of the ECB (see Section 3.8.1).

The other 92% of the euro banknotes are issued by the NCBs in proportion to their respective shares in the capital key of the ECB. The difference between each NCB's share of total banknotes in circulation and the amount of banknotes it has

The successful launch of the euro banknotes and coins on 1 January 2002 was the culmination of long and detailed preparations that had started in the early 1990s.

Euro banknotes

Work on the first series of euro banknotes was carried out by the EMI, as part of its preparatory work for Stage Three of EMU, and finalised by the ECB.

The preliminary work had actually started in 1992 under the auspices of the Committee of Governors. The long lead times for banknote production had led the Committee to set up a Working Group on the Printing and Issuing of a European Banknote (BNWG) comprising chief cashiers and general managers of the NCB printing works.

In June 1995 the EMI Council took advice from art historians and graphics and marketing experts and selected two themes for the banknote designs:

• "Ages and styles of Europe", representing seven distinct architectural periods of European history: classical, Romanesque, Gothic, Renaissance, baroque and rococo, the age of iron and glass, and modern twentieth century architecture;

• an abstract or modern design.

The EMI Council also concluded that the seven denominations of the banknotes should be €5, €10, €20, €50, €100, €200 and €500.

A design competition was launched on 12 February 1996 and ran for seven months. When the competition closed in mid-September, the NCBs first checked the designs for printability and compliance with the design brief and then sent the approved designs to a notary in Frankfurt am Main, who replaced the authorship identification with a secret three-digit code. The anonymous designs were then released to the EMI.

A jury of 14 independent experts in marketing, design and art history met at the EMI on 26 and 27 September 1996 under the chairmanship of the EMI's Secretary General. The jury members, who represented all the EU Member States except Denmark (Danmarks Nationalbank did not propose an expert because Denmark had decided not to join the euro area), assessed the designs on the basis of various criteria: creativity, aesthetics, functionality, public perception, gender equality and avoidance of national bias. After careful deliberations, the jury was able to draw up two shortlists of the five best design series for each theme.

Between 7 and 13 October 1996, Gallup Europe carried out a public survey on the ten shortlisted designs involving more than 2,000 people from all EU Member States except Denmark. The survey results, the jury appraisal and a technical assessment by the BNWG were submitted to the EMI Council in December 1996.

provisions and other legal acts adopted before the start of Stage Three. This secondary legislation defines three things:

- the entities from which the ECB is entitled to collect statistical information;
- the confidentiality regime;
- the provisions for enforcement.

Scope of the ECB's statistical function

The main areas of the ECB's statistical activity are:

- money, banking and financial market statistics, including statistics on monetary aggregates and their counterparts, interest rates, debt securities and quoted shares, and non-monetary financial intermediaries;

- balance of payments statistics and statistics on the Eurosystem's international reserves, on the international investment position of the euro area as a whole, and on nominal and real effective euro exchange rates;

- financial accounts (including government finance statistics); full sectoral accounts (in preparation).

The ECB publishes a wide range of data in these areas, together with statistics on the HICP, other prices, costs, output and labour markets, which are mainly compiled by the Statistical Office of the European Communities (Eurostat).

Statistical cooperation with Community institutions and international organisations

In carrying out its statistical activities, the ECB is required to *"cooperate with the Community institutions or bodies and with the competent authorities of the Member States or third countries and with international organisations"* (Article 5.1 of the Statute of the ESCB). To this end, the ECB cooperates most closely with Eurostat. On 10 March 2003 this cooperation was confirmed in a Memorandum of Understanding[18] between Eurostat and the ECB's statistics department. The Memorandum assigns statistical responsibilities as follows:

- the ECB is responsible for money and banking statistics at the EU level;

- the ECB and the Commission share responsibility for balance of payments statistics and related statistics, and for financial accounts statistics;

- the Commission is responsible for price and cost and other economic statistics.

---

[18] The Memorandum of Understanding on economic and financial statistics between the Directorate General Statistics of the European Central Bank (DG Statistics) and the Statistical Office of the European Communities (Eurostat) of 10 March 2003 is published on the ECB's website (http://www.ecb.int). It replaces a similar agreement between the EMI Statistics Division and Eurostat of 26 July 1995, which had been drawn up on the basis of the conclusions reached in the CMFB in the early 1990s.

The ECB and the Commission also cooperate bilaterally or through committees (in particular the Committee on Monetary, Financial and Balance of Payments Statistics (CMFB)) on all matters of common statistical interest, including any initiation of or consultation on relevant Community legislation.

The ECB also maintains close relationships with other international organisations, such as the IMF, in statistical matters. Wherever possible, ECB statistics conform to international statistical standards. Thus, the ECB also complies with the requirement to *"contribute to the harmonisation, where necessary, of the rules and practices governing the collection, compilation and distribution of statistics in the areas within its fields of competence"*, as laid down in Article 5.3 of the Statute of the ESCB.

Assistance by NCBs

Under Article 5.2 of the Statute of the ESCB, the NCBs are required to help the ECB in compiling statistics. In practice, the NCBs (and, in some cases, other national authorities) collect data from credit institutions and other sources in their respective countries and calculate national aggregates. The ECB then uses these data to compile the aggregates for the euro area.

It is worth noting that these provisions apply to all EU Member States and require the authorities of the non-euro area countries to cooperate with the ECB in performing statistical tasks. Article 47.2 of the Statute of the ESCB states that *"the General Council shall contribute to the collection of statistical information as referred to in Article 5"*. Although legal instruments adopted by the ECB have no binding force in non-euro area countries, the General Council, and therefore the NCBs of non-participating Member States, must involve themselves in the ECB's statistical work.

3.6 ECONOMIC RESEARCH

High-quality research has become an activity of growing importance in modern central banking. This applies in particular to the ECB which has to cope with the unprecedented challenges associated with conducting a single monetary policy in a multi-country area.

The goal of economic research at the ECB is to provide a strong conceptual and empirical basis for policy-making and to better communicate policy to the markets and the public. To this end, economic research within the Eurosystem is geared to increase knowledge of the functioning of the euro area economy and to provide models, tools and analyses relevant to the conduct of monetary policy and other tasks of the Eurosystem.

In many instances, ECB research is conducted within the framework of organised networks. These are groups of researchers jointly engaged in broad, multi-purpose projects. They may include economists from the ECB, euro area NCBs, other central banks and policy-making organisations, and academics. The ECB participates and provides coordination and organisational support, alone or with other institutions.

Another joint activity of the ECB and the euro area NCBs is the macroeconomic modelling of the euro area. Econometric models are used in the monetary policy decision-making process (for example in preparing the Eurosystem staff macroeconomic projections). Furthermore, model-building has been a catalyst for the development of new statistical data. Finally, Eurosystem research work is complemented by the organisation of central bank conferences, such as the ECB Central Banking Conferences and the conferences of the International Research Forum on Monetary Policy.

3.7 THE ECB'S CONTRIBUTION TO PRUDENTIAL SUPERVISION AND FINANCIAL STABILITY

Article 105(5) of the EC Treaty gives the Eurosystem the task of contributing *"to the smooth conduct of policies pursued by the competent authorities relating to the prudential supervision of credit institutions and the stability of the financial system".*

Institutional framework

The institutional framework for banking supervision established by Community legislation relies on two building blocks:

• national competence based on the principles of "home country control", minimum harmonisation of basic concepts and "mutual recognition";

• cooperation among the competent authorities.

Home country control and mutual recognition

According to the principle of home country control, the supervision of a credit institution is the responsibility of the competent authorities of the Member State where it was licensed. The principle of mutual recognition means that any licensed credit institution may provide local branch or cross-border banking services throughout the European Union on the basis of EU-wide mutual recognition of bank licensing and supervisory practices. For these purposes, Community legislation provides for the minimum harmonisation of basic concepts, such as the notion of a credit institution, criteria for bank licensing and common standards of prudential supervision and accounting principles.

Supervisory responsibilities are therefore carried out at the national level and are allocated according to institutional arrangements specific to each Member State. In some countries, the respective NCB is entrusted with banking supervision, either extensively or even exclusively. In other Member States, separate bodies perform banking supervision, but cooperate with the respective central bank.

EMU has introduced a separation between the jurisdiction over monetary policy (now the whole euro area) and that over national supervisory policies (the home country), which has led recently to substantial changes in the national institutional and operational arrangements in several EU Member States. The same applies to the scope of the supervisory functions beyond the banking sector. As a result, more and more supervision in all financial market segments is being concentrated within a single supervisory body.

Cooperation among national supervisory authorities

The need for cooperation among supervisory authorities was recognised at an early stage of progressing globalisation in financial market activity and the increasing scope of cross-border activity. Back in the 1970s two fora for multilateral cooperation in the field of banking supervision were created at the European level:

- the *Groupe de Contact*, a Committee of the European Economic Area (EEA) banking supervisory authorities, was set up to address issues relating to the implementation of banking regulation and supervisory practices, including the discussion of individual cases.

- the *Banking Supervisory Group* was created by the Committee of Governors and foreshadowed the current arrangements that are organised by the ECB.

The authors of the Maastricht Treaty were aware that EMU would heighten the need for cooperation in the supervisory field. However, in the absence of a clear vision of enhanced cooperation at that time, the Treaty left all options open. The mandate for the ESCB was formulated in a very general manner without specification of instruments, and the ECB's involvement was limited to advisory tasks. Under the enabling clause of Article 105(6) of the EC Treaty and Article 25.2 of the Statute of the ESCB, the EU Council, with the assent of the European Parliament, may confer upon the ECB *"specific tasks concerning policies relating to the prudential supervision of credit institutions and other financial institutions with the exception of insurance undertakings"*.

The enabling clause has not been activated in the recent reform of the EU's institutional arrangements for financial stability, which was undertaken to enhance cooperation within EMU and the Single Market. Cooperation in the field of financial regulation, supervision and stability was rearranged in 2004. The *Lamfalussy framework*, which had already been implemented in the securities sector, has been extended to all other financial sectors. The adoption of the new framework is expected to enhance the flexibility and efficiency of the regulatory process. It distinguishes between "level 1 legislation" (to be adopted by the EU Council and the European Parliament through the co-decision procedure) and "level 2 legislation" which consists of implementing measures that can be adopted more quickly and flexibly by regulatory committees ("level 2 committees"). Supervisory committees ("level 3 committees") ensure a more consistent implementation of Community directives and strive for convergence of supervisory practices.

In the field of banking legislation and supervision, the new Committees are the European Banking Committee (level 2), which has replaced the Banking Advisory Committee, and the Committee of European Banking Supervisors (level 3), which incorporates the Groupe de Contact. A Financial Services Committee provides advice and oversight on financial market issues for the ECOFIN Council.

The ECB's contribution

The ECB's contribution *"to the smooth conduct of policies pursued by the competent authorities relating to the prudential supervision of credit institutions and the stability of the financial system"* consists in:

• promoting cooperation among central banks and supervisory authorities on policy issues of common interest in the field of prudential supervision and financial stability;

• performing its advisory function under Articles 4 and 25.1 of the Statute of the ESCB;

• cooperating with other relevant fora operating in Europe.

The ECB promotes cooperation among central banks and supervisory authorities by hosting and supporting the Banking Supervision Committee (BSC). The BSC is an ESCB committee (see Section 2.5.2) established by the Governing Council of the ECB in 1998 to take over the functions previously performed by the Banking Supervisory Sub-Committee, created by the Committee of Governors in 1990 and subsequently established at the EMI in 1994. The BSC brings together high-ranking representatives of the ECB and the NCBs and supervisory authorities of the EU Member States. Its mandate, which was reviewed in 2004, is to assist the Eurosystem in carrying out its statutory tasks in the field of the prudential supervision of credit institutions and in ensuring the stability of the financial system.

By facilitating cooperation between the Eurosystem and national supervisory authorities, the BSC helps to provide a euro area-wide perspective on a variety of issues. In so doing it complements national views on financial stability issues and fosters the emergence of common stances on the challenges of an increasingly integrated banking system. Its joint analysis focuses mainly on the structural changes affecting banking business, the soundness of banking and financial structures, and possible threats to stability. In addition, the BSC serves as a channel for bilateral flows of information between the Eurosystem and national supervisory authorities.

The BSC also helps the ECB to perform its advisory tasks in the field of banking supervision and financial stability. Draft Community and national legislation in this field are subject to consultation of the ECB under Article 4 of the Statute. Furthermore, Article 25.1 of the Statute states that the ECB may offer advice on the scope and implementation of Community legislation relating to banking supervision and financial stability.

Finally, the ECB cooperates with other relevant fora operating in the field of prudential supervision and financial stability. In addition to the existing links with the Basel Committee (see Section 5.4.5), the ECB, assisted by the BSC, will contribute to the new EU structure for financial regulation, supervision and stability through its participation in the European Securities Committee and the two new committees mentioned above.

3.8 INTRA-EUROSYSTEM FINANCIAL RELATIONSHIPS

All euro area NCBs enjoy financial autonomy and generally perform Eurosystem tasks at their own cost and risk. However, intra-system financial relationships exist in two respects:

i.   the euro area NCBs have paid up their shares in the capital of the ECB, have endowed the ECB with foreign reserve assets and share the ECB's financial results;

ii.   the euro area NCBs share out among themselves the "monetary income", i.e. the income that accrues to them in performing the Eurosystem's monetary policy function.

Box 16   Key for subscription to the ECB's capital

The key for subscription to the ECB's capital not only determines the subscriptions of the EU central banks to the capital of the ECB (Article 28 of the Statute of the ESCB). Adjusted for the shares of the non-euro area NCBs it also serves as a yardstick for the distribution of the following financial rights and obligations among euro area NCBs.

• the contributions to the ECB's foreign reserve assets (Article 30 of the Statute);

• the allocation of euro banknotes in circulation among the NCBs and the allocation of monetary income (Article 32 of the Statute);

• the appropriation of the annual financial results of the ECB (Article 33 of the Statute);

• the weighting of voting rights in the Governing Council for decisions on financial issues specified in Articles 28, 30, 32 and 33 of the Statute.

Under Article 29 of the Statute, the shares of the NCBs in the ECB's capital key are weighted according to an equal measure of the shares of the NCBs' Member States in the population and GDP of the EU, as established and notified to the ECB by the European Commission in line with EU Council rules.

The key was first calculated in 1998, when the ECB was established, and is adjusted every five years. The first adjustment of the ECB's capital key took effect on 1 January 2004 and a further adjustment was made on 1 May 2004 in the light of EU enlargement.[19]

---

[19] See the ECB's Press Releases of 30 December 2003 and 26 April 2004 on the Key for subscription of the ECB's capital.

Table 4 Capital key of the ECB (%)

NCB	1 June 1998 to 31 Dec. 2003	1 Jan. 2004 to 30 Apr. 2004	from 1 May 2004
Nationale Bank van België/ Banque Nationale de Belgique	2.8658	2.8297	2.5502
Deutsche Bundesbank	24.4935	23.4040	21.1364
Bank of Greece	2.0564	2.1614	1.8974
Banco de España	8.8935	8.7801	7.7758
Banque de France	16.8337	16.5175	14.8712
Central Bank & Financial Services Authority of Ireland	0.8496	1.0254	0.9219
Banca d'Italia	14.8950	14.5726	13.0516
Banque centrale du Luxembourg	0.1492	0.1708	0.1568
De Nederlandsche Bank	4.2780	4.4323	3.9955
Oesterreichische Nationalbank	2.3594	2.3019	2.0800
Banco de Portugal	1.9232	2.0129	1.7653
Suomen Pankki – Finlands Bank	1.3970	1.4298	1.2887
Subtotal for euro area NCBs	*80.9943*	*79.6384*	*71.4908*
Česká národní banka	-	-	1.4584
Danmarks Nationalbank	1.6709	1.7216	1.5663
Eesti Pank	-	-	0.1784
Central Bank of Cyprus	-	-	0.1300
Latvijas Banka	-	-	0.2978
Lietuvos bankas	-	-	0.4425
Magyar Nemzeti Bank	-	-	1.3884
Central Bank of Malta	-	-	0.0647
Narodowy Bank Polski	-	-	5.1380
Banka Slovenije	-	-	0.3345
Národná banka Slovenska	-	-	0.7147
Sveriges Riksbank	2.6537	2.6636	2.4133
Bank of England	14.6811	15.9764	14.3822
Subtotal for non-euro area NCBs	*19.0057*	*20.3616*	*28.5092*
Total	**100.0000**	**100.0000**	**100.0000**

The resulting rights and obligations of the euro area NCBs are apportioned among them on the basis of the key for subscription to the ECB's capital. The method for establishing and revising this key is described in Box 16.

3.8.1 Financial resources of the ECB

The financial resources of the ECB consist mainly of its own funds, its foreign reserve assets and its claims on the NCBs resulting from the ECB's share in the issue of euro banknotes.

Own funds

The ECB's own funds are the counterparts of its paid-up capital and general reserve fund. The purpose of own funds is to generate revenue to cover the ECB's administrative expenditure and to serve as a buffer against losses which may result from the holding of risk-bearing financial assets, in particular foreign exchange assets.

The capital of the ECB

The capital of the ECB has been subscribed by the ESCB NCBs in proportion to their shares in the capital key of the ECB (see Box 16). Article 28 of the Statute of the ESCB set the initial amount of capital at €5,000 million. Under Article 49.3 of the Statute, as amended recently by the Treaty of Accession, the ECB's subscribed capital was increased on 1 May 2004 in proportion to the weight of the NCBs of the new Member States in the expanded capital key, and now stands at €5,564,669,247. This increase ensured that the weighting of the new NCBs in the capital key did not make it necessary to materially reduce the amount of capital paid up by the NCBs before 1 May 2004.

The euro area NCBs have fully paid up their subscriptions. Currently, the fully paid-up subscriptions of the euro area NCBs to the capital of the ECB amount to a total of €3,978,226,562.

In line with Article 48 of the Statute, the non-euro area NCBs are not required to pay up their subscriptions. Instead, they have to make contributions to cover the operational costs incurred by the ECB in connection with tasks performed for the non-euro area NCBs. These contributions were set by the General Council at 7% of the amount which would be payable if these countries were to participate in EMU.

Currently, the contributions made by the non-euro area NCBs amount to a total of €111,050,988. They do not entitle the non-euro area NCBs to any share in the income of the ECB, nor do they make them liable to fund any losses of the ECB.

Under Article 28.2 of the Statute of the ESCB and a Council Regulation of 8 May 2000[20], the capital of the ECB may be increased by an additional amount of up to €5,000 million. In line with the Regulation, the Governing Council may only decide on such an increase *"in order to sustain the adequacy of the capital base needed to support the operations of the ECB"*.

General reserve fund

Article 33 of the Statute of the ESCB states that the Governing Council may decide to transfer up to 20% of the ECB's net profit to a general reserve fund subject to a limit equal to 100% of the ECB's capital. This was done for the net profits earned by the ECB in 2000 and 2001. At the end of 2002, the general reserve fund of the ECB amounted to €773 million. It has now fallen to €296

---

[20] Council Regulation (EC) No 1009/2000 of 8 May 2000 concerning capital increases of the European Central Bank (OJ L 115, 16.5.2000, p. 1).

million because part of the accumulated reserves were used to cover the loss incurred by the ECB in 2003.

Foreign reserve assets

The foreign reserve assets mainly stem from the transfers made by the euro area NCBs under Article 30.1 of the Statute (see Section 3.2.2). Their value has varied since then as a result of foreign exchange transactions and valuation changes. At the end of 2003, the ECB held foreign reserve assets equivalent to around €38 billion.

As the counterpart of the initial transfer of foreign reserve assets, the ECB incurred liabilities vis-à-vis the euro area NCBs totalling some €40 billion. These liabilities are denominated in euro and determined by the value of the assets at the time of their transfer.[21] They are remunerated at the latest available marginal rate of the Eurosystem's main refinancing operations, adjusted to reflect a zero return on the gold component.

The foreign reserve assets and the related liabilities represent a very large share of the assets and liabilities sides of the ECB balance sheet and are a source of sizeable exchange rate and interest rate risks. Such risks materialised in 2000 and 2003: in 2000, the ECB recorded high profits from intervention sales of US dollars and Japanese yen; in 2003, however, it incurred sizeable losses when the US dollar weakened sharply against the euro and the exchange rate fell below the acquisition cost of the ECB's foreign currency holdings.

Claims and liabilities from the issue of euro banknotes

Since 2002 the ECB has been allocated a share of 8% in the total value of euro banknotes in circulation (see Section 3.4). This share is disclosed under the balance sheet liability item "Banknotes in circulation" and, at the end of 2003, amounted to €35 billion.

The ECB's share of the total banknote issue is backed by claims on the NCBs, which put ECB banknotes into circulation. These claims bear interest at the latest available marginal rate of the Eurosystem's main refinancing operations. This remuneration is the ECB's seigniorage income, but is distributed to the NCBs separately in the form of quarterly interim distributions. It is distributed in full unless the ECB's net profit for the year is less than its income earned on euro banknotes in circulation[22]. Conversely, if the estimates for the ECB's financial results suggest a shortfall the Governing Council may decide that the ECB's seigniorage income is retained partly or in full in order to offset the shortfall.

---

[21] The total liability to NCBs is subject to adjustment with the revision of the ECB's capital key, as the weightings of the Eurosystem NCBs change relative to those of the non-euro area NCBs in order to leave headroom for the latter to acquire claims of an appropriate weight in due course without breaking the prescribed limit of the euro value of reserve assets that may be transferred to the ECB.

[22] See Decision ECB/2002/9 of 21 November 2002 on the distribution of the income of the European Central Bank on euro banknotes in circulation to the national central banks of the participating Member States (OJ L 323, 28.11.2002, p. 49).

Allocation of profits and shortfalls

Given the particular structure of the ECB's balance sheet, with a very large foreign exchange component on the assets side, the ECB's financial results are heavily influenced by exchange rate and interest rate variations. For example, a depreciation of the US dollar against the euro by only 100 basis points reduces the ECB's net profit by some €300 million, which amounts to more or less the total administrative expenses of the ECB for 2003.

Under Article 33.1 of the Statute of the ESCB, the ECB's net profits, reduced by the interim distribution of its seigniorage income and a possible transfer of a portion to the general reserve fund, are distributed to the euro area NCBs in proportion to their paid-up shares.

If the ECB incurs a loss, however, Article 33.2 of the Statute provides that the shortfall may be offset against the general reserve fund of the ECB and, if necessary, following a decision by the Governing Council, against the monetary income of the relevant financial year in proportion and up to the amounts allocated to the NCBs (see Section 3.8.2). Thus, the net loss incurred by the ECB in the financial year 2003 (€476 million) was covered by drawing on the general reserve fund. The second option has not had to be used thus far. It is relevant in cases where the ECB's net income (including its share of 8% in the monetary income of the Eurosystem) is insufficient to cover losses.

3.8.2 Monetary income sharing

Under Article 32 of the Statute of the ESCB, the "monetary income" – i.e. the income that accrues to the NCBs in the performance of the Eurosystem's monetary policy function – is distributed to the NCBs in line with their respective shares in the capital of the ECB.

Intra-Eurosystem income sharing is limited to monetary income; all other income earned by NCBs (such as earnings on their own financial resources) remains with the NCB which earned it. In conceptual terms, monetary income is earned on those assets of the NCBs that are the counterpart of their liabilities in respect of both the banknotes they issue and deposits of credit institutions. Since deposits of credit institutions held with the NCBs are remunerated at or close to market rates and thus do not generate a significant amount of income for the Eurosystem, monetary income consists mainly of seigniorage income. This is the income arising as the result of the exclusive right of the ECB and the NCBs to issue non-interest-bearing banknotes with legal tender status.

It is necessary to share the monetary income because, in a single currency area, NCBs' monetary liabilities can shift freely and autonomously from one NCB to another. This applies especially to the NCBs' euro banknotes liabilities which are the main source of monetary income. As mentioned in Section 3.4, euro banknotes are legal tender throughout the euro area and are not repatriated. Furthermore, in the integrated euro money market, credit institutions are free to cover their needs in central bank money either by borrowing from their domestic NCB or other domestic money market counterparties or by raising funds from cross-border money market counterparties. This freedom of choice has an impact on the type of assets which an individual NCB acquires against the issue of base money and accordingly on the level of its actual monetary income. Thus, the creation of central bank money can only be controlled at the Eurosystem level; no individual NCB has control over the size and nature of its monetary assets and liabilities.

Monetary income sharing is important in two respects: it ensures a fair allocation of the Eurosystem's income among its members, and safeguards the system's functional integrity. It is intended to ensure that monetary income accrues to the NCB of the country that generated it, and not of the country that initially received it. The capital key of the ECB, which is based on a combination of the shares in Eurosystem GDP and population size (see Box 16), is used as a proxy for the wealth-generating contribution of a Member State to the total monetary income of the Eurosystem. Its application also ensures that the income which results from non-euro area residents holding euro banknotes is apportioned equitably among the euro area countries.

Sharing monetary income is also a means of ensuring the functional integrity of the Eurosystem. By assigning each euro area NCB a pre-determined share in the system's monetary income, the arrangement ensures that each NCB is in a position to carry out the decentralised operations of the Eurosystem and avoids incentives for competition that would conflict with the singleness of the ECB's policies.

The monetary income of the NCBs is calculated by earmarking specified assets to be offset against monetary liabilities and measuring the income that arises on such assets in line with rules laid down by the Governing Council.[23] Assets for earmarking include those that are directly affected by the monetary policy operations of the Eurosystem;[24] a limited amount of gold can also be earmarked. Income arising from these assets is pooled by NCBs after the deduction of interest paid on deposits of credit institutions, of interest paid on intra-Eurosystem liabilities (which are a substitute for monetary liabilities) and, exceptionally, of specific losses that may arise as the result of monetary policy operations carried out by an NCB on behalf of the Eurosystem.

The rules outlined above will be phased in progressively over the next few years and will become fully effective in 2008. Until that date, the monetary income allocation within the Eurosystem is subject to a transitional arrangement which mitigates the impact of the full effect of the arrangements on NCBs' relative income positions.[25]

[23] Decision ECB/2001/16 of 6 December 2001 on the allocation of monetary income of the national central banks of participating Member States from the financial year 2002 (OJ L 337, 20.12.2001, p. 55), as amended by Decision ECB/2003/22 of 18 December 2003 (OJ L 9, 15.1.2004, p. 39).

[24] These are loans to credit institutions, and net claims on other participating NCBs, which arise as the result of cross border shifts of money via the TARGET system and the arrangements for the allocation of banknotes in circulation among Eurosystem central banks.

[25] The transitional regime smoothes differences in earned monetary income that NCBs incur because their respective shares in banknotes issued in the euro area before 2002 were higher or lower than their respective shares in the ECB's capital. The amount of monetary income to be pooled by each NCB is adjusted accordingly on the basis of compensating factors related to their average shares in the total Eurosystem banknotes in circulation between mid-1999 and mid-2001. These compensating factors will be progressively reduced to zero by 2008, when all income on banknotes will be allocated fully in accordance with the ECB's capital key.

Jean-Claude Trichet, President
of the ECB, during a hearing
at the European Parliament in
2004.
Credit: European Parliament.

4 THE ECB AND THE EUROPEAN COMMUNITY

In accordance with Article 108 of the EC Treaty, the ECB acts totally independently and on its own behalf within the limits of the powers assigned to it by the Treaty. However, as an organisation created by Community law that performs a policy function under the EC Treaty, the ECB is associated with the institutional framework of the Community.

The Treaty therefore combines the ECB's independence (and that of the NCBs) in fulfilling the objectives of the Eurosystem with provisions that ensure:

• the ECB's democratic accountability;

• effective dialogue and cooperation between the ECB and the Community institutions and bodies;

• judicial control of the ECB's legal acts by the European Court of Justice;

• the external scrutiny of the ECB's financial management and integrity.

4.1 INDEPENDENCE

A cornerstone of monetary order in the euro area is the independence of the ECB and euro area NCBs from political influence. This independence has been enshrined in both the EC Treaty and the Statute of the ESCB, rather than in secondary legislation, and thus has "constitutional" status.

The ECB's independence is a corollary to its primary objective of maintaining price stability and its exclusive competence for the monetary policy and related functions in the euro area. The ECB needs to be shielded from all types of influence that might be adverse to the achievement of its primary objective. An independent central bank is not only in a better position to pursue the primary objective of price stability; it is also perceived by the public to be more credible than a central bank which is a dependent on a government. Indeed, governments have to pursue many objectives and are not perceived by the financial markets and the general public to always give priority to the objective of price stability where there is a conflict of objectives.

The independence of the ECB is not therefore an end in itself, but rather an indispensable element of a monetary order that gives priority to the objective of price stability.

The concept of independence includes:

- institutional independence;
- legal independence;
- personal independence of the members of its decision-making bodies;
- functional and operational independence;
- financial and organisational independence.

Given their specific role in the Eurosystem, the concept of independence also extends to the NCBs and their decision-making bodies. The meaning of this concept for the organic laws of the NCBs was specified by the EMI and confirmed by the ECB in their respective convergence reports drawn up under Articles 121(2) and 122(2) of the EC Treaty (see Section 1.2.2).

4.1.1 Institutional independence

Article 108 is the key Treaty provision establishing the independence of the ECB. Its first sentence states explicitly that, *"when exercising their powers and carrying out their tasks and duties, neither the ECB nor an NCB nor any member of their decision-making bodies shall seek or take instructions from Community institutions or bodies, from any government of a Member State or from any other body"*. The wording of Article 108 makes it illegal to accept or seek instructions from any body, be it public or private, national or international, with the emphasis on the term "instruction". Article 108 does not preclude seeking relevant information or dialoguing with the aforementioned bodies.

The prohibition on the acceptance of instructions is complemented by a self-commitment of the Community institutions and bodies and the governments of the Member States. The second sentence states that these bodies *"have undertaken to respect this principle and not to seek to influence the members of the decision-making bodies of the ECB or of the NCBs in the performance of their tasks."* Thus, they are obliged to abstain from attempting to give instructions to the members of the decision-making bodies of the ECB and the NCBs and to abstain from influencing them.

4.1.2 Legal independence

The ECB and NCBs enjoy their own legal personality (see Section 2.1), which is a prerequisite for the independence of the members of the Eurosystem. For the ECB, legal independence includes the right to bring actions before the European Court of Justice (ECJ) in order to uphold its prerogatives if they are impaired by a Community institution or Member State.

4.1.3 Personal independence

To substantiate the institutional independence, the Statute protects the personal independence of the members of the ECB's decision-making bodies. It stipulates, in particular, relatively long fixed terms of office:

- a minimum term of office of five years for the NCB governors, which is renewable;

- a non-renewable term of office of eight years for the members of the Executive Board.[1]

A member of the ECB's decision-making bodies may not be dismissed in a discretionary manner on the grounds of past policy performance. Instead members may only be removed from office if they become unable to fulfil the conditions required for the performance of their duties or if they are found guilty of serious misconduct. In such cases, the Governing Council or the Executive Board may apply to the ECJ to have the member of the Executive Board *compulsorily retired* (Article 11.4 of the Statute of the ESCB).

In the same circumstances, an NCB governor may be *relieved from office* by the competent national authority in line with the procedures specified in the statute of their respective NCB. However, the governor concerned or the Governing Council may refer the matter to the Court, which has jurisdiction in such cases (Article 14.2 of the Statute of the ESCB).

The statutes of the NCBs (as amended in line with Article 109 of the EC Treaty) extend the protection against discretionary dismissals to the other members of the NCBs' decision-making bodies; however, the other members do not enjoy the right to refer the matter to the ECJ.

4.1.4 Functional and operational independence

Functional and operational independence is substantiated in several provisions of the Statute of the ESCB. To this end, the ECB has been assigned all necessary competences and powers to achieve its primary objective of price stability. For example, the Eurosystem is endowed with the exclusive competence for monetary policy and has a monopoly on banknote issuing. The Member States' right to mint coins is restricted to low denominations and the volume of coins issued is subject to approval by the ECB. No legal tender may therefore be created against the ECB's will, and this gives the ECB full control over the money base in the euro area.

---

[1] When the ECB was established in 1998, a system of staggered terms of office was applied for appointments to the Executive Board to ensure continuity. The first ECB President was appointed for eight years and the first Vice-President for four years. The other four members of the Executive Board were appointed respectively for five, six, seven and eight years. When this system has run its course in 2007, all members of the Executive Board will have been appointed for eight years.

The institutional arrangements in the field of exchange rate policy ensure consistency with the objective of price stability for both the single monetary policy and the exchange rate policy (Article 4 of the EC Treaty). To the same end, official foreign reserve holdings are concentrated within the Eurosystem; the ECB controls the use of these holdings as well as Member States' residual working balances in foreign currencies (see Section 3.2).

In addition, Article 101 of the EC Treaty prohibits the Eurosystem from lending to the public sector. This prohibition, which came into force at the start of Stage Two of EMU, shields the Eurosystem against pressure from the public sector to grant monetary financing using central bank money, and includes the purchase by the Eurosystem of public debt on the primary market. The ECB regularly monitors the market for possible circumventions of this prohibition involving purchases of public debt on the secondary market.

The Eurosystem may freely use a wide range of instruments for the implementation of its policies. This range of instruments includes regulatory powers and the right to impose enforceable sanctions in case of non-compliance with ECB regulations and decisions (see Section 2.5.3).

4.1.5 Financial and organisational independence

The ECB and the NCBs have their own financial resources and income and enjoy organisational autonomy. Their financial and organisational autonomy enables the Eurosystem to perform its tasks as required.

The capital of the ECB is subscribed and paid up by the NCBs. The ECB has its own budget, independent from that of the EU. The Statute also allows the ECB to adopt autonomously the conditions of employment for its staff and to organise its internal structure as it sees fit.

In addition, as a supranational organisation, the ECB enjoys in the territories of the Member States the privileges and immunities that are necessary for the performance of its tasks. Chapter 1 of the Protocol on the privileges and immunities of the European Communities of 8 April 1965 guarantees, among other things, that the premises and archives of the ECB are inviolable and that its property and assets are intangible. The Protocol states further that these must not be subject to any administrative or legal measure of constraint without the authorisation of the ECJ.

As regards the NCBs' financial and budgetary autonomy and the autonomy of their staff, the Member States have a certain influence over NCBs' budgets and the distribution of profits and staffing, be it as (sometimes sole) shareholder of their respective NCB or as national legislator. However, in line with the statutes of the NCBs, the Member States' rights are subject to the proviso that their exercise is not allowed to impede on the NCBs' capacity to perform their Eurosystem-related functions.

4.2 DEMOCRATIC ACCOUNTABILITY

Given its exclusive competence for the monetary policy of the euro area, the ECB has been entrusted with a core aspect of monetary sovereignty. Respect for the fundamental principles of democratic societies requires that the ECB is held accountable to the citizens and their democratically elected representatives. Consequently, both the Treaty and the Statute of the ESCB contain a number of provisions that require the ECB, just like any other independent central bank, to subject its actions and decisions to public scrutiny. It is of course in the ECB's own interest anyway to ensure that its decisions are properly explained and justified so as to foster public support for its policies.

4.2.1 Accountability as a core element of legitimacy

Accountability is a basic precondition for democratic legitimacy and a core element of democratic structures. In a democracy, all power emanates from its citizens and all decisions that bind and affect a community have to be legitimised by the will of the electorate. Thus, public policy decisions are legitimate if they are the direct or indirect expression of that will – this is often referred to as "input legitimacy" or "legitimacy by procedure" – or if they meet the justified expectations and needs of the citizens – a notion referred to as "output legitimacy" or "legitimacy by result".

As an organisation established by the EC Treaty, which was signed and ratified by all Member States in accordance with their constitutional requirements, the ECB enjoys **"input legitimacy"**. The EU Member States (acting through their elected representatives) took a sovereign decision to transfer responsibility for monetary policy and the related tasks to a new Community organisation and to endow it with independence from political interference. Competency for monetary policy is transferred within the limits and the conditions of a mandate which clearly defines the objective of monetary policy and thus limits the amount of legally permitted discretion that the decision-making bodies of the ECB can use in conducting monetary policy.

Further "input legitimacy" is derived from the procedure for appointing the members of the ECB's decision-making bodies; they are all appointed by the democratically elected representatives of the Member States. As already stated, Executive Board members are appointed by common accord of the Member States at the level of the Heads of State or Government (after consultation of the European Parliament); the other members of the Governing Council are appointed by their respective national authorities in line with prevailing procedures.

However, the ECB can also derive **"output legitimacy"** by successfully performing the tasks entrusted to it. The conduct of monetary policy and the performance of other tasks have been made subject to independent decision-making for a specific purpose, i.e. maintaining price stability in the euro area. As mentioned in Section 4.1 above, the experience of a number of central banks in the post-war period has shown that this objective can be best achieved by having an independent central bank that acts within a clear and binding mandate. In this way, despite its intentional distance from the normal political process, an independent central bank can enjoy full output legitimacy.

In addition, the legitimacy of independent central banks rests on a comprehensive framework for holding them accountable. Independence and accountability are two sides of the same coin. Thus, the ECB is called on to explain and justify to the European citizens and their elected representatives how it uses the powers and prerogatives it has been entrusted with.

4.2.2 Nature and scope of the ECB's accountability

The term "accountability" refers to a concept deeply rooted in the democratic and institutional conventions of English-speaking countries[2]. In a European context, the notion of "being accountable" is understood to mean being held responsible for one's decisions and actions and being required to justify and explain them. This concept necessarily refers to an ex post justification and explanation. Indeed, if any political body – such as a parliament or government – were able to intervene or influence directly the policy-making of the central bank, they would actually be taking part in the decision-making process itself and hence would share the responsibility for the policy outcomes. This would not only contradict the independent status of the central bank, but it would also render the concept of accountability meaningless.

To a large extent, accountability goes hand in hand with transparency. Transparency means not only releasing information, but also structuring that information in such a way that the public can understand it. Transparency thus facilitates the process of holding an independent central bank accountable.

The Treaty provisions for holding the ECB accountable and the practices and procedures established over the years have been adapted to the specific political, economic and institutional circumstances in which the ECB operates. As already discussed in Section 1.2.2, the ECB is a supranational central bank that carries out its tasks for the multi-country economy of the euro area; its audience is not genuinely European, but rather multinational. The ECB has also been given a specific institutional structure with the ex officio participation of the NCB governors in its decision-making.

Despite institutional and political differences, the provisions and procedures for holding the ECB accountable ensure that the ECB fulfils its accountability obligations no less effectively and adequately than a "conventional" central bank in a national context.

---

[2] For a comparison with the US Federal Reserve System, the Bank of England and the Bank of Japan, see the Article entitled "The accountability of the ECB" in the November 2002 issue of the ECB's *Monthly Bulletin*.

4.2.3 Discharge of the accountability obligation

Collective accountability of the ECB's decision-making bodies

As explained in Section 2.5.1, the ECB's main decision-making bodies – the Governing Council and the Executive Board – are collegiate bodies in which all members are collectively responsible for the proper fulfilment of the ECB's tasks and functions. The members of both these bodies take decisions with exclusive regard to the objectives of the Eurosystem and on the basis of conditions prevailing in the euro area as a whole, and without reference to developments in any particular country.

The decision-making bodies of the ECB are therefore held collectively accountable for all decisions they take. By contrast, a system of individual responsibility, such as that in force in the US Federal Reserve System, the Bank of England and the Bank of Japan, cannot be applied to the ECB as it would be inconsistent with the institutional structure and policy substance.

For example, it would be inconsistent to have a system whereby all the members of the Governing Council were held individually accountable to the European Parliament because the EU institutions and bodies are not involved in appointing the governors of any NCB. It would also be inconsistent for NCB governors to give accounts of their actions as members of the Governing Council to their national parliaments; indeed, national parliaments lack the legitimacy to judge how NCB governors have performed their "European" duties – duties which explicitly preclude them from acting as defenders of national interests.

Accountability for the ECB's statutory mandate

The ECB is held accountable for all activities and tasks which the EC Treaty has assigned to the Eurosystem and, in particular, for the conduct of monetary policy. By setting a quantitative definition of price stability, the ECB has created a benchmark against which its performance can be assessed.

The ECB is also held accountable for all other functions that are performed through the Eurosystem at its behest. By contrast, it cannot be held accountable for non-Eurosystem functions that the NCBs perform under Article 14.4 of the Statute of the ESCB. Indeed, the NCBs concerned perform these functions under their own responsibility and liability and are held accountable for them by the national authorities under the legal and constitutional provisions of the relevant Member State.

To whom is the ECB accountable?

As a body established by the Treaty, and acting within the limits of the powers conferred on it, the ECB is accountable first and foremost to citizens of the EU Member States which have concluded and ratified the Treaty. The Treaty contains extensive reporting obligations (see the next section below) which provide a framework for the ECB to be directly scrutinised by the European public. The

ECB explains and justifies its decisions directly to the public through publications in all official Community languages and speeches given by members of the ECB decision-making bodies in all euro area member countries and elsewhere.

In addition, the EC Treaty provides for regular dialogue with the elected representatives of the European citizens, i.e. the European Parliament (see Section 4.3.1); just as the national legislative bodies of the United States, Japan and the United Kingdom are the principal addressees of democratic accountability for the central banks of those countries.

Over and above the accountability provisions of the EC Treaty, national legislation may require NCBs to present annual reports and may empower the respective parliaments to ask NCB governors to appear before plenary sessions or the relevant parliamentary committees upon request or at the governors' own initiative. National parliaments, however, may only hold NCBs accountable for the functions performed outside the Eurosystem, whereas the ECB is solely accountable for the Eurosystem functions.

Nevertheless, although NCB contacts with their national political authorities do not, strictly speaking, form part of the accountability obligation, they do offer prime opportunities to explain the ECB's decisions and inform national policy-makers of the conduct of the single monetary policy and the reasoning behind it.

Means of discharging the accountability obligation

In theory, approval and reward (if the mandate is successfully fulfilled) and sanctions (in the event of sub-optimal performance) may appear a suitable means of enforcing central bank accountability. In practice, however, the specific nature of monetary policy means that certain qualifications should be added.

As mentioned in Section 3.1.1, given the time lags in the transmission process, monetary policy can only affect the price level over the medium term. It is therefore impossible for the central bank to offset unanticipated shocks to the price level (such as those caused by changes in commodity prices) in the short run. Moreover, given the uncertainty surrounding the transmission mechanism, and given that the appropriate response of monetary policy depends on the nature, duration and size of economic shocks, it does not seem appropriate to specify a fixed horizon for assessing monetary policy.

A measurement of the central bank's performance therefore always requires a balanced and differentiated assessment. The use of formal sanction mechanisms would simply be too blunt and may prevent the central bank from fulfilling its mandate properly. Hence, constant scrutiny of the central bank's actions by parliament and the general public would seem to be the most appropriate method for holding an independent central bank accountable.

The ECB is subject to extensive reporting requirements:

• Article 113 of the EC Treaty requires the ECB to present an annual report on the activities of the ESCB and the monetary policy of both the previous and current year to the European Parliament, the EU Council, the Commission and the European Council;

• Article 15 of the Statute of the ESCB calls for the publication of quarterly reports and weekly consolidated financial statements for the Eurosystem.

The ECB actually exceeds these statutory obligations by producing a Monthly Bulletin (rather than just quarterly reports) and by publishing Working Papers and other publications on its website.

However, unlike the US Federal Reserve System, the Bank of England and the Bank of Japan, the ECB does not publish the minutes of the meetings of its main policy-making body, nor does it publish details of how the members of the Governing Council voted. This is consistent with the clear stipulations of Article 10.4 of the Statute of the ESCB, which states that *"the proceedings of the meetings shall be confidential"*.

Non-disclosure of voting behaviour also protects the independence of Governing Council members. The publication of individual voting behaviour could lead to pressure and speculation about the motives behind the decisions of the individual members of the Governing Council. It would even enable the public to see whether any attempts to exercise influence on voting behaviour had had the intended result. Although such concerns might not be particularly relevant to central banks operating in "conventional" nation states, NCB governors in the euro area are associated with their home countries. There is therefore a risk that the respective NCB governor may be perceived as a "national representative" within the Governing Council and may lead to unjustified attempts to influence them.

However, Article 10.4 of the Statute also states that *"the Governing Council may decide to make the outcome of its deliberations public"*. To this end, the President and Vice-President of the ECB hold a press conference immediately after the first Governing Council meeting of each month, a transcript of which is published on the ECB's website, and the ECB regularly provides comprehensive assessments of monetary and economic issues in its Monthly Bulletin. In terms of timeliness and detail, these communications appear no less capable of explaining policy decisions (and the reasoning behind them) than what other central banks would classify as "summary records".

4.3 DIALOGUE AND COOPERATION WITH COMMUNITY INSTITUTIONS AND BODIES

Although the EC Treaty clearly divides the policy responsibilities within the framework of EMU, at the same time it also promotes dialogue and cooperation between the different policy-makers through a number of formalised contacts between the ECB and Community institutions and bodies.

Working relations between the ECB and other policy-making bodies within the EU are necessary for the Eurosystem to fulfil its tasks properly. This is self-evident for all those tasks where the ECB shares its competences with Community bodies. In these cases, the Treaty calls for cooperation between the ECB and the institutions or bodies concerned (e.g. in the field of exchange rate policy, representation of the euro area and statistics). However, given the interaction between the single monetary policy and the economic policies in the Community, the ECB also has an interest in maintaining a fruitful dialogue with other policy-makers, such as governments or social partners. Regular dialogue between the ECB and other policy-making bodies provides an opportunity to explain the course of monetary policy and improve outsiders' understanding of the ECB's activities. In this way, the ECB can provide a reliable reference parameter for the decisions of individual actors with the aim of stabilising inflation expectations.

4.3.1 European Parliament

The dialogue between the ECB and the European Parliament is mainly concerned with the fulfilment of the ECB's mandate and tasks. As discussed in Section 4.2 above, the European Parliament plays a key role in holding the ECB accountable for the conduct of monetary policy and related tasks.

Deliberation on the ECB's Annual Reports
Under Article 113(3) of the EC Treaty, the President of the ECB is required to present the ECB's Annual Report to the European Parliament at its plenary session. After the presentation, Parliament adopts a resolution, which provides a comprehensive assessment of the ECB's activities and policy conduct.

Testimony before the European Parliament
Also under Article 113(3) of the Treaty, the President of the ECB and the other members of the Executive Board may, at the request of the European Parliament or on their own initiative, be heard by the competent committees of the Parliament. In line with this provision, the President of the ECB appears four times a year before Parliament's Committee on Economic and Monetary Affairs. Under Parliament's Rules of Procedure, this Committee was designated as the committee responsible for relations with the ECB. During these hearings, the President explains the ECB's policy decisions and answers questions from Committee members. As a result, these quarterly testimonies have become the mainstay of Parliament's activities in holding the ECB accountable.

Other members of the ECB's Executive Board also appear before the Committee on Economic and Monetary Affairs. Over recent years, the Vice-President has generally been invited to present the ECB's Annual Report to the Committee when preparing the subsequent deliberation in the plenary session. Moreover, once a year, the Committee invites the Executive Board member responsible for economics and research to present the ECB's views on the Commission's annual review of the EU economy and the draft Broad Economic Policy Guidelines. On occasion, the Committee has also invited and heard other members of the Executive Board on specific topics relating to the ECB's competences and tasks.

Committee meetings are normally open to the public and a verbatim report of proceedings is put on the website of the European Parliament shortly after the testimony. Moreover, the ECB's Annual Report contains a specific chapter on accountability and the ECB's relationship with Parliament, which highlights the main issues discussed in the course of this regular dialogue.

Written questions

Further to direct interaction and exchange of views between the ECB's President and members of the Committee on Economic and Monetary Affairs, Parliament's Rules of Procedure (new Rule 40a "Questions for written answer to the European Central Bank") also allow all Members of the European Parliament (MEPs) to submit further questions in writing to the ECB via the Committee's Chair. These questions, together with the answers prepared by the ECB, are subsequently published in the Official Journal of the European Union. They are thereby made available to the public in all official Community languages.

Even though neither the Treaty nor the Statute of the ESCB contains any obligations in this respect, the ECB has agreed to this procedure. However, it has emphasised that this should in no way lessen the importance of the regular testimonies where the principal questions regarding the ECB's policy decisions should continue to be discussed.

Other areas of interaction

There are three further important areas of interaction between the ECB and the European Parliament:

1. Parliament is consulted on the appointment of the ECB's President, Vice-President and other members of the Executive Board, (Article 112(2) of the EC Treaty). The Committee on Economic and Monetary Affairs conducts hearings with the nominees and the plenum of the European Parliament adopts an opinion.

2. Parliament is involved in Community legislation to amend and complement the Statute of the ESCB (Articles 10.6, 41 and 42 of the Statute). Its assent is required for amendments to the Statute in line with Article 41 of the Statute, and it must be consulted on amendments to voting rights under Article 10.6 and proposed complementary legislation in line with Article 42.

3. Parliament is also involved in other law-making in areas that fall within the ECB's responsibility.

4.3.2 EU Council and Eurogroup

The ECB shares responsibility with the EU Council for exchange rate matters and the international representation of the euro area. Furthermore, it liaises with the Council on economic policy cooperation at the euro area level. Respect for the ECB's independence and the recognition of its responsibilities, however, implies that the ECB's relations with the Council and the Eurogroup in the field of economic policies can only be a non-binding dialogue; it cannot imply coordinating monetary policy ex ante with other policies.

It should also be noted that it is the Council's responsibility to recommend to the Heads of State or Government the appointments of the President, Vice-President and other members of the Executive Board of the ECB.

EU Council

Legally speaking, there is only one EU Council; however, the Council actually meets in various compositions, depending on the subject under consideration. For very important EMU decisions, such as the accession of EU Member States to the euro area or amendments to Article 10.2 of the Statute of the ESCB, the Council meets in the composition of the Heads of State or Government[3]. By contrast, current EMU matters fall within the sphere of the Council of Economics and Finance Ministers (ECOFIN Council). In this context, paragraph 44 of the Presidency Conclusions of the Luxembourg European Council of 12 and 13 December 1997 stated explicitly that the ECOFIN Council was *"the centre for the coordination of the Member States' economic policies"* and that it was *"empowered to act in the relevant areas"*.

Although not all EU Member States are part of the euro area, representatives of all Member States (including those not participating in Stage Three of EMU) take part in EU Council deliberations on EMU matters. However, the voting rights of the representatives of the non-participating countries are suspended in most EMU matters, though not all. Exceptions where all members vote include Community legislation that the EU Council adopts on the basis of Article 107 of the EC Treaty, namely legislation amending and complementing the Statute of the ESCB (see Section 2.5.4).

Under Article 113(2) of the EC Treaty, the ECB President is invited to participate in meetings of the ECOFIN Council whenever matters relating to the objectives and tasks of the ESCB are on the agenda. Such topics include the Broad Economic Policy Guidelines, currency issues, reforms in the European financial sector and the external representation of the Community within EMU, as well as issues related to foreign exchange policy.

---

[3] The EU Council meeting in the composition of the Heads of State or Government should not be confused with the European Council. The latter, which brings together the Heads of State or Government of the EU Member States and the President of the European Commission, provides the European Union with the necessary impetus for its development and defines the general political guidelines. The decisions of the Heads of State or Government to appoint the members of the Executive Board and to determine the seat of the ECB are of an intergovernmental nature.

The ECB also participates in ECOFIN Council meetings when it is discussing "complementary legislation" or amendments to certain provisions of the Statute of the ESCB. On these occasions, the ECB is also represented in the relevant Council sub-structures when preparing the ECOFIN Council session. Moreover, the ECB is generally invited to observe the preparation of other Community legislation in areas of particular relevance. Finally, the ECB has also been involved in the activities of specific bodies dealing with issues of interest or direct relevance to the ECB, such as the Financial Services Committee or the Committee of Wise Men on the Regulation of European Securities Markets.

The President of the ECB regularly attends the informal, biannual meetings of the ECOFIN Council, which provide an opportunity for open discussion on topical issues, free from the usual procedural constraints of formal Council sessions. The NCB governors are also invited to these meetings, at which they accompany their respective ministers.

The ECB also has important reporting obligations towards the ECOFIN Council. For example, the President of the ECB presents the ECB's Annual Report to the Council and reports to the Council as part of the biennial convergence exercise required under Article 122 of the EC Treaty.

Eurogroup

As already mentioned, the EU Council deliberates on EMU matters in full composition, albeit mostly with suspended voting rights for the representatives from the non-participating countries. The Treaty does not provide for a body that brings together the finance ministers of euro area member countries to discuss issues of common concern relating to the euro area and the single currency. To remedy this situation, the Luxembourg European Council of December 1997 decided to establish the "Eurogroup": an informal body composed of the finance ministers of euro area countries and the Commissioner for Economic and Monetary Affairs. The ECB is invited to participate in Eurogroup meetings "when appropriate"; so far, the ECB has indeed been regularly invited and has participated in all meetings.

The Eurogroup establishes a communication channel at the euro area level, similar to the informal contacts that traditionally exist between governments and central banks within nation states. The informal character of the Eurogroup makes it possible for an open discussion of all issues relevant to the euro area. The climate of openness and trust is bolstered by the fact that the Eurogroup meetings are restricted to the ministers, the relevant Commissioner and the ECB President (each with one accompanying person); this is in stark contrast to the large number that usually attend formal EU Council sessions.

The Eurogroup generally meets once a month before the ECOFIN Council meetings. Discussions within the Eurogroup focus on the overall functioning of the euro area economy, in particular the overall economic outlook for the euro area, budgetary developments in individual euro area member countries and ways of providing political impulses for further efforts to bring about structural reform.

In addition, the Eurogroup also discusses developments in the euro exchange rate and the external perception of the euro area as an entity in its own right.

4.3.3 European Commission

The European Commission is also involved in the dialogue between the ECB and the ECOFIN Council. The Commissioner for Economic and Monetary Affairs attends the respective meetings of the ECOFIN Council and the Eurogroup as well as the meetings of the ECB's Governing Council.

In addition to this policy dialogue at the highest level, the Commission and the ECB also maintain close working relations, which are reinforced by frequent contacts in multilateral settings, such as the Economic and Financial Committee or the Economic Policy Committee (see below), and in bilateral meetings. This contact is particularly important given the central role the Commission plays in the process of economic policy-making in the Community. In particular, the Commission is entrusted with a number of specific tasks relating to EMU. These include:

• formulating recommendations for the Broad Economic Policy Guidelines (BEPGs);

• monitoring the budgetary situation in the Member States and reporting on this to the ECOFIN Council;

• preparing, at least once every two years, a convergence report examining to what extent those Member States that have yet to adopt the euro have fulfilled the convergence criteria.

In addition, the European Commission has initiated, or is at least involved in, a wide range of specific activities that are either related to or have an impact on the Eurosystem's tasks and activities. In many cases, such activities can often benefit substantially from, or even necessitate, the ECB's direct involvement.

• Eurostat and the ECB cooperate closely in the area of statistics, both bilaterally and within the relevant statistical committees of the Community, in particular the Committee on Monetary, Financial and Balance of Payments Statistics (CMFB) (see Section 3.5).

• In other areas, too, the ECB is involved in a number of specialised working groups and regulatory committees. Such bodies deal with a wide range of topics, for example financial market integration (e.g. the "Giovannini Group") or prudential supervision and financial stability (e.g. the European Banking Committee and the Committee of European Banking Supervisors).

• Finally, the Commission and the ECB have worked, and will continue to work, closely together on EU enlargement-related issues within the ECB's areas of responsibility and expertise.

4.3.4 Economic and Financial Committee

The Economic and Financial Committee (EFC) was established under Article 114(2) of the EC Treaty to provide the ECOFIN Council with preparatory analyses of, and advice on, a wide range of economic and financial questions. In paragraph 12 of its Resolution on economic policy coordination in Stage 3 of EMU, the Luxembourg European Council of December 1997 also assigned the EFC the task of providing *"the framework within which the dialogue* [between the Council and the ECB] *can be prepared and continued at the level of senior officials* [from ministries, NCBs, the Commission and the ECB]."

The Treaty states that the Member States, the Commission and the ECB must each appoint no more than two members to the Committee. By tradition, the two representatives of each Member State are one senior official from the administration and one senior official from the respective central bank. However, now that the EU has 25 Member States, the EFC generally meets in restricted composition with only one representative per Member State (usually a senior official from the administration) and two representatives each from the Commission and the ECB. The ECB's representatives are currently the Vice-President and the member of the Executive Board who is in charge of economics; their alternates are the Directors General for international relations and economics, respectively.

As a result of its participation in the EFC, the ECB has become involved in discussions on the Broad Economic Policy Guidelines, the surveillance of fiscal policies on the basis of Member States' annual Stability and Convergence Programmes and the preparation of European positions on international issues. The ECB also participates in other activities of the EFC, which range from technical subjects, such as the minting of euro coins, to institutional reform and the external representation of the Community within EMU.

Discussions within the EFC also serve to prepare the dialogue between the euro area finance ministers and the ECB, which takes place within the Eurogroup. A core feature of the ECB's participation in the EFC involves preparing assessments of the overall economic outlook for the euro area and exchange rate developments. Moreover, it includes an ongoing review of the sustainability of public finances and the appropriateness of the general orientations of fiscal policy.

The ECB's involvement in the EFC is based on full respect for its independence and exclusive responsibility for the single monetary policy. The ECB participates fully in discussions and express its views on all issues, but it does not participate in any voting procedures. Moreover, the EFC consciously refrains from discussing the conduct of monetary policy. The same applies to statements on the single monetary policy made at the meetings of international organisations and forums, such as the IMF or G7. In line with the division of responsibilities, the preparation and presentation of such statements are the exclusive competence of the ECB.

4.3.5 Economic Policy Committee

The Economic Policy Committee (EPC) was established in 1974 by a Council Decision[4] and is composed of two representatives and two alternates from each of the Member States, the Commission and the ECB.

Like the EFC, the EPC is involved in preparing the Eurogroup and ECOFIN Council meetings; however, its work focuses particularly on structural reforms. As part of the "Cardiff process" (see Section 1.2.2), the Committee conducts annually an in-depth peer review of economic reforms in the Member States. Moreover, the EPC is closely involved in the "Luxembourg process" (see Section 1.2.2), which serves as a platform for coordination among Member States in the area of employment policies. The Committee also deals with a variety of long-term structural issues, such as the budgetary implications of ageing populations.

Since the ECB attaches the utmost importance to structural reforms in the Member States as the main means of combating unemployment and fully exploiting the growth potential of the euro area, the ECB's participation in the EPC offers a useful opportunity to contribute to the Committee's work. As with the EFC, the ECB's involvement in the work of the EPC is based on full respect for the Bank's independence.

4.3.6 Macroeconomic Dialogue

The purpose of the Macroeconomic Dialogue is to foster greater understanding of EMU-related policy requirements and thereby to improve the conditions for non-inflationary and employment-generating growth. This twice-yearly dialogue is commonly known as the "Cologne process", having been established in 1999 by the Cologne European Council (see Section 1.2.2) and takes place at both a political and a technical level. It is based on a full respect for the independence of all actors involved, in particular the independence of the social partners in the process of wage formation and that of the ECB in relation to the single monetary policy. The recognition of the assignment of separate policy responsibilities and related obligations help to focus awareness on the fact that it is the task of each policy actor to ensure the successful implementation of policies within their own fields of competence.

4.4 THE ECB'S LINGUISTIC REGIME

As a Community organisation, the ECB addresses itself to a multilingual audience and has multinational decision-making bodies and staff. The linguistic plurality of the EU requires that the ECB communicate in many languages with a view to reaching the widest possible audience. The ECB follows a pragmatic approach that reconciles respect for linguistic diversity in the EU with the principle of efficiency and timeliness of communication.

---

[4] Council Decision 74/112/EEC of 18 February 1974 setting up an Economic Policy Committee (OJ L 63, 5.3.1974, p. 21).

Since 1 May 2004 there have been 20 official Community languages.[5] The ECB's linguistic regime for its legal acts and relations with third parties and the general public follows the principles of multilingualism enshrined in Community law.[6] Regulations and other legal acts with general applicability are published in all official languages. The same applies to statutory publications (e.g. Annual Reports, Monthly Bulletins) and a number of press releases. Legal acts addressed to individual third parties are issued in the language of the addressee. Third parties who address the ECB in one of the official Community languages can expect to receive an answer written in the language used.

For most other types of communication and, in particular, for the internal workings of the ECB and intra-ESCB relations, only one "vehicle language" – English – is used. Exceptions are the proceedings of the Governing and General Councils and the ESCB Committees, where simultaneous interpretation is provided in a number of languages. The use of a single vehicle language meets the need for speedy, effective and fully reliable communication within the ECB and the Eurosystem in the formulation and implementation of the single monetary policy and related tasks.

4.5 JUDICIAL REVIEW BY THE EUROPEAN COURT OF JUSTICE

As already discussed, the ECB enjoys extensive powers under the Treaty and the Statute of the ESCB, which include regulatory powers and the right to impose sanctions and penalties on undertakings in the event that they do not comply with the regulations and decisions of the ECB. Hence, Article 35.1 of the Statute of the ESCB provides for judicial review of the acts and omissions of the ECB under the conditions laid down in Articles 230 to 233 of the EC Treaty. Accordingly, the EU Council, the Commission or any Member State may initiate proceedings before the European Court of Justice (ECJ) against acts of the ECB that are intended to produce legal effects vis-à-vis third parties. The ECJ has jurisdiction in such actions *"on grounds of lack of competence, infringement of an essential procedural requirement, infringement of* [the] *Treaty or of any rule of law relating to its application, or misuse of powers"* (second paragraph of Article 230 of the Treaty). Moreover, any natural or legal person may, under the same conditions, initiate proceedings against a decision of the ECB that is of direct and individual concern to that person (fourth paragraph of Article 230).

Under Article 232 of the Treaty, the ECB may also be taken to the ECJ by a Community institution or a Member State for infringing the Treaty by failure to act. Similarly, any natural and legal person may complain to the Court that the ECB has failed to address to that person an act required by the Treaty or the Statute of the ESCB.

---

[5] In the alphabetical order of the languages: Spanish, Czech, Danish, German, Greek, English, Estonian, French, Italian, Latvian, Lithuanian, Hungarian, Maltese, Dutch, Polish, Portuguese, Slovak, Slovene, Finnish and Swedish.

[6] EEC Council Regulation No 1 determining the languages to be used by the European Economic Community (OJ B 17, 6.10.1958, p. 385).

If the action is well-founded, the ECJ declares the act to be void or, in the case of an omission, states that the failure to act was contrary to the Treaty. In those cases, the ECB is required to take the necessary measures to comply with its judgement. Such a situation arose in 2003 when the ECJ declared the ECB's own anti-fraud regime to be void and instead ruled that the ECB should be subject to the Community's anti-fraud scheme (see Section 4.6).

The ECJ not only reviews the acts and omissions of the ECB, but is also competent to rule in actions brought by the ECB against a Community institution or a Member State for the purpose of protecting its prerogatives or against a Community institution because of the latter's failure to act (Articles 230 and 232 respectively). In the same vein, the ECB may bring action against an NCB if it fails to fulfil its Treaty and Statute obligations (Article 237(d) of the Treaty).

The ECJ also has jurisdiction in disputes between the ECB and its staff (see Section 6.4.1) and in all cases where jurisdiction has been conferred on the Court by agreement between the ECB and its contractual partners.

4.6 SCRUTINY OF FINANCIAL MANAGEMENT AND INTEGRITY

Sound financial management of the Eurosystem is a matter of public concern; after all, the ECB and the NCBs exercise a public function that ultimately involves the taxpayer's money. Accordingly, the Treaty contains several provisions which subject the ECB's financial management and integrity to scrutiny.

The ECB discharges its accountability obligation by drawing up its Annual Accounts and publishing them as part of its Annual Reports. The Annual Accounts of the ECB and all the Eurosystem NCBs are examined by independent external auditors. Under Article 27.1 of the Statute of the ESCB, these external auditors are recommended by the Governing Council and approved by the EU Council. The legal provisions and associated practices developed by the ECB were deemed to be in line with the IMF's Code of Good Practices on Transparency in Monetary and Financial Policies, which was adopted in 1999 and last reviewed in August 2000.

In addition to the independent external audit, the ECB's financial management is also scrutinised by the European Court of Auditors. Under Article 27.2 of the Statute, the Court of Auditors examines the operational efficiency of the management of the ECB and publishes an Annual Report in the Official Journal of the European Union.

Finally, following the ruling of the ECJ of 10 July 2003[7], the ECB falls within the scope of the anti-fraud scheme that was set up by the European Community on the

---

[7] Regulation (EC) No 1073/1999 of the European Parliament and of the Council of 25 May 1999 concerning investigations conducted by the European Anti-Fraud Office (OJ L 136, 31.5.1999, p. 1).

basis of Article 280 of the EC Treaty.[8] This scheme entitles the European Anti-Fraud Office (OLAF), which is an independent investigation service within the Commission[9], to investigate fraud and other irregular action at the ECB in the case of a reasoned suspicion. In the light of the ECJ's ruling, the ECB has adapted its internal rules and procedures to the legal framework provided by the ECJ in its judgement, and has adopted the necessary measures to ensure close coordination with OLAF in combating fraud.[10]

[8] Case C-11/00 Commission of the European Communities v European Central Bank [2003] ECR I-07147.
[9] Commission Decision of 28 April 1999 establishing the European Anti-Fraud Office (OJ L 136, 31.5.1999, p. 20).
[10] Decision (ECB/2004/11) of the European Central Bank of 3 June 2004 concerning the terms and conditions for European Anti-Fraud Office investigations of the European Central Bank in relation to the prevention of fraud, corruption and any other illegal activities detrimental to the European Communities' financial interests and amending the Conditions of Employment for Staff of the European Central Bank (OJ L 230, 30.6.2004, p. 56).

BANK FOR INTERNATIONAL S

Press conference with the
ECB President, Jean-Claude
Trichet, at the Bank for
International Settlements in
Basel on 26 June 2004.
Credit: BIS.

5 THE ECB'S INVOLVEMENT IN INTERNATIONAL COOPERATION

The ECB is involved in representing the euro area at the international level, which means representing the European Community with respect to EMU matters in international organisations and fora where the tasks entrusted to the Eurosystem are concerned. The precise nature of such involvement hinges on the division of powers within the Community and between the Community and its Member States. Thus, depending on the topic under discussion, the ECB's involvement in international organisations and fora may range from the exclusive representation of European Community policy positions to the formulation of the ECB's own positions alongside those of other policy-makers at the Community and national level.

5.1 BACKGROUND

As monetary and exchange rate policy was transferred to the Community level, it became necessary to devise arrangements that would allow the ECB to participate in monetary and financial cooperation at the international level. These arrangements had to take into account the following four aspects.

i. The division of powers within the Community
Article 111(3) and (4) of the EC Treaty entitles the EU Council to decide on the arrangements for negotiating and concluding agreements with non-EU countries or international organisations on monetary and foreign exchange regime matters and as regards the position and representation of the Community at the international level with respect to EMU matters, *"in compliance with the allocation of powers"* within the Community. Until now, the provisions of Article 111(3) have only been used to conclude agreements between the European Community and certain non-EU countries on monetary and exchange rate matters[1]; the other provisions have not yet been used. Instead, current arrangements for the international representation of the Community are based on an understanding reached at the European Council meetings in Luxembourg in December 1997 and Vienna in December 1998. The Presidency Conclusions of the Luxembourg European Council state that the ECB and the ECOFIN Council *"will carry out their tasks in representing the Community at the international level in an efficient manner and in compliance with the distribution of powers laid down in the Treaty"*.

ii. The division of responsibilities within the Eurosystem
Under Articles 6.1 and 12.5 of the Statute of the ESCB, it is up to the Governing Council to decide how the Eurosystem should be represented at the international

---

[1] This is the case for the four Council Decisions concerning monetary relations with the Principality of Monaco, the Republic of San Marino, the Principality of Andorra and the Vatican City, as well as the two Council Decisions on exchange rate matters relating to the Cape Verde escudo and the CFA franc and Comorian franc.

level. The ECB is entitled to participate in international monetary institutions, as are the NCBs, subject to Governing Council approval. The Governing Council has decided that the NCBs should continue to take part in international organisations and fora, depending on the extent to which their respective countries are involved in such bodies, whereas the ECB should ensure that the Eurosystem is consistently represented where necessary and appropriate.

iii. The division of powers between the Community and the euro area countries

As discussed in Section 1.2.2, the individual euro area countries remain responsible for all economic policies except for monetary and exchange rate policies. This means that the involvement of the ECB, the Community and individual EU Member States in the process of international cooperation varies depending on the mandates of the relevant international organisations and fora.

iv. The institutional set-up of the individual international organisations and fora

The transfer of monetary sovereignty posed some unique questions for the institutional framework for international relations, as the arrangements in place at the time were not tailored to the involvement of a monetary union as large as the euro area. The existing array of international organisations and fora has been designed to promote cooperation among sovereign states that had full competence for the conduct of their economic, monetary and financial policies. To become effective, the provisions governing the international relations of the Community and the ECB required the negotiation of adjustments to the rules and procedures on which international relations are based. Until now such adjustments have largely been based on pragmatism. This is in line with the Presidency Conclusions of the Vienna European Council of December 1998, which stated that *"a pragmatic approach might be the most successful which could minimise the adaptation of current rules and practices provided, of course, that such an approach resulted in an outcome which recognised properly the role of the euro"*.

The pragmatic solutions that have been devised so far allow ECB participation in international organisations and fora where the tasks entrusted to the Eurosystem are concerned.

• Whenever international cooperation concerns the **single monetary policy**, the ECB is the sole institution entitled to represent policy positions of the European Community, since the single monetary policy is an exclusive competence of the ECB's main decision-making bodies, the Governing Council and the Executive Board.

• As regards the **euro exchange rate**, the ECB shares responsibility with the EU Council (ECOFIN) and the Eurogroup. Thus, both the President of the ECB and the President of the Eurogroup are involved in consultations with third parties – for example at the G7 level – and communication policy.

- In the area of **payment systems**, the ECB may formulate positions at the international level on issues related to the Eurosystem's responsibility for promoting the smooth and efficient operation of payment and settlement systems. The euro area NCBs, which participate in international organisations and fora alongside the ECB, may also express views reflecting their own responsibility and experience in managing and overseeing domestic payment and settlement systems.

- In **statistical matters**, the Statute of the ESCB imposes a general obligation on the ECB to cooperate with international organisations. This provision, which takes into account the fact that statistical work is carried out in a global context, allows the ECB to formulate positions along with other competent Community bodies (e.g. Eurostat).

- In the area of **prudential supervision** and **financial stability**, the ECB may participate in relevant international meetings and state its positions alongside those of the national authorities that have competence in this field (e.g. NCBs and national supervisory agencies).

5.2 POLICY CONTENT OF THE ECB'S INTERNATIONAL RELATIONS

The ECB's main activities in the field of international cooperation involve exchanging information and views with other policy-makers within multilateral organisations and fora. Peer review of the economic developments and policies in major economic areas is particularly important in this context as it enhances the ECB's ability to analyse the impact of external developments on the euro area economy. Exchanges of information and views are further complemented by surveillance carried out by independent organisations, such as the International Monetary Fund (IMF) and the Organisation for Economic Co-operation and Development (OECD).

The ECB also participates in the efforts of the international community to develop common understandings on a number of best practices and rules designed to make policy-making more efficient and transparent. Best practices are usually laid down in core principles, standards and codes to be implemented in each individual country on a voluntary basis. The identification of best practices encourages emulation and transparency among policy-makers, thus making the notion of good public governance a central component of international cooperation.

However, the policy content of the ECB's international cooperation does not include ex ante coordination of its monetary and exchange rate policy with the policies carried out by non-euro area countries. This could easily become incompatible with its mandate and independent status: attempts to coordinate ex ante would not only blur the specific responsibilities of policy-makers, but also reduce their accountability.

5.3 ECB RELATIONS WITH INTERNATIONAL ORGANISATIONS

The ECB has established relations with the International Monetary Fund (IMF) and the Organisation for Economic Co-operation and Development (OECD). Both these organisations regularly monitor and assess economic and policy developments in their member countries.

5.3.1 International Monetary Fund

The IMF, which was established in 1944 under the Bretton Woods Agreement, currently has 184 Member States. Its main tasks are to foster global monetary cooperation, secure exchange rate stability, facilitate international trade and promote economic growth. The scope of its mandate places the IMF at the centre of the international monetary and financial system.

In view of the importance of member countries' economic policies to the stability of the global economic system, surveillance lies at the heart of the IMF's activities. IMF surveillance consists in monitoring and assessing economic and financial developments and policies of member countries as part of consultations with member countries under Article IV of the IMF's Articles of Agreement (known as Article IV consultations). Surveillance also comprises an assessment of the global implications of national policies in an increasingly integrated world economic and financial system (multilateral surveillance).

Observer status of the ECB

Given the respective mandates of the IMF and the ECB, it was considered essential for the ECB to be represented at the IMF on those issues which fall within the ECB's fields of competence. On 21 December 1998 the IMF Executive Board decided to grant observer status to the ECB. This was a pragmatic solution that avoided the need to amend the IMF's Articles of Agreement, which restrict membership to countries. The arrangement extends a standing invitation to the ECB to participate as an observer in all IMF Executive Board meetings where issues of direct relevance to the ECB are to be discussed. These issues are the following agenda items:

• Article IV consultations on euro area policies;

• Article IV consultations with individual euro area countries;

• the role of the euro in the international monetary system;

• multilateral surveillance, i.e. the biannual discussion of the IMF's World Economic Outlook and the Global Financial Stability Report and regular discussions on world economic and market developments.

In all these discussions of the IMF Executive Board, as far as the monetary policy of the euro area is concerned, the ECB Observer presents the policy positions of the European Community. On exchange rate matters, the Executive Director representing the Eurogroup Presidency and the ECB Observer both present the

Community position, reflecting the regular exchange of views which takes place at the euro area level, for example at Eurogroup meetings (see Section 4.3.2).

In addition to the standing invitation, the ECB Observer may also be invited to attend meetings on an ad hoc basis for agenda items which both the ECB and the IMF consider to be of mutual interest for the performance of their respective mandates. It has now become common practice for the ECB Observer to be invited to attend Article IV discussions concerning EU Member States that have not yet adopted the euro, given that the ECB is involved in monetary policy coordination procedures with the NCBs of these countries. Likewise, the ECB Observer attends annual Article IV consultation discussions on the United States and Japan.

Also under the observer arrangements, the President of the ECB is invited to attend, as an observer, meetings of the International Monetary and Financial Committee (IMFC). The IMFC meets twice a year alongside the IMF's spring and annual meetings to advise and report to the IMF Board of Governors on the supervision of the international monetary and financial system. It also provides guidance on the policy work of the IMF Executive Board.

Article IV consultations with the ECB and euro area countries

Since the introduction of the euro, Article IV consultations with euro area member countries have been split into two distinct parts: one part of the Article IV process concerns mainly monetary and exchange rate issues in the euro area; the other deals with individual euro area countries and all economic policies apart from monetary and exchange rate policies (e.g. fiscal or structural policies). This two-pronged approach reflects the adaptation of IMF procedures which was made necessary by the division of competences within the euro area.

An IMF delegation visits the ECB twice a year to discuss recent developments and matters relevant to monetary and exchange rate policy in the euro area. In this context, the IMF mission also holds discussions with European Community bodies that have a coordinating role for national policies (e.g. in the framework of the Broad Economic Policy Guidelines and the Stability and Growth Pact), such as the European Commission, the Economic and Financial Committee and the Eurogroup. These discussions focus on economic developments and policies (e.g. fiscal and structural policies) in the euro area as a whole which are of relevance for monetary policy and exchange rate developments.

In the second part of the Article IV process, which concerns the economic policies of individual member countries, the IMF visits the individual countries to meet the national policy-makers.

Other fields of cooperation

The ECB is also involved in a number of IMF initiatives to strengthen the international financial architecture. This was the case for the Code of Good Practices on Transparency in Monetary and Financial Policies, which contains broad principles for the transparency and accountability of authorities in the field of monetary policy and related central bank tasks. These cover payment systems and supervision, the guidelines on the management of foreign exchange reserves and the Reports on the Observance of Standards and Codes (ROSC), which are all part of broader efforts by the international community to foster the implementation of internationally agreed standards and codes. The ROSCs assess the observance by countries of these standards and codes in order to identify potential weaknesses that may contribute to economic and financial vulnerability.

The ECB has also developed working relationships with the IMF in other areas. In particular, the ECB actively participates in the application and development of international statistical standards – such as those laid down in the IMF's Balance of Payments Manual (fifth edition) – as part of the revised System of National Accounts (SNA 93). Working relationships have also been developed in the framework of the Special Data Dissemination Standard (SDDS), which was established in 1996 to ensure that member countries provide timely, reliable and comprehensive data to both the public and the IMF for surveillance purposes. Likewise the ECB is regularly involved in IMF technical assistance activities.

5.3.2 Organisation for Economic Co-operation and Development

The OECD is an intergovernmental organisation which currently has 30 member countries and links with 70 others. It provides a forum for its members to consult each other, compare experiences and cooperate in order to achieve the highest possible sustainable growth and improve economic and social well-being in line with the principles of a market economy. The OECD covers all areas of public policy, including monetary and other economic policies. The ECB takes part in all OECD activities related to the tasks of the Eurosystem.

Although OECD membership is restricted to countries, the European Community is permanently represented at the OECD, and takes part in relevant work. This arrangement is based on Supplementary Protocol No. 1 to Article 13 of the OECD Convention of 14 December 1960. Since 1999 the ECB has participated in all relevant OECD meetings alongside the European Commission as part of the delegation of the European Community, whereby both the ECB and the Commission express their own views within their respective fields of competence.

The OECD Committees and Working Parties in which the ECB participates include the following:

• the Economic and Development Review Committee;
• the Economic Policy Committee and its Working Parties;
• the Committee on Financial Markets.

The **Economic and Development Review Committee (EDRC)**, which was established in 1961, is responsible for conducting regular reviews of the economic situation and policies of each OECD member country. It publishes economic surveys based on these reviews, which include a number of policy recommendations. Member countries may decide to take these recommendations into account in their policy-making processes. In 2001, the EDRC also started conducting an annual review of the euro area.

The **Economic Policy Committee (EPC)** focuses on the global economic situation, in particular the implications of developments in three major OECD regions (the euro area, the United States and Japan). It examines a wide range of issues related to both economic outlooks and policy requirements in the OECD area and thus provides OECD members with a comprehensive assessment of the situation. The EPC is supported by a number of Working Parties:

i.   Working Party No. 1 deals with economic issues and policies of a more structural nature (e.g. the links between policies and long-term growth, the criteria for the surveillance of public expenditure and the role of automatic stabilisers).

ii. Working Party No. 3 monitors and assesses major macroeconomic developments (e.g. exchange rate developments, imbalances in the external and/or budget positions, and systemic financial risks).

iii. The Working Party on Short-Term Economic Prospects (STEP) assists the EPC in formulating economic projections.

Finally, the **Committee on Financial Markets** examines structural developments in OECD financial markets.

5.4 ECB PARTICIPATION IN INFORMAL FORA FOR FINANCE MINISTERS AND CENTRAL BANK GOVERNORS

5.4.1 G7 finance ministers and central bank governors

As part of the broader framework of *cooperation* within the Group of Seven countries[2] (G7), finance ministers and central bank governors meet regularly to discuss key international economic and financial issues. Their meetings are mainly concerned with economic and financial developments and prospects in their respective countries, exchange rate issues and the global economy. In addition, they address issues of common interest related to international monetary and financial policy. These informal exchanges of views may help participants to achieve a greater understanding of the different issues involved, and may also be of use in the discussion and decision-making processes of international organisations such as the IMF, the World Bank or the OECD, providing possible guidance or political impetus for their work.

Up to the start of Stage Three of EMU, participation in the meetings of G7 finance ministers and central bank governors was restricted to the respective national authorities of the G7 countries. With the transfer of monetary and exchange rate policy from the national to the Community level, arrangements in

---

[2] Canada, France, Germany, Italy, Japan, the United Kingdom and the United States form the Group of Seven (G7) and with Russia the Group of Eight (G8). Heads of State or Government and foreign ministers meet in the G8 composition and finance ministers in the G7 composition.

the euro area were adapted to take account of the new allocation of competences. As a result, both the President of the ECB and the President of the Eurogroup participate in those parts of the meetings that deal with macroeconomic surveillance and exchange rate issues. The three central bank governors of the euro area G7 countries (France, Germany and Italy) do not participate in this part of the meetings. However, they continue to take part when the G7 discusses other issues, e.g. the international financial architecture and debt initiatives for poor countries.

In terms of actual roles and responsibilities, the ECB President presents the views of the Eurosystem on monetary policy in the euro area and the President of the Eurogroup participates in the discussions on other economic developments and policies in the euro area. Given that the ECB and the EU Council share responsibility for exchange rate matters, the views presented at the G7 reflect prior consultations between them.

5.4.2 G10 finance ministers and central bank governors

The work of the Group of Ten[3] (G10) ministers and governors is closely linked to the activities of the IMF. It dates back to the creation of the General Arrangements to Borrow (GAB), which were established in 1962 to complement the IMF's ordinary resources. In recent years, the main focus of the G10 has been on preventing and managing international financial crises.

The President of the ECB participates as an observer in the annual meetings of ministers and governors, which are organised alongside the IMF's annual meeting. Meetings are complemented by ad hoc meetings at the deputy level, which the ECB also attends as an observer.

5.4.3 G20 finance ministers and central bank governors

The Group of 20[4] (G20) is an informal forum of finance ministers and central bank governors set up in 1999 to involve key emerging market countries in the dialogue on international economic and financial policy issues. It aims to facilitate an open exchange of views on those matters and thus promote consensus-building on issues discussed by the relevant decision-making bodies, such as the IMF and the World Bank.

---

[3] The G10 comprises Belgium, Canada, France, Germany, Italy, Japan, Netherlands, Sweden, the United Kingdom and the United States. Switzerland is an associate member of the G10.

[4] The members of the Group of 20 are the finance ministers and central bank governors of Argentina, Australia, Brazil, Canada, China, France, Germany, India, Indonesia, Italy, Japan, Korea, Mexico, Russia, Saudi Arabia, South Africa, Turkey, the United Kingdom and the United States. Another member is the European Community, represented by the President of the EU Council and the President of the ECB. The managing director of the IMF and the President of the World Bank, plus the chairpersons of the International Monetary and Financial Committee and Development Committee of the IMF and World Bank, also participate in the talks as ex officio members.

The ECB and the EU Presidency are members of the G20. Both participate in the meetings of G20 ministers and governors as well as in the preparatory meetings at the deputy level. The participation of both the ECB and the EU Presidency makes it possible to bring a euro area-wide perspective to the issues under consideration. The contributions of the ECB and/or the EU Presidency to the G20 discussions are coordinated, to the extent appropriate, in line with the allocation of competences provided for by the Treaty.

5.4.4 Financial Stability Forum

In February 1999 the G7 finance ministers and central bank governors decided to set up a Financial Stability Forum (FSF) with the following objectives:

i.   to assess vulnerabilities of the international financial system;

ii. to identify activities for promoting international financial stability through enhanced information exchange and international cooperation in financial supervision and surveillance.

Administrative support for the FSF is provided by a secretariat located at the BIS. A member of the ECB's Executive Board (Tommaso Padoa-Schioppa) attended the early FSF meetings as an observer and, since June 2000, has attended FSF meetings as a regular member, notably in his capacity as Chairman of the BIS Committee on Payment and Settlement Systems.

5.4.5 Bank for International Settlements and central bank fora

Established in 1930, the BIS is the world's oldest international monetary and financial organisation. A major objective of the BIS is to *"promote the cooperation of central banks"* (Article 3 of the Statute of the BIS). The ECB takes part in all BIS-based *cooperation* activities, including statistical work. Since 2000, the ECB has also been a shareholder of the BIS with voting and representation rights at its Annual General Meeting.

The President of the ECB participates[5] in the meetings of the G10 central bank governors, which are usually held at the BIS headquarters in Basel every two months. Within this forum, the governors discuss key international economic, monetary and financial issues (e.g. economic trends both in industrial countries and in emerging market economies, potential threats to global financial stability and longer-term monetary and financial developments). Meetings are increasingly being opened to the central banks of the emerging market economies that are of systemic importance.

---

[5] Since November 2003, the ECB President has chaired the G10 meetings.

The G10 central bank governors have set up a number of permanent committees and ad hoc Working Parties. Four permanent committees are of particular relevance for the ECB:

i.   The ECB has observer status at the meetings of the **Basel Committee on Banking Supervision (BCBS)**. The BCBS, which is a permanent forum for cooperation among the G10 countries, is an internationally recognised standard-setter for banking regulation, supervision and best practices. Given the importance of the Committee's work for the activities of the ECB and the Eurosystem in the field of prudential supervision and financial stability, the ECB also participates in some of the BCBS' subgroups (e.g. the Electronic Banking Group, the Capital Group, the Research Task Force and the Risk Management Group).

ii. The **Committee on Payment and Settlement Systems (CPSS)** has been chaired by a member of the ECB's Executive Board (Tommaso Padoa-Schioppa) since June 2000. The CPSS is at the forefront of efforts to promote efficient and robust payment and settlement arrangements.

iii. The ECB is also a member of the **Committee on the Global Financial System (CGFS)**. The activities of the CGFS are designed to identify and assess potential sources of stress in the global financial environment, to further understanding of the functioning of financial markets and to promote their efficiency and stability.

iv. Finally, the ECB is a member of the **Markets Committee**, which brings together senior central bank representatives to regularly review developments in the financial markets, focusing in particular on foreign exchange markets.

The Eurotower,
the ECB's
headquarters in
Frankfurt am Main.
Credit:
ECB/Martin Starl.

6 THE ECB AS A CORPORATE ENTITY

As a central bank, the ECB has features of both the public and private sectors. Its legal foundations and mission make it a public authority; at the same time, its policies are mainly implemented by financial operations and its organisational set-up and working methods are similar to those of a private sector bank. The ECB is therefore a public authority *sui generis* with some corporate characteristics.

6.1 MISSION STATEMENT

In August 2003 the Executive Board adopted the ECB's mission statement reflecting its aims and position within the Eurosystem.

"The European Central Bank and the national central banks together constitute the Eurosystem, the central banking system of the euro area. The main objective of the Eurosystem is to maintain price stability: safeguarding the value of the euro.

We at the European Central Bank are committed to performing all central bank tasks entrusted to us effectively. In so doing, we strive for the highest level of integrity, competence, efficiency and transparency."

The first part of the mission statement emphasises the ECB's vital relationship with the NCBs of the euro area and the primary objective of the Eurosystem. The second part stresses the ECB's commitment to performing its tasks in an effective manner, and the values which the staff and management of the ECB regard as especially important for the performance of their duties. The values of integrity, competence, efficiency and transparency were given particular prominence in an ECB staff survey, the results of which served as direct input for the formulation of the mission statement.

These values are reflected in the way in which the ECB has organised its internal structure and working procedures. These structural and procedural features are not static but continually evolving with a view to developing the best practices and standards.

6.2 CORPORATE GOVERNANCE

The term "corporate governance" can have a number of different connotations and definitions. In an ECB context, however, it denotes:

• the rules and procedures for making decisions on the ECB's corporate affairs;

• the arrangements for monitoring compliance with these decisions and with applicable legislation.

Since the ECB is an independent organisation, the ECB's corporate governance is primarily the responsibility of its decision-making bodies, in particular the Governing Council and the Executive Board. In addition, there are several external and internal control layers.

6.2.1 The role of the Governing Council and the Executive Board in corporate governance

As the supreme decision-making body for the administration and functioning of the ECB, the Governing Council adopts the Rules of Procedure of the ECB and is responsible, in particular, for its finances. On a proposal from the Executive Board, it adopts the annual budget of the ECB and takes all decisions relating to the endowment of the ECB with financial resources and the appropriation of the annual financial results. It also determines the conditions of employment of both the Executive Board members (see Section 2.5.1) and the ECB staff.

In line with its statutory task of managing the current business of the ECB, the Executive Board exercises organisational and managerial powers. Having consulted the Governing Council, the Board decides on the internal structure of the ECB, i.e. the number, name and responsibilities of its functional units. The main functional units, or "business areas", are placed under the direct managerial control of the Executive Board. The Board then decides on the individual responsibilities of its members with respect to given business areas and informs both the Governing Council and General Council. Such decisions are taken in the presence of all Board members and may not be taken against the vote of the President.[1]

The Executive Board is also responsible for all staff matters. It adopts the Staff Rules (to implement the Conditions of Employment determined by the Governing Council) and takes all necessary decisions with respect to the selection, appointment and promotion of the staff of the ECB.

6.2.2 External and internal control layers

As mentioned in Section 4.6, the ECB's financial management and integrity is scrutinised externally by independent auditors, the European Court of Auditors and the European Anti-Fraud Office (OLAF). These external control layers are supplemented by several internal control mechanisms and procedures which are described below.

Budget Committee

The Budget Committee, which was established by the Governing Council under Article 15 of the ECB's Rules of Procedure, assists the Governing Council in matters related to the ECB budget. It is composed of representatives of the Eurosystem central banks, one of whom acts as chairperson. The Committee in particular examines the draft annual budgets of the ECB and submits an opinion to the Governing Council before the latter adopts the budgets. Likewise, the Committee submits its view to the Governing Council on the execution of the annual budgets.

[1] Article 10.2 of the Rules of Procedure of the ECB.

Internal control structure

The internal control structure is based on a functional approach, with each business area responsible for its own internal control and efficiency. The business areas establish and implement a set of operational control procedures within their sphere of responsibility. In addition, the ECB's Directorate Planning and Controlling and the Risk Management Division advise the Executive Board on specific bank-wide control issues.

Internal Audit

The Directorate Internal Audit reports directly to the Executive Board. Its mandate is defined in the ECB Audit Charter, which was drawn up by the Executive Board on the basis of international professional standards, in particular those of the Institute of Internal Auditors.

Codes of conduct and insider trading prevention

One of the core values of the ECB is to promote the highest level of integrity. Accordingly, the ECB has established rules and procedures to demonstrate its commitment to this aim.

The **Code of Conduct for the members of the Governing Council**, adopted in May 2002[2], reflects the responsibility of all Governing Council members to safeguard the integrity and reputation of the Eurosystem and maintain the effectiveness of its operations. An adviser, appointed by the Governing Council, provides guidance on some aspects of professional conduct

The **Code of Conduct of the European Central Bank**[3] gives guidance and sets benchmarks for the staff of the ECB and the members of the Executive Board, all of whom are encouraged to maintain high standards of professional ethics in performing their duties.

Insider trading rules[4] have been drawn up to prevent abuse of sensitive financial market information. Under these rules, all ECB staff and Board members are prohibited from taking direct or indirect advantage of inside information when conducting private financial activities at their own risk and for their own account or at the risk and for the account of a third party.

An Ethics Adviser, appointed by the Executive Board, provides guidance on all aspects of professional conduct and also ensures a consistent interpretation of the insider trading rules.

Data Protection Officer

In line with a European Parliament and Council Regulation[5], the Executive Board has appointed a Data Protection Officer (DPO), who took up his position on

[2] OJ C 123, 24.5.2002, p. 9.
[3] OJ C 76, 8.3.2001, p. 12.
[4] OJ C 236, 22.8.2001, p. 13.
[5] Regulation (EC) No 45/2001 of the European Parliament and of the Council of 18 December 2000 on the protection of individuals with regard to the processing of personal data by the Community institutions and bodies and on the free movement of such data (OJ L 8, 12.1.2001, p. 1).

1 January 2002. The DPO ensures that personal data collected or processed by the ECB are kept confidential.

Procurement rules

In its procurement of goods and services, the ECB gives due regard to the principles of publicity, transparency, equal access, non-discrimination and efficient administration. Its procurement rules are in line with the principles of the Community Public Procurement Directives. They stipulate that derogations from these principles may only be made in cases of urgency, for reasons of security or secrecy, where there is a sole supplier, for supplies from NCBs to the ECB, or to ensure the continuity of a supplier.

6.2.3 Access to the ECB's archives

Public access to the ECB's archives is governed by the provisions of the ECB Decision of 4 March 2004[6]. This Decision grants the public the right of access to ECB documents in line with the resolutions of the Birmingham (1992) and Copenhagen (1993) European Council meetings in order to bring the Community closer to its citizens and in recognition of citizens' legitimate interest in following the organisation and functioning of institutions and bodies that are financed with public funds.

The term "document" means any content, whatever its medium, drawn up or held by the ECB and relating to its policies, activities or decisions. Thus the public also has access to the documents originating from the EMI and the Committee of Governors, which are contained in the ECB's archives.

Access to a document is not granted where its disclosure would not be in the public interest as regards the confidentiality of the proceedings of the ECB's decision-making bodies. The confidentiality of these and related documents is maintained for a maximum period of 30 years. The rationale for keeping such documents confidential (see Section 4.2.2) prevails over the public's interest in information. However, keeping these documents confidential does not harm the public interest since the ECB informs the public extensively of the outcome of the meetings of its decision-making bodies.

Applications for access to ECB documents are to be addressed to the ECB's Directorate General Secretariat and Linguistic Services which manages the ECB's archives. A refusal of the application may be referred to the Executive Board. If the ECB rejects an application outright, the matter may be referred to the European Ombudsman and the Court of Justice under Articles 195 and 230 of the EC Treaty.

---

[6] Decision ECB/2004/3 of 4 March 2004 on public access to European Central Bank documents (OJ L 80, 18.3.2004, p. 42).

6.3 ORGANISATIONAL STRUCTURE

The Executive Board determines the organisational structure of the ECB. Under Article 10.2 of the ECB's Rules of Procedure, the Governing Council needs to be consulted prior to any changes to the organisational structure.

The ECB is currently divided into 17 business areas (see Chart 3). The flat organisational structure reflects both the breadth of the functions of the ECB and the wish to avoid too deep a hierarchy. Each business area is headed by a senior manager (Director General or Director) who reports to a member of the Executive Board. Several area heads also chair ESCB committees in their respective fields of competence (see Section 2.5.2).

Several internal ECB committees have been established to facilitate the performance of cross-departmental functions. In 2003 the Executive Board also established a Management Committee, which advises and assists the Executive Board on issues relating to the management of the ECB, its strategic planning and the annual budget process. The Management Committee is chaired by a member of the Executive Board and composed of senior managers.

Until now, the ECB's priorities have been to establish its functions, formulate and implement the single monetary policy and introduce the euro. After the successful completion of these processes and with a steady increase in the number of staff (from some 400 in 1998 to around 1,200 in 2003), the ECB has increased its focus on strengthening its internal organisation. In this context, it has embarked on a process called "ECB in Motion", which aims to strengthen the internal functioning of the ECB. As a result of this process, a number of measures have been introduced

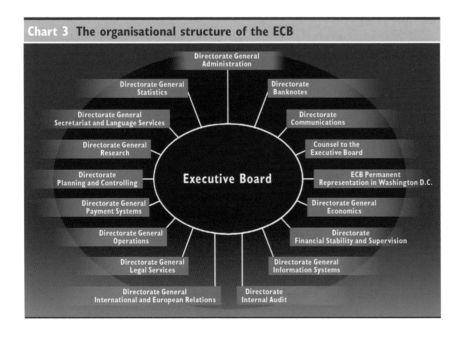

Chart 3 The organisational structure of the ECB

Directorate General Administration
Directorate General Statistics
Directorate Banknotes
Directorate General Secretariat and Language Services
Directorate Communications
Directorate General Research
Counsel to the Executive Board
Directorate Planning and Controlling
Executive Board
ECB Permanent Representation in Washington D.C.
Directorate General Payment Systems
Directorate General Economics
Directorate General Operations
Directorate Financial Stability and Supervision
Directorate General Legal Services
Directorate General Information Systems
Directorate General International and European Relations
Directorate Internal Audit

to improve the functioning of internal management, to enhance professional development opportunities and internal communication and to reduce bureaucracy[7].

6.4 STAFF AND STAFF RELATIONS

The ECB has the power to define its staff policy autonomously. This autonomy forms part of the ECB's independence as guaranteed by Article 108 of the EC Treaty and substantiated in Article 36 of the Statute of the ESCB.

6.4.1 Staff

The ECB employs staff originating from all EU Member States. At the end of 2003, it employed 1,213 people, The bulk of ECB staff are professionally qualified and are involved in analysis and research, and corporate management. As core and leader of the Eurosystem, the ECB has created a large number of job opportunities requiring managerial and analytical skills. Most of these professionals have studied economics at graduate or postgraduate level.

ECB staff are selected, appointed and promoted on the basis of professional qualifications, and with due regard to publicity, transparency, equal access and non-discrimination. In line with these principles, the recruitment rules adopted by the Executive Board[8] lay down a selection process that is geared towards securing highly qualified and able individuals with impeccable standards of integrity. While observing this principle, the selection process also aims to secure the broadest possible geographical basis from among nationals of EU Member States, without regard to racial or ethnic origin, religion or belief, sexual orientation or disability. The ECB does not apply quotas by nationality. Instead, its policy to advertise EU-wide with specific information campaigns ensure a level playing-field for all EU nationalities.

The conditions of employment of ECB staff, as determined by the Governing Council and implemented by the Staff Rules adopted by the Executive Board, form an integral part of the individual contracts of employment between the ECB and its staff members. In principle, individual contracts are concluded for an indefinite period.

The salaries and social benefits of ECB staff members are comparable with those at other European and European-based international organisations. The ECB has programmes in place to support members of staff recruited throughout the EU in moving themselves and their families to Frankfurt am Main. In addition, the ECB offers its staff childcare and international education facilities. Since September 2002 the children of ECB staff have been able to attend the new European School, which has been established in the north-west of Frankfurt.[9]

---

[7] See the ECB's Annual Report 2003, Chapter 8, Section 2.2.
[8] ECB (2004), Administrative Circular 05/2004 of 18 May 2004.
[9] The European Schools are a joint undertaking of the EU Member States and the European Community and have been set up primarily for the benefit of the staff of Community institutions and bodies.

The salaries paid by the ECB, including the emoluments of the members of the Executive Board, are subject to income tax levied by the European Community for the benefit of its budget.

The rights of the ECB staff are protected by the legal system of the European Community. Under the Treaty, the European Court of Justice has jurisdiction in any dispute between the ECB and its staff. The rights of staff include the right to take strike action.

An independent Social Counsellor provides confidential counselling to staff members on work-related matters and mediates in interpersonal conflicts at the workplace. The ECB has also appointed an independent Equal Opportunities Adviser to advise on issues related to equal opportunities in the broadest sense, for example with regard to gender, nationality and age.

6.4.2 ECB staff representation

The ECB's Conditions of Employment stipulate that staff representation should be organised through a Staff Committee. This Committee represents the general interests of all members of staff on matters related to contracts of employment; staff regulations and remuneration; employment, working, health and safety conditions at the ECB; and social security cover and pension schemes. Its members are elected by secret ballot of all staff members.

Under the Conditions of Employment, the ECB Staff Committee is given full consultation rights in such matters, rights with which the ECB scrupulously complies. In addition, the ECB has provided the Staff Committee with all the facilities necessary to enable it to perform its duties effectively. For example, its members are granted partial dispensation from work equivalent to 2.3 full-time positions. In addition, the ECB pays for secretarial and logistical support and legal advice.

Some ECB staff are members of the Union of the Staff of the ECB (USE). The USE is also involved by the ECB in matters related to social and working conditions. However, in 2002 the Court of First Instance found the request of the USE and an external trade union, the International and European Public Services Organisation (IPSO), for recognition as partners in the negotiation of collective labour agreements to be inadmissible. The appeal initiated by IPSO before the European Court of Justice was subsequently withdrawn.

6.4.3 Social Dialogue with regard to the ESCB

In 1999 the ECB established a voluntary Social Dialogue with the European trade union federations representing employees at the ESCB central banks:

• UNI-Europe (formerly Eurofiet);
• the Standing Committee of the Unions of central bank staff (SCUCB);
• the European Public Sector Union (EPSU).

The Social Dialogue was set up at the request of the European trade union federations and involves employee representatives from each of the ESCB central banks. It addresses various aspects of decisions (e.g. substance, rationale, timing) that have a major impact on the level and the quality of employment in the NCBs. It ensures that staff representatives from all EU NCBs and the ECB can express their views before the decision-making bodies of the ECB take a decision.

The Social Dialogue does not interfere with local staff relations at the ECB and the NCBs; this was stated explicitly in a document signed by the relevant parties in December 1999. Such relations are exclusively a matter for the ECB and the individual NCBs and are dealt with at the local level.

6.5 SEAT AND PREMISES

By common accord of the Heads of State or Government of the EU Member States of 29 October 1993, Frankfurt am Main became the seat of the ECB.[10] A Headquarters Agreement with the Federal Republic of Germany was signed on 18 September 1998 and entered into force on 4 March 1999. It deals with practical and technical aspects of the application of the Protocol on Privileges and Immunities of the European Communities.

The ECB is currently located in three rented buildings in the centre of Frankfurt. However, it has decided to construct its own premises. In March 2002 the ECB purchased land in the eastern part of Frankfurt on which to build; the site currently houses Frankfurt's *Grossmarkthalle* (wholesale market), which is a listed building and is to be incorporated into the design of the new premises.

In November 2002 the ECB launched an international urban and architectural design competition for its new premises.[11] The ECB received applications from more than 300 architects from 31 countries and five continents. A Pre-Selection Committee consisting of five ECB experts supported by five architects chose 80 candidates, 70 established and 10 emerging young architects.

An international jury chaired by the ECB's Vice-President Lucas D. Papademos and composed of 12 members (three members from the ECB, three members from the NCBs, five internationally renowned architects and one representative from the City of Frankfurt) shortlisted three winning designs in February 2004.[12] The selection was made on the basis of predetermined criteria such as the quality of the architectural design, originality, inspiration and innovation of the concept and its integration into the surrounding area.

---

[10] Decision taken by common Agreement between the Representatives of the Governments of the Member States, meeting at Head of State and Government level, on the location of the seats of certain bodies and departments of the European Communities and of Europol (OJ C 323, 30.11.1993, p. 1).

[11] See the ECB's Press Release of 26 November 2002.

[12] See the ECB's Press Release of 13 February 2004.

The prizes were awarded as follows:

• 1st prize: Coop Himmelb(l)au, Vienna, Austria;

• 2nd prize: ASP Schweger Assoziierte, Berlin, Germany;

• 3rd prize: 54f architekten/T. R. Hamzah & Yeang, Darmstadt,
  Germany/Selangor, Malaysia.

All three prizewinners were then invited to participate in the project's revision phase, which requires the architecture offices to review their design proposals to take account of the specific recommendations and requirements of the jury, the ECB and the City of Frankfurt. In October 2004, at the end of the revision phase, the Governing Council is expected to award the contract for planning the ECB's new premises to one of the three prizewinning architecture offices. The planning process will start thereafter and construction is scheduled to begin in 2006.

The new building will not only enhance the ECB's functionality and efficiency, but will also reflect the ECB's core values as Europe's monetary authority.

ANNEX I

EXCERPTS FROM
THE TREATY ESTABLISHING THE EUROPEAN COMMUNITY

PART ONE

PRINCIPLES

Article 2
The Community shall have as its task, by establishing a common market and an economic and monetary union and by implementing common policies or activities referred to in Articles 3 and 4, to promote throughout the Community a harmonious, balanced and sustainable development of economic activities, a high level of employment and of social protection, equality between men and women, sustainable and non-inflationary growth, a high degree of competitiveness and convergence of economic performance, a high level of protection and improvement of the quality of the environment, the raising of the standard of living and quality of life, and economic and social cohesion and solidarity among Member States.

Article 3
1. For the purposes set out in Article 2, the activities of the Community shall include, as provided in this Treaty and in accordance with the timetable set out therein:

(a) the prohibition, as between Member States, of customs duties and quantitative restrictions on the import and export of goods, and of all other measures having equivalent effect;

(b) a common commercial policy;

(c) an internal market characterised by the abolition, as between Member States, of obstacles to the free movement of goods, persons, services and capital;

(d) measures concerning the entry and movement of persons as provided for in Title IV;

(e) a common policy in the sphere of agriculture and fisheries;

(f) a common policy in the sphere of transport;

(g) a system ensuring that competition in the internal market is not distorted;

(h) the approximation of the laws of Member States to the extent required for the functioning of the common market;

(i)   the promotion of coordination between employment policies of the Member States with a view to enhancing their effectiveness by developing a coordinated strategy for employment;

(j)   a policy in the social sphere comprising a European Social Fund;

(k)   the strengthening of economic and social cohesion;

(l)   a policy in the sphere of the environment;

(m) the strengthening of the competitiveness of Community industry;

(n)   the promotion of research and technological development;

(o)   encouragement for the establishment and development of trans-European networks;

(p)   a contribution to the attainment of a high level of health protection;

(q)   a contribution to education and training of quality and to the flowering of the cultures of the Member States;

(r)   a policy in the sphere of development cooperation;

(s)   the association of the overseas countries and territories in order to increase trade and promote jointly economic and social development;

(t)   a contribution to the strengthening of consumer protection;

(u)   measures in the spheres of energy, civil protection and tourism.

2. In all the activities referred to in this Article, the Community shall aim to eliminate inequalities, and to promote equality, between men and women.

Article 4
1. For the purposes set out in Article 2, the activities of the Member States and the Community shall include, as provided in this Treaty and in accordance with the timetable set out therein, the adoption of an economic policy which is based on the close coordination of Member States' economic policies, on the internal market and on the definition of common objectives, and conducted in accordance with the principle of an open market economy with free competition.

2. Concurrently with the foregoing, and as provided in this Treaty and in accordance with the timetable and the procedures set out therein, these activities shall include the irrevocable fixing of exchange rates leading to the introduction of a single currency, the ecu, and the definition and conduct of a single monetary policy and exchange-rate policy the primary objective of both of which shall be to maintain price stability and, without prejudice to this objective, to support the

general economic policies in the Community, in accordance with the principle of an open market economy with free competition.

3. These activities of the Member States and the Community shall entail compliance with the following guiding principles: stable prices, sound public finances and monetary conditions and a sustainable balance of payments.

Article 8
A European system of central banks (hereinafter referred to as 'ESCB') and a European Central Bank (hereinafter referred to as 'ECB') shall be established in accordance with the procedures laid down in this Treaty; they shall act within the limits of the powers conferred upon them by this Treaty and by the Statute of the ESCB and of the ECB (hereinafter referred to as 'Statute of the ESCB') annexed thereto.

PART THREE

COMMUNITY POLICIES

Title VII
Economic and monetary policy

CHAPTER I

ECONOMIC POLICY

Article 98
Member States shall conduct their economic policies with a view to contributing to the achievement of the objectives of the Community, as defined in Article 2, and in the context of the broad guidelines referred to in Article 99(2). The Member States and the Community shall act in accordance with the principle of an open market economy with free competition, favouring an efficient allocation of resources, and in compliance with the principles set out in Article 4.

Article 99
1. Member States shall regard their economic policies as a matter of common concern and shall coordinate them within the Council, in accordance with the provisions of Article 98.

2. The Council shall, acting by a qualified majority on a recommendation from the Commission, formulate a draft for the broad guidelines of the economic policies of the Member States and of the Community, and shall report its findings to the European Council.

The European Council shall, acting on the basis of the report from the Council, discuss a conclusion on the broad guidelines of the economic policies of the Member States and of the Community.

On the basis of this conclusion, the Council shall, acting by a qualified majority, adopt a recommendation setting out these broad guidelines. The Council shall inform the European Parliament of its recommendation.

3. In order to ensure closer coordination of economic policies and sustained convergence of the economic performances of the Member States, the Council shall, on the basis of reports submitted by the Commission, monitor economic developments in each of the Member States and in the Community as well as the consistency of economic policies with the broad guidelines referred to in paragraph 2, and regularly carry out an overall assessment.

For the purpose of this multilateral surveillance, Member States shall forward information to the Commission about important measures taken by them in the field of their economic policy and such other information as they deem necessary.

4. Where it is established, under the procedure referred to in paragraph 3, that the economic policies of a Member State are not consistent with the broad guidelines referred to in paragraph 2 or that they risk jeopardising the proper functioning of economic and monetary union, the Council may, acting by a qualified majority on a recommendation from the Commission, make the necessary recommendations to the Member State concerned. The Council may, acting by a qualified majority on a proposal from the Commission, decide to make its recommendations public.

The President of the Council and the Commission shall report to the European Parliament on the results of multilateral surveillance. The President of the Council may be invited to appear before the competent committee of the European Parliament if the Council has made its recommendations public.

5. The Council, acting in accordance with the procedure referred to in Article 252, may adopt detailed rules for the multilateral surveillance procedure referred to in paragraphs 3 and 4 of this Article.

Article 100
1. Without prejudice to any other procedures provided for in this Treaty, the Council, acting by a qualified majority on a proposal from the Commission, may decide upon the measures appropriate to the economic situation, in particular if severe difficulties arise in the supply of certain products.

2. Where a Member State is in difficulties or is seriously threatened with severe difficulties caused by exceptional occurrences beyond its control, the Council, acting by a qualified majority on a proposal from the Commission, may grant, under certain conditions, Community financial assistance to the Member State concerned. The President of the Council shall inform the European Parliament of the decision taken.

Article 101
1. Overdraft facilities or any other type of credit facility with the ECB or with the central banks of the Member States (hereinafter referred to as 'national central

banks') in favour of Community institutions or bodies, central governments, regional, local or other public authorities, other bodies governed by public law, or public undertakings of Member States shall be prohibited, as shall the purchase directly from them by the ECB or national central banks of debt instruments.

2. Paragraph 1 shall not apply to publicly owned credit institutions which, in the context of the supply of reserves by central banks, shall be given the same treatment by national central banks and the ECB as private credit institutions.

Article 102
1. Any measure, not based on prudential considerations, establishing privileged access by Community institutions or bodies, central governments, regional, local or other public authorities, other bodies governed by public law, or public undertakings of Member States to financial institutions, shall be prohibited.

2. The Council, acting in accordance with the procedure referred to in Article 252, shall, before 1 January 1994, specify definitions for the application of the prohibition referred to in paragraph 1.

Article 103
1. The Community shall not be liable for or assume the commitments of central governments, regional, local or other public authorities, other bodies governed by public law, or public undertakings of any Member State, without prejudice to mutual financial guarantees for the joint execution of a specific project. A Member State shall not be liable for or assume the commitments of central governments, regional, local or other public authorities, other bodies governed by public law, or public undertakings of another Member State, without prejudice to mutual financial guarantees for the joint execution of a specific project.

2. If necessary, the Council, acting in accordance with the procedure referred to in Article 252, may specify definitions for the application of the prohibition referred to in Article 101 and in this Article.

Article 104
1. Member States shall avoid excessive government deficits.

2. The Commission shall monitor the development of the budgetary situation and of the stock of government debt in the Member States with a view to identifying gross errors. In particular it shall examine compliance with budgetary discipline on the basis of the following two criteria:

(a) whether the ratio of the planned or actual government deficit to gross domestic product exceeds a reference value, unless:

  – either the ratio has declined substantially and continuously and reached a level that comes close to the reference value;

  – or, alternatively, the excess over the reference value is only exceptional and temporary and the ratio remains close to the reference value;

(b) whether the ratio of government debt to gross domestic product exceeds a reference value, unless the ratio is sufficiently diminishing and approaching the reference value at a satisfactory pace.

The reference values are specified in the Protocol on the excessive deficit procedure annexed to this Treaty.

3. If a Member State does not fulfil the requirements under one or both of these criteria, the Commission shall prepare a report. The report of the Commission shall also take into account whether the government deficit exceeds government investment expenditure and take into account all other relevant factors, including the medium-term economic and budgetary position of the Member State.

The Commission may also prepare a report if, notwithstanding the fulfilment of the requirements under the criteria, it is of the opinion that there is a risk of an excessive deficit in a Member State.

4. The Committee provided for in Article 114 shall formulate an opinion on the report of the Commission.

5. If the Commission considers that an excessive deficit in a Member State exists or may occur, the Commission shall address an opinion to the Council.

6. The Council shall, acting by a qualified majority on a recommendation from the Commission, and having considered any observations which the Member State concerned may wish to make, decide after an overall assessment whether an excessive deficit exists.

7. Where the existence of an excessive deficit is decided according to paragraph 6, the Council shall make recommendations to the Member State concerned with a view to bringing that situation to an end within a given period. Subject to the provisions of paragraph 8, these recommendations shall not be made public.

8. Where it establishes that there has been no effective action in response to its recommendations within the period laid down, the Council may make its recommendations public.

9. If a Member State persists in failing to put into practice the recommendations of the Council, the Council may decide to give notice to the Member State to take, within a specified time limit, measures for the deficit reduction which is judged necessary by the Council in order to remedy the situation.

In such a case, the Council may request the Member State concerned to submit reports in accordance with a specific timetable in order to examine the adjustment efforts of that Member State.

10. The rights to bring actions provided for in Articles 226 and 227 may not be exercised within the framework of paragraphs 1 to 9 of this Article.

11. As long as a Member State fails to comply with a decision taken in accordance with paragraph 9, the Council may decide to apply or, as the case may be, intensify one or more of the following measures:

– to require the Member State concerned to publish additional information, to be specified by the Council, before issuing bonds and securities;

– to invite the European Investment Bank to reconsider its lending policy towards the Member State concerned;

– to require the Member State concerned to make a non-interest-bearing deposit of an appropriate size with the Community until the excessive deficit has, in the view of the Council, been corrected;

– to impose fines of an appropriate size.

The President of the Council shall inform the European Parliament of the decisions taken.

12. The Council shall abrogate some or all of its decisions referred to in paragraphs 6 to 9 and 11 to the extent that the excessive deficit in the Member State concerned has, in the view of the Council, been corrected. If the Council has previously made public recommendations, it shall, as soon as the decision under paragraph 8 has been abrogated, make a public statement that an excessive deficit in the Member State concerned no longer exists.

13. When taking the decisions referred to in paragraphs 7 to 9, 11 and 12, the Council shall act on a recommendation from the Commission by a majority of two thirds of the votes of its members weighted in accordance with Article 205(2), excluding the votes of the representative of the Member State concerned.

14. Further provisions relating to the implementation of the procedure described in this Article are set out in the Protocol on the excessive deficit procedure annexed to this Treaty.

The Council shall, acting unanimously on a proposal from the Commission and after consulting the European Parliament and the ECB, adopt the appropriate provisions which shall then replace the said Protocol.

Subject to the other provisions of this paragraph, the Council shall, before 1 January 1994, acting by a qualified majority on a proposal from the Commission and after consulting the European Parliament, lay down detailed rules and definitions for the application of the provisions of the said Protocol.

CHAPTER 2

MONETARY POLICY

Article 105

1. The primary objective of the ESCB shall be to maintain price stability. Without prejudice to the objective of price stability, the ESCB shall support the general economic policies in the Community with a view to contributing to the achievement of the objectives of the Community as laid down in Article 2. The ESCB shall act in accordance with the principle of an open market economy with free competition, favouring an efficient allocation of resources, and in compliance with the principles set out in Article 4.

2. The basic tasks to be carried out through the ESCB shall be:

– to define and implement the monetary policy of the Community;

– to conduct foreign-exchange operations consistent with the provisions of Article 111;

– to hold and manage the official foreign reserves of the Member States;

– to promote the smooth operation of payment systems.

3. The third indent of paragraph 2 shall be without prejudice to the holding and management by the governments of Member States of foreign-exchange working balances.

4. The ECB shall be consulted:

– on any proposed Community act in its fields of competence;

– by national authorities regarding any draft legislative provision in its fields of competence, but within the limits and under the conditions set out by the Council in accordance with the procedure laid down in Article 107(6).

The ECB may submit opinions to the appropriate Community institutions or bodies or to national authorities on matters in its fields of competence.

5. The ESCB shall contribute to the smooth conduct of policies pursued by the competent authorities relating to the prudential supervision of credit institutions and the stability of the financial system.

6. The Council may, acting unanimously on a proposal from the Commission and after consulting the ECB and after receiving the assent of the European Parliament, confer upon the ECB specific tasks concerning policies relating to the prudential supervision of credit institutions and other financial institutions with the exception of insurance undertakings.

Article 106
1. The ECB shall have the exclusive right to authorise the issue of banknotes within the Community. The ECB and the national central banks may issue such notes. The banknotes issued by the ECB and the national central banks shall be the only such notes to have the status of legal tender within the Community.

2. Member States may issue coins subject to approval by the ECB of the volume of the issue. The Council may, acting in accordance with the procedure referred to in Article 252 and after consulting the ECB, adopt measures to harmonise the denominations and technical specifications of all coins intended for circulation to the extent necessary to permit their smooth circulation within the Community.

Article 107
1. The ESCB shall be composed of the ECB and of the national central banks.

2. The ECB shall have legal personality.

3. The ESCB shall be governed by the decision-making bodies of the ECB which shall be the Governing Council and the Executive Board.

4. The Statute of the ESCB is laid down in a Protocol annexed to this Treaty.

5. Articles 5.1, 5.2, 5.3, 17, 18, 19.1, 22, 23, 24, 26, 32.2, 32.3, 32.4, 32.6, 33.1(a) and 36 of the Statute of the ESCB may be amended by the Council, acting either by a qualified majority on a recommendation from the ECB and after consulting the Commission or unanimously on a proposal from the Commission and after consulting the ECB. In either case, the assent of the European Parliament shall be required.

6. The Council, acting by a qualified majority either on a proposal from the Commission and after consulting the European Parliament and the ECB or on a recommendation from the ECB and after consulting the European Parliament and the Commission, shall adopt the provisions referred to in Articles 4, 5.4, 19.2, 20, 28.1, 29.2, 30.4 and 34.3 of the Statute of the ESCB.

Article 108
When exercising the powers and carrying out the tasks and duties conferred upon them by this Treaty and the Statute of the ESCB, neither the ECB, nor a national central bank, nor any member of their decision-making bodies shall seek or take instructions from Community institutions or bodies, from any government of a Member State or from any other body. The Community institutions and bodies and the governments of the Member States undertake to respect this principle and not to seek to influence the members of the decision-making bodies of the ECB or of the national central banks in the performance of their tasks.

Article 109
Each Member State shall ensure, at the latest at the date of the establishment of the ESCB, that its national legislation including the statutes of its national central bank is compatible with this Treaty and the Statute of the ESCB.

Article 110

1. In order to carry out the tasks entrusted to the ESCB, the ECB shall, in accordance with the provisions of this Treaty and under the conditions laid down in the Statute of the ESCB:

– make regulations to the extent necessary to implement the tasks defined in Article 3.1, first indent, Articles 19.1, 22 and 25.2 of the Statute of the ESCB and in cases which shall be laid down in the acts of the Council referred to in Article 107(6);

– take decisions necessary for carrying out the tasks entrusted to the ESCB under this Treaty and the Statute of the ESCB;

– make recommendations and deliver opinions.

2. A regulation shall have general application. It shall be binding in its entirety and directly applicable in all Member States.

Recommendations and opinions shall have no binding force.

A decision shall be binding in its entirety upon those to whom it is addressed.

Articles 253, 254 and 256 shall apply to regulations and decisions adopted by the ECB.

The ECB may decide to publish its decisions, recommendations and opinions.

3. Within the limits and under the conditions adopted by the Council under the procedure laid down in Article 107(6), the ECB shall be entitled to impose fines or periodic penalty payments on undertakings for failure to comply with obligations under its regulations and decisions.

Article 111

1. By way of derogation from Article 300, the Council may, acting unanimously on a recommendation from the ECB or from the Commission, and after consulting the ECB in an endeavour to reach a consensus consistent with the objective of price stability, after consulting the European Parliament, in accordance with the procedure in paragraph 3 for determining the arrangements, conclude formal agreements on an exchange-rate system for the ecu in relation to non-Community currencies. The Council may, acting by a qualified majority on a recommendation from the ECB or from the Commission, and after consulting the ECB in an endeavour to reach a consensus consistent with the objective of price stability, adopt, adjust or abandon the central rates of the ecu within the exchange-rate system. The President of the Council shall inform the European Parliament of the adoption, adjustment or abandonment of the ecu central rates.

2. In the absence of an exchange-rate system in relation to one or more non-Community currencies as referred to in paragraph 1, the Council, acting by a qualified majority either on a recommendation from the Commission and after

consulting the ECB or on a recommendation from the ECB, may formulate general orientations for exchange-rate policy in relation to these currencies. These general orientations shall be without prejudice to the primary objective of the ESCB to maintain price stability.

3. By way of derogation from Article 300, where agreements concerning monetary or foreign-exchange regime matters need to be negotiated by the Community with one or more States or international organisations, the Council, acting by a qualified majority on a recommendation from the Commission and after consulting the ECB, shall decide the arrangements for the negotiation and for the conclusion of such agreements. These arrangements shall ensure that the Community expresses a single position. The Commission shall be fully associated with the negotiations.

Agreements concluded in accordance with this paragraph shall be binding on the institutions of the Community, on the ECB and on Member States.

4. Subject to paragraph 1, the Council, acting by a qualified majority on a proposal from the Commission and after consulting the ECB, shall decide on the position of the Community at international level as regards issues of particular relevance to economic and monetary union and on its representation, in compliance with the allocation of powers laid down in Articles 99 and 105.

5. Without prejudice to Community competence and Community agreements as regards economic and monetary union, Member States may negotiate in international bodies and conclude international agreements.

CHAPTER 3

INSTITUTIONAL PROVISIONS

Article 112
1. The Governing Council of the ECB shall comprise the members of the Executive Board of the ECB and the Governors of the national central banks.

2. (a) The Executive Board shall comprise the President, the Vice-President and four other members.

(b) The President, the Vice-President and the other members of the Executive Board shall be appointed from among persons of recognised standing and professional experience in monetary or banking matters by common accord of the governments of the Member States at the level of Heads of State or Government, on a recommendation from the Council, after it has consulted the European Parliament and the Governing Council of the ECB.

Their term of office shall be eight years and shall not be renewable.

Only nationals of Member States may be members of the Executive Board.

Article 113

1. The President of the Council and a member of the Commission may participate, without having the right to vote, in meetings of the Governing Council of the ECB.

The President of the Council may submit a motion for deliberation to the Governing Council of the ECB.

2. The President of the ECB shall be invited to participate in Council meetings when the Council is discussing matters relating to the objectives and tasks of the ESCB.

3. The ECB shall address an annual report on the activities of the ESCB and on the monetary policy of both the previous and current year to the European Parliament, the Council and the Commission, and also to the European Council. The President of the ECB shall present this report to the Council and to the European Parliament, which may hold a general debate on that basis.

The President of the ECB and the other members of the Executive Board may, at the request of the European Parliament or on their own initiative, be heard by the competent committees of the European Parliament.

Article 114

1. In order to promote coordination of the policies of Member States to the full extent needed for the functioning of the internal market, a Monetary Committee with advisory status is hereby set up.

It shall have the following tasks:

– to keep under review the monetary and financial situation of the Member States and of the Community and the general payments system of the Member States and to report regularly thereon to the Council and to the Commission;

– to deliver opinions at the request of the Council or of the Commission, or on its own initiative for submission to those institutions;

– without prejudice to Article 207, to contribute to the preparation of the work of the Council referred to in Articles 59, 60, 99(2), (3), (4) and (5), 100, 102, 103, 104, 116(2), 117(6), 119, 120, 121(2) and 122(1);

– to examine, at least once a year, the situation regarding the movement of capital and the freedom of payments, as they result from the application of this Treaty and of measures adopted by the Council; the examination shall cover all measures relating to capital movements and payments; the Committee shall report to the Commission and to the Council on the outcome of this examination.

The Member States and the Commission shall each appoint two members of the Monetary Committee.

2. At the start of the third stage, an Economic and Financial Committee shall be set up. The Monetary Committee provided for in paragraph 1 shall be dissolved.

The Economic and Financial Committee shall have the following tasks:

– to deliver opinions at the request of the Council or of the Commission, or on its own initiative for submission to those institutions;

– to keep under review the economic and financial situation of the Member States and of the Community and to report regularly thereon to the Council and to the Commission, in particular on financial relations with third countries and international institutions;

– without prejudice to Article 207, to contribute to the preparation of the work of the Council referred to in Articles 59, 60, 99(2), (3), (4) and (5), 100, 102, 103, 104, 105(6), 106(2), 107(5) and (6), 111, 119, 120(2) and (3), 122(2), 123(4) and (5), and to carry out other advisory and preparatory tasks assigned to it by the Council;

– to examine, at least once a year, the situation regarding the movement of capital and the freedom of payments, as they result from the application of this Treaty and of measures adopted by the Council; the examination shall cover all measures relating to capital movements and payments; the Committee shall report to the Commission and to the Council on the outcome of this examination.

The Member States, the Commission and the ECB shall each appoint no more than two members of the Committee.

3. The Council shall, acting by a qualified majority on a proposal from the Commission and after consulting the ECB and the Committee referred to in this Article, lay down detailed provisions concerning the composition of the Economic and Financial Committee. The President of the Council shall inform the European Parliament of such a decision.

4. In addition to the tasks set out in paragraph 2, if and as long as there are Member States with a derogation as referred to in Articles 122 and 123, the Committee shall keep under review the monetary and financial situation and the general payments system of those Member States and report regularly thereon to the Council and to the Commission.

Article 115
For matters within the scope of Articles 99(4), 104 with the exception of paragraph 14, 111, 121, 122 and 123(4) and (5), the Council or a Member State may request the Commission to make a recommendation or a proposal, as appropriate. The Commission shall examine this request and submit its conclusions to the Council without delay.

CHAPTER 4

TRANSITIONAL PROVISIONS

Article 119
1. Where a Member State is in difficulties or is seriously threatened with difficulties as regards its balance of payments either as a result of an overall disequilibrium in its balance of payments, or as a result of the type of currency at its disposal, and where such difficulties are liable in particular to jeopardise the functioning of the common market or the progressive implementation of the common commercial policy, the Commission shall immediately investigate the position of the State in question and the action which, making use of all the means at its disposal, that State has taken or may take in accordance with the provisions of this Treaty. The Commission shall state what measures it recommends the State concerned to take.

If the action taken by a Member State and the measures suggested by the Commission do not prove sufficient to overcome the difficulties which have arisen or which threaten, the Commission shall, after consulting the Committee referred to in Article 114, recommend to the Council the granting of mutual assistance and appropriate methods therefor.

The Commission shall keep the Council regularly informed of the situation and of how it is developing.

2. The Council, acting by a qualified majority, shall grant such mutual assistance; it shall adopt directives or decisions laying down the conditions and details of such assistance, which may take such forms as:

(a) a concerted approach to or within any other international organisations to which Member States may have recourse;

(b) measures needed to avoid deflection of trade where the State which is in difficulties maintains or reintroduces quantitative restrictions against third countries;

(c) the granting of limited credits by other Member States, subject to their agreement.

3. If the mutual assistance recommended by the Commission is not granted by the Council or if the mutual assistance granted and the measures taken are insufficient, the Commission shall authorise the State which is in difficulties to take protective measures, the conditions and details of which the Commission shall determine.

Such authorisation may be revoked and such conditions and details may be changed by the Council acting by a qualified majority.

4. Subject to Article 122(6), this Article shall cease to apply from the beginning of the third stage.

Article 120

1. Where a sudden crisis in the balance of payments occurs and a decision within the meaning of Article 119(2) is not immediately taken, the Member State concerned may, as a precaution, take the necessary protective measures. Such measures must cause the least possible disturbance in the functioning of the common market and must not be wider in scope than is strictly necessary to remedy the sudden difficulties which have arisen.

2. The Commission and the other Member States shall be informed of such protective measures not later than when they enter into force. The Commission may recommend to the Council the granting of mutual assistance under Article 119.

3. After the Commission has delivered an opinion and the Committee referred to in Article 114 has been consulted, the Council may, acting by a qualified majority, decide that the State concerned shall amend, suspend or abolish the protective measures referred to above.

4. Subject to Article 122(6), this Article shall cease to apply from the beginning of the third stage.

Article 121

1. The Commission and the EMI shall report to the Council on the progress made in the fulfilment by the Member States of their obligations regarding the achievement of economic and monetary union. These reports shall include an examination of the compatibility between each Member State's national legislation, including the statutes of its national central bank, and Articles 108 and 109 of this Treaty and the Statute of the ESCB. The reports shall also examine the achievement of a high degree of sustainable convergence by reference to the fulfilment by each Member State of the following criteria:

– the achievement of a high degree of price stability; this will be apparent from a rate of inflation which is close to that of, at most, the three best performing Member States in terms of price stability;

– the sustainability of the government financial position; this will be apparent from having achieved a government budgetary position without a deficit that is excessive as determined in accordance with Article 104(6);

– the observance of the normal fluctuation margins provided for by the exchange-rate mechanism of the European Monetary System, for at least two years, without devaluing against the currency of any other Member State;

– the durability of convergence achieved by the Member State and of its participation in the exchange-rate mechanism of the European Monetary System being reflected in the long-term interest-rate levels.

The four criteria mentioned in this paragraph and the relevant periods over which they are to be respected are developed further in a Protocol annexed to this Treaty. The reports of the Commission and the EMI shall also take account of the development of the ecu, the results of the integration of markets, the situation and development of the balances of payments on current account and an examination of the development of unit labour costs and other price indices.

2.   On the basis of these reports, the Council, acting by a qualified majority on a recommendation from the Commission, shall assess:

– for each Member State, whether it fulfils the necessary conditions for the adoption of a single currency;

– whether a majority of the Member States fulfils the necessary conditions for the adoption of a single currency,

and recommend its findings to the Council, meeting in the composition of the Heads of State or Government. The European Parliament shall be consulted and forward its opinion to the Council, meeting in the composition of the Heads of State or Government.

3. Taking due account of the reports referred to in paragraph 1 and the opinion of the European Parliament referred to in paragraph 2, the Council, meeting in the composition of the Heads of State or Government, shall, acting by a qualified majority, not later than 31 December 1996:

– decide, on the basis of the recommendations of the Council referred to in paragraph 2, whether a majority of the Member States fulfils the necessary conditions for the adoption of a single currency;

– decide whether it is appropriate for the Community to enter the third stage, and if so:

– set the date for the beginning of the third stage.

4.   If by the end of 1997, the date for the beginning of the third stage has not been set, the third stage shall start on 1 January 1999. Before 1 July 1998, the Council, meeting in the composition of the Heads of State or Government, after a repetition of the procedure provided for in paragraphs 1 and 2, with the exception of the second indent of paragraph 2, taking into account the reports referred to in paragraph 1 and the opinion of the European Parliament, shall, acting by a qualified majority and on the basis of the recommendations of the Council referred to in paragraph 2, confirm which Member States fulfil the necessary conditions for the adoption of a single currency.

Article 122
1. If the decision has been taken to set the date in accordance with Article 121(3), the Council shall, on the basis of its recommendations referred to in Article 121(2), acting by a qualified majority on a recommendation from the

Commission, decide whether any, and if so which, Member States shall have a derogation as defined in paragraph 3 of this Article. Such Member States shall in this Treaty be referred to as 'Member States with a derogation'.

If the Council has confirmed which Member States fulfil the necessary conditions for the adoption of a single currency, in accordance with Article 121(4), those Member States which do not fulfil the conditions shall have a derogation as defined in paragraph 3 of this Article. Such Member States shall in this Treaty be referred to as 'Member States with a derogation'.

2. At least once every two years, or at the request of a Member State with a derogation, the Commission and the ECB shall report to the Council in accordance with the procedure laid down in Article 121(1). After consulting the European Parliament and after discussion in the Council, meeting in the composition of the Heads of State or Government, the Council shall, acting by a qualified majority on a proposal from the Commission, decide which Member States with a derogation fulfil the necessary conditions on the basis of the criteria set out in Article 121(1), and abrogate the derogations of the Member States concerned.

3. A derogation referred to in paragraph 1 shall entail that the following articles do not apply to the Member State concerned: Articles 104(9) and (11), 105(1), (2), (3) and (5), 106, 110, 111, and 112(2)(b). The exclusion of such a Member State and its national central bank from rights and obligations within the ESCB is laid down in Chapter IX of the Statute of the ESCB.

4. In Articles 105(1), (2) and (3), 106, 110, 111 and 112(2)(b), 'Member States' shall be read as 'Member States without a derogation'.

5. The voting rights of Member States with a derogation shall be suspended for the Council decisions referred to in the articles of this Treaty mentioned in paragraph 3. In that case, by way of derogation from Articles 205 and 250(1), a qualified majority shall be defined as two thirds of the votes of the representatives of the Member States without a derogation weighted in accordance with Article 205(2), and unanimity of those Member States shall be required for an act requiring unanimity.

6. Articles 119 and 120 shall continue to apply to a Member State with a derogation.

Article 123
1. Immediately after the decision on the date for the beginning of the third stage has been taken in accordance with Article 121(3), or, as the case may be, immediately after 1 July 1998:

– the Council shall adopt the provisions referred to in Article 107(6);

– the governments of the Member States without a derogation shall appoint, in accordance with the procedure set out in Article 50 of the Statute of the ESCB, the President, the Vice-President and the other members of the Executive Board of the ECB. If there are Member States with a derogation, the number of members of the Executive Board may be smaller than provided for in Article 11.1 of the Statute of the ESCB, but in no circumstances shall it be less than four.

As soon as the Executive Board is appointed, the ESCB and the ECB shall be established and shall prepare for their full operation as described in this Treaty and the Statute of the ESCB. The full exercise of their powers shall start from the first day of the third stage.

2. As soon as the ECB is established, it shall, if necessary, take over tasks of the EMI. The EMI shall go into liquidation upon the establishment of the ECB; the modalities of liquidation are laid down in the Statute of the EMI.

3. If and as long as there are Member States with a derogation, and without prejudice to Article 107(3) of this Treaty, the General Council of the ECB referred to in Article 45 of the Statute of the ESCB shall be constituted as a third decision-making body of the ECB.

4. At the starting date of the third stage, the Council shall, acting with the unanimity of the Member States without a derogation, on a proposal from the Commission and after consulting the ECB, adopt the conversion rates at which their currencies shall be irrevocably fixed and at which irrevocably fixed rate the ecu shall be substituted for these currencies, and the ecu will become a currency in its own right. This measure shall by itself not modify the external value of the ecu.

The Council, acting by a qualified majority of the said Member States, on a proposal from the Commission and after consulting the ECB, shall take the other measures necessary for the rapid introduction of the ecu as the single currency of those Member States. The second sentence of Article 122(5) shall apply.

5. If it is decided, according to the procedure set out in Article 122(2), to abrogate a derogation, the Council shall, acting with the unanimity of the Member States without a derogation and the Member State concerned, on a proposal from the Commission and after consulting the ECB, adopt the rate at which the ecu shall be substituted for the currency of the Member State concerned, and take the other measures necessary for the introduction of the ecu as the single currency in the Member State concerned.

Article 124
1. Until the beginning of the third stage, each Member State shall treat its exchange-rate policy as a matter of common interest. In so doing, Member States shall take account of the experience acquired in cooperation within the framework of the European Monetary System (EMS) and in developing the ecu, and shall respect existing powers in this field.

2. From the beginning of the third stage and for as long as a Member State has a derogation, paragraph 1 shall apply by analogy to the exchange-rate policy of that Member State.

ANNEX 2

PROTOCOL ON THE STATUTE OF THE EUROPEAN SYSTEM OF CENTRAL BANKS AND OF THE EUROPEAN CENTRAL BANK*

THE HIGH CONTRACTING PARTIES,

DESIRING to lay down the Statute of the European System of Central Banks and of the European Central Bank provided for in Article 8 of the Treaty establishing the European Community,

HAVE AGREED upon the following provisions, which shall be annexed to the Treaty establishing the European Community.

CHAPTER I

CONSTITUTION OF THE ESCB

Article 1
The European System of Central Banks
1.1.   The European System of Central Banks (ESCB) and the European Central Bank (ECB) shall be established in accordance with Article 8 of this Treaty; they shall perform their tasks and carry on their activities in accordance with the provisions of this Treaty and of this Statute.

1.2.   In accordance with Article 107(1) of this Treaty, the ESCB shall be composed of the ECB and of the central banks of the Member States ('national central banks'). The Institut monétaire luxembourgeois will be the central bank of Luxembourg.

CHAPTER II

OBJECTIVES AND TASKS OF THE ESCB

Article 2
Objectives
In accordance with Article 105(1) of this Treaty, the primary objective of the ESCB shall be to maintain price stability. Without prejudice to the objective of price stability, it shall support the general economic policies in the Community

---

* Protocol annexed to the Treaty establishing the European Community (OJ C 191, 29.7.1992, p. 68), as amended by the Treaty of Amsterdam (OJ C 340, 10.11.1997, p. 1), the Treaty of Nice (OJ C 80, 10.3.2001, p. 1), Council Decision 2003/223/EC (OJ L 83, 1.4.2003, p. 66) and the Act concerning the conditions of Accession of the Czech Republic, the Republic of Estonia, the Republic of Cyprus, the Republic of Latvia, the Republic of Lithuania, the Republic of Hungary, the Republic of Malta, the Republic of Poland, the Republic of Slovenia and the Slovak Republic and the adjustments to the Treaties on which the European Union is founded (OJ L 236, 23.9.2003, p. 33) – unofficial consolidated version.

with a view to contributing to the achievement of the objectives of the Community as laid down in Article 2 of this Treaty. The ESCB shall act in accordance with the principle of an open market economy with free competition, favouring an efficient allocation of resources, and in compliance with the principles set out in Article 4 of this Treaty.

Article 3
Tasks
3.1.   In accordance with Article 105(2) of this Treaty, the basic tasks to be carried out through the ESCB shall be:

– to define and implement the monetary policy of the Community;

– to conduct foreign-exchange operations consistent with the provisions of Article 111 of this Treaty;

– to hold and manage the official foreign reserves of the Member States;

– to promote the smooth operation of payment systems.

3.2.   In accordance with Article 105(3) of this Treaty, the third indent of Article 3.1 shall be without prejudice to the holding and management by the governments of Member States of foreign-exchange working balances.

3.3.   In accordance with Article 105(5) of this Treaty, the ESCB shall contribute to the smooth conduct of policies pursued by the competent authorities relating to the prudential supervision of credit institutions and the stability of the financial system.

Article 4
Advisory functions
In accordance with Article 105(4) of this Treaty:

(a) the ECB shall be consulted:

   – on any proposed Community act in its fields of competence;

   – by national authorities regarding any draft legislative provision in its fields of competence, but within the limits and under the conditions set out by the Council in accordance with the procedure laid down in Article 42;

(b) the ECB may submit opinions to the appropriate Community institutions or bodies or to national authorities on matters in its fields of competence.

Article 5
Collection of statistical information
5.1.   In order to undertake the tasks of the ESCB, the ECB, assisted by the national central banks, shall collect the necessary statistical information either from the competent national authorities or directly from economic agents. For

these purposes it shall cooperate with the Community institutions or bodies and with the competent authorities of the Member States or third countries and with international organizations.

5.2.   The national central banks shall carry out, to the extent possible, the tasks described in Article 5.1.

5.3.   The ECB shall contribute to the harmonization, where necessary, of the rules and practices governing the collection, compilation and distribution of statistics in the areas within its fields of competence.

5.4.   The Council, in accordance with the procedure laid down in Article 42, shall define the natural and legal persons subject to reporting requirements, the confidentiality regime and the appropriate provisions for enforcement.

Article 6
International cooperation
6.1.   In the field of international cooperation involving the tasks entrusted to the ESCB, the ECB shall decide how the ESCB shall be represented.

6.2.   The ECB and, subject to its approval, the national central banks may participate in international monetary institutions.

6.3.   Articles 6.1 and 6.2 shall be without prejudice to Article 111(4) of this Treaty.

CHAPTER III

ORGANIZATION OF THE ESCB

Article 7
Independence
In accordance with Article 108 of this Treaty, when exercising the powers and carrying out the tasks and duties conferred upon them by this Treaty and this Statute, neither the ECB, nor a national central bank, nor any member of their decision-making bodies shall seek or take instructions from Community institutions or bodies, from any government of a Member State or from any other body. The Community institutions and bodies and the governments of the Member States undertake to respect this principle and not to seek to influence the members of the decision-making bodies of the ECB or of the national central banks in the performance of their tasks.

Article 8
General principle
The ESCB shall be governed by the decision-making bodies of the ECB.

Article 9
The European Central Bank
9.1.   The ECB which, in accordance with Article 107(2) of this Treaty, shall have legal personality, shall enjoy in each of the Member States the most extensive legal capacity accorded to legal persons under its law; it may, in particular, acquire or dispose of movable and immovable property and may be a party to legal proceedings.

9.2.   The ECB shall ensure that the tasks conferred upon the ESCB under Article 105(2), (3) and (5) of this Treaty are implemented either by its own activities pursuant to this Statute or through the national central banks pursuant to Articles 12.1 and 14.

9.3.   In accordance with Article 107(3) of this Treaty, the decision-making bodies of the ECB shall be the Governing Council and the Executive Board.

Article 10
The Governing Council
10.1.   In accordance with Article 112(1) of this Treaty, the Governing Council shall comprise the members of the Executive Board of the ECB and the governors of the national central banks.

10.2.[1] Each member of the Governing Council shall have one vote. As from the date on which the number of members of the Governing Council exceeds 21, each member of the Executive Board shall have one vote and the number of governors with a voting right shall be 15. The latter voting rights shall be assigned and shall rotate as follows:

– as from the date on which the number of governors exceeds 15, until it reaches 22, the governors shall be allocated to two groups, according to a ranking of the size of the share of their national central bank's Member State in the aggregate gross domestic product at market prices and in the total aggregated balance sheet of the monetary financial institutions of the Member States which have adopted the euro. The shares in the aggregate gross domestic product at market prices and in the total aggregated balance sheet of the monetary financial institutions shall be assigned weights of 5/6 and 1/6, respectively. The first group shall be composed of five governors and the second group of the remaining governors. The frequency of voting rights of the governors allocated to the first group shall not be lower than the frequency of voting rights of those of the second group. Subject to the previous sentence, the first group shall be assigned four voting rights and the second group eleven voting rights;

– as from the date on which the number of governors reaches 22, the governors shall be allocated to three groups according to a ranking based on the above criteria. The first group shall be composed of five governors and shall be assigned four voting rights. The second group shall be composed of half of the total number of governors, with any fraction rounded up to the nearest integer,

[1]   As amended by Council Decision 2003/223/EC.

and shall be assigned eight voting rights. The third group shall be composed of the remaining governors and shall be assigned three voting rights;

– within each group, the governors shall have their voting rights for equal amounts of time;

– for the calculation of the shares in the aggregate gross domestic product at market prices Article 29.2 shall apply. The total aggregated balance sheet of the monetary financial institutions shall be calculated in accordance with the statistical framework applying in the European Community at the time of the calculation;

– whenever the aggregate gross domestic product at market prices is adjusted in accordance with Article 29.3, or whenever the number of governors increases, the size and/or composition of the groups shall be adjusted in accordance with the above principles;

– the Governing Council, acting by a two-thirds majority of all its members, with and without a voting right, shall take all measures necessary for the implementation of the above principles and may decide to postpone the start of the rotation system until the date on which the number of governors exceeds 18.

The right to vote shall be exercised in person. By way of derogation from this rule, the Rules of Procedure referred to in Article 12.3 may lay down that members of the Governing Council may cast their vote by means of teleconferencing. These rules shall also provide that a member of the Governing Council who is prevented from attending meetings of the Governing Council for a prolonged period may appoint an alternate as a member of the Governing Council.

The provisions of the previous paragraphs are without prejudice to the voting rights of all members of the Governing Council, with and without a voting right, under Articles 10.3, 10.6 and 41.2.

Save as otherwise provided for in this Statute, the Governing Council shall act by a simple majority of the members having a voting right. In the event of a tie, the President shall have the casting vote.

In order for the Governing Council to vote, there shall be a quorum of two-thirds of the members having a voting right. If the quorum is not met, the President may convene an extraordinary meeting at which decisions may be taken without regard to the quorum.

10.3. For any decisions to be taken under Articles 28, 29, 30, 32, 33 and 51, the votes in the Governing Council shall be weighted according to the national central banks' shares in the subscribed capital of the ECB. The weights of the votes of the members of the Executive Board shall be zero. A decision requiring a qualified majority shall be adopted if the votes cast in favour represent at least two thirds of the subscribed capital of the ECB and represent at least half of the shareholders. If a Governor is unable to be present, he may nominate an alternate to cast his weighted vote.

10.4. The proceedings of the meetings shall be confidential. The Governing Council may decide to make the outcome of its deliberations public.

10.5. The Governing Council shall meet at least 10 times a year.

10.6.[2] Article 10.2 may be amended by the Council meeting in the composition of the Heads of State or Government, acting unanimously either on a recommendation from the ECB and after consulting the European Parliament and the Commission, or on a recommendation from the Commission and after consulting the European Parliament and the ECB. The Council shall recommend such amendments to the Member States for adoption. These amendments shall enter into force after having been ratified by all the Member States in accordance with their respective constitutional requirements.

A recommendation made by the ECB under this paragraph shall require a decision by the Governing Council acting unanimously.

Article 11
The Executive Board
11.1. In accordance with Article 112(2)(a) of this Treaty, the Executive Board shall comprise the President, the Vice-President and four other members.

The members shall perform their duties on a full-time basis. No member shall engage in any occupation, whether gainful or not, unless exemption is exceptionally granted by the Governing Council.

11.2. In accordance with Article 112(2)(b) of this Treaty, the President, the Vice-President and the other members of the Executive Board shall be appointed from among persons of recognized standing and professional experience in monetary or banking matters by common accord of the governments of the Member States at the level of the Heads of State or Government, on a recommendation from the Council after it has consulted the European Parliament and the Governing Council.

Their term of office shall be eight years and shall not be renewable.

Only nationals of Member States may be members of the Executive Board.

11.3. The terms and conditions of employment of the members of the Executive Board, in particular their salaries, pensions and other social security benefits shall be the subject of contracts with the ECB and shall be fixed by the Governing Council on a proposal from a Committee comprising three members appointed by the Governing Council and three members appointed by the Council. The members of the Executive Board shall not have the right to vote on matters referred to in this paragraph.

[2] As inserted by Article 5 of the Treaty of Nice.

11.4. If a member of the Executive Board no longer fulfils the conditions required for the performance of his duties or if he has been guilty of serious misconduct, the Court of Justice may, on application by the Governing Council or the Executive Board, compulsorily retire him.

11.5. Each member of the Executive Board present in person shall have the right to vote and shall have, for that purpose, one vote. Save as otherwise provided, the Executive Board shall act by a simple majority of the votes cast. In the event of a tie, the President shall have the casting vote. The voting arrangements shall be specified in the Rules of Procedure referred to in Article 12.3.

11.6. The Executive Board shall be responsible for the current business of the ECB.

11.7. Any vacancy on the Executive Board shall be filled by the appointment of a new member in accordance with Article 11.2.

Article 12
Responsibilities of the decision-making bodies
12.1. The Governing Council shall adopt the guidelines and take the decisions necessary to ensure the performance of the tasks entrusted to the ESCB under this Treaty and this Statute. The Governing Council shall formulate the monetary policy of the Community including, as appropriate, decisions relating to intermediate monetary objectives, key interest rates and the supply of reserves in the ESCB, and shall establish the necessary guidelines for their implementation.

The Executive Board shall implement monetary policy in accordance with the guidelines and decisions laid down by the Governing Council. In doing so the Executive Board shall give the necessary instructions to national central banks. In addition the Executive Board may have certain powers delegated to it where the Governing Council so decides.

To the extent deemed possible and appropriate and without prejudice to the provisions of this Article, the ECB shall have recourse to the national central banks to carry out operations which form part of the tasks of the ESCB.

12.2. The Executive Board shall have responsibility for the preparation of meetings of the Governing Council.

12.3. The Governing Council shall adopt Rules of Procedure which determine the internal organization of the ECB and its decision-making bodies.

12.4. The Governing Council shall exercise the advisory functions referred to in Article 4.

12.5. The Governing Council shall take the decisions referred to in Article 6.

Article 13
The President
13.1. The President or, in his absence, the Vice-President shall chair the Governing Council and the Executive Board of the ECB.

13.2. Without prejudice to Article 39, the President or his nominee shall represent the ECB externally.

Article 14
National central banks
14.1. In accordance with Article 109 of this Treaty, each Member State shall ensure, at the latest at the date of the establishment of the ESCB, that its national legislation, including the statutes of its national central bank, is compatible with this Treaty and this Statute.

14.2. The statutes of the national central banks shall, in particular, provide that the term of office of a Governor of a national central bank shall be no less than five years.

A Governor may be relieved from office only if he no longer fulfils the conditions required for the performance of his duties or if he has been guilty of serious misconduct. A decision to this effect may be referred to the Court of Justice by the Governor concerned or the Governing Council on grounds of infringement of this Treaty or of any rule of law relating to its application. Such proceedings shall be instituted within two months of the publication of the decision or of its notification to the plaintiff or, in the absence thereof, of the day on which it came to the knowledge of the latter, as the case may be.

14.3. The national central banks are an integral part of the ESCB and shall act in accordance with the guidelines and instructions of the ECB. The Governing Council shall take the necessary steps to ensure compliance with the guidelines and instructions of the ECB, and shall require that any necessary information be given to it.

14.4. National central banks may perform functions other than those specified in this Statute unless the Governing Council finds, by a majority of two thirds of the votes cast, that these interfere with the objectives and tasks of the ESCB. Such functions shall be performed on the responsibility and liability of national central banks and shall not be regarded as being part of the functions of the ESCB.

Article 15
Reporting commitments
15.1. The ECB shall draw up and publish reports on the activities of the ESCB at least quarterly.

15.2. A consolidated financial statement of the ESCB shall be published each week.

15.3. In accordance with Article 113(3) of this Treaty, the ECB shall address an annual report on the activities of the ESCB and on the monetary policy of both the previous and the current year to the European Parliament, the Council and the Commission, and also to the European Council.

15.4. The reports and statements referred to in this Article shall be made available to interested parties free of charge.

Article 16
Banknotes
In accordance with Article 106(1) of this Treaty, the Governing Council shall have the exclusive right to authorize the issue of banknotes within the Community. The ECB and the national central banks may issue such notes. The banknotes issued by the ECB and the national central banks shall be the only such notes to have the status of legal tender within the Community.

The ECB shall respect as far as possible existing practices regarding the issue and design of banknotes.

CHAPTER IV

MONETARY FUNCTIONS AND OPERATIONS OF THE ESCB

Article 17
Accounts with the ECB and the national central banks
In order to conduct their operations, the ECB and the national central banks may open accounts for credit institutions, public entities and other market participants and accept assets, including book entry securities, as collateral.

Article 18
Open market and credit operations
18.1. In order to achieve the objectives of the ESCB and to carry out its tasks, the ECB and the national central banks may:

– operate in the financial markets by buying and selling outright (spot and forward) or under repurchase agreement and by lending or borrowing claims and marketable instruments, whether in Community or in non-Community currencies, as well as precious metals;

– conduct credit operations with credit institutions and other market participants, with lending being based on adequate collateral.

18.2. The ECB shall establish general principles for open market and credit operations carried out by itself or the national central banks, including for the announcement of conditions under which they stand ready to enter into such transactions.

Article 19
Minimum reserves
19.1. Subject to Article 2, the ECB may require credit institutions established in Member States to hold minimum reserve on accounts with the ECB and national central banks in pursuance of monetary policy objectives. Regulations concerning the calculation and determination of the required minimum reserves may be established by the Governing Council. In cases of non-compliance the ECB shall be entitled to levy penalty interest and to impose other sanctions with comparable effect.

19.2. For the application of this Article, the Council shall, in accordance with the procedure laid down in Article 42, define the basis for minimum reserves and the maximum permissible ratios between those reserves and their basis, as well as the appropriate sanctions in cases of non-compliance.

Article 20
Other instruments of monetary control
The Governing Council may, by a majority of two thirds of the votes cast, decide upon the use of such other operational methods of monetary control as it sees fit, respecting Article 2.

The Council shall, in accordance with the procedure laid down in Article 42, define the scope of such methods if they impose obligations on third parties.

Article 21
Operations with public entities
21.1. In accordance with Article 101 of this Treaty, overdrafts or any other type of credit facility with the ECB or with the national central banks in favour of Community institutions or bodies, central governments, regional, local or other public authorities, other bodies governed by public law, or public undertakings of Member States shall be prohibited, as shall the purchase directly from them by the ECB or national central banks of debt instruments.

21.2. The ECB and national central banks may act as fiscal agents for the entities referred to in Article 21.1.

21.3. The provisions of this Article shall not apply to publicly owned credit institutions which, in the context of the supply of reserves by central banks, shall be given the same treatment by national central banks and the ECB as private credit institutions.

Article 22
Clearing and payment systems
The ECB and national central banks may provide facilities, and the ECB may make regulations, to ensure efficient and sound clearing and payment systems within the Community and with other countries.

Article 23
External operations
The ECB and national central banks may:

– establish relations with central banks and financial institutions in other countries and, where appropriate, with international organizations;

– acquire and sell spot and forward all types of foreign exchange assets and precious metals; the term 'foreign exchange asset' shall include securities and all other assets in the currency of any country or units of account and in whatever form held;

– hold and manage the assets referred to in this Article;

– conduct all types of banking transactions in relations with third countries and international organizations, including borrowing and lending operations.

Article 24
Other operations
In addition to operations arising from their tasks, the ECB and national central banks may enter into operations for their administrative purposes or for their staff.

CHAPTER V

PRUDENTIAL SUPERVISION

Article 25
Prudential supervision
25.1. The ECB may offer advice to and be consulted by the Council, the Commission and the competent authorities of the Member States on the scope and implementation of Community legislation relating to the prudential supervision of credit institutions and to the stability of the financial system.

25.2. In accordance with any decision of the Council under Article 105(6) of this Treaty, the ECB may perform specific tasks concerning policies relating to the prudential supervision of credit institutions and other financial institutions with the exception of insurance undertakings.

CHAPTER VI

FINANCIAL PROVISIONS OF THE ESCB

Article 26
Financial accounts
26.1. The financial year of the ECB and national central banks shall begin on the first day of January and end on the last day of December.

26.2. The annual accounts of the ECB shall be drawn up by the Executive Board, in accordance with the principles established by the Governing Council. The accounts shall be approved by the Governing Council and shall thereafter be published.

26.3. For analytical and operational purposes, the Executive Board shall draw up a consolidated balance sheet of the ESCB, comprising those assets and liabilities of the national central banks that fall within the ESCB.

26.4. For the application of this Article, the Governing Council shall establish the necessary rules for standardizing the accounting and reporting of operations undertaken by the national central banks.

Article 27
Auditing
27.1. The accounts of the ECB and national central banks shall be audited by independent external auditors recommended by the Governing Council and approved by the Council. The auditors shall have full power to examine all books and accounts of the ECB and national central banks and obtain full information about their transactions.

27.2. The provisions of Article 248 of this Treaty shall only apply to an examination of the operational efficiency of the management of the ECB.

Article 28
Capital of the ECB
28.1. The capital of the ECB, which shall become operational upon its establishment, shall be ECU 5 000 million. The capital may be increased by such amounts as may be decided by the Governing Council acting by the qualified majority provided for in Article 10.3, within the limits and under the conditions set by the Council under the procedure laid down in Article 42.

28.2. The national central banks shall be the sole subscribers to and holders of the capital of the ECB. The subscription of capital shall be according to the key established in accordance with Article 29.

28.3. The Governing Council, acting by the qualified majority provided for in Article 10.3, shall determine the extent to which and the form in which the capital shall be paid up.

28.4. Subject to Article 28.5, the shares of the national central banks in the subscribed capital of the ECB may not be transferred, pledged or attached.

28.5. If the key referred to in Article 29 is adjusted, the national central banks shall transfer among themselves capital shares to the extent necessary to ensure that the distribution of capital shares corresponds to the adjusted key. The Governing Council shall determine the terms and conditions of such transfers.

Article 29
Key for capital subscription
29.1. When in accordance with the procedure referred to in Article 123(1) of this Treaty the ESCB and the ECB have been established, the key for subscription of the ECB's capital shall be established. Each national central bank shall be assigned a weighting in this key which shall be equal to the sum of:

– 50% of the share of its respective Member State in the population of the Community in the penultimate year preceding the establishment of the ESCB;

– 50% of the share of its respective Member State in the gross domestic product at market prices of the Community as recorded in the last five years preceding the penultimate year before the establishment of the ESCB.

The percentages shall be rounded up to the nearest multiple of 0.05 percentage points.

29.2. The statistical data to be used for the application of this Article shall be provided by the Commission in accordance with the rules adopted by the Council under the procedure provided for in Article 42.

29.3. The weightings assigned to the national central banks shall be adjusted every five years after the establishment of the ESCB by analogy with the provisions laid down in Article 29.1. The adjusted key shall apply with effect from the first day of the following year.

29.4. The Governing Council shall take all other measures necessary for the application of this Article.

Article 30
Transfer of foreign reserve assets to the ECB
30.1. Without prejudice to Article 28, the ECB shall be provided by the national central banks with foreign reserve assets, other than Member States' currencies, ECUs, IMF reserve positions and SDRs, up to an amount equivalent to ECU 50 000 million. The Governing Council shall decide upon the proportion to be called up by the ECB following its establishment and the amounts called up at later dates. The ECB shall have the full right to hold and manage the foreign reserves that are transferred to it and to use them for the purposes set out in this Statute.

30.2. The contributions of each national central bank shall be fixed in proportion to its share in the subscribed capital of the ECB.

30.3. Each national central bank shall be credited by the ECB with a claim equivalent to its contribution. The Governing Council shall determine the denomination and remuneration of such claims.

30.4. Further calls of foreign reserve assets beyond the limit set in Article 30.1 may be effected by the ECB, in accordance with Article 30.2, within the limits and under the conditions set by the Council in accordance with the procedure laid down in Article 42.

30.5. The ECB may hold and manage IMF reserve positions and SDRs and provide for the pooling of such assets.

30.6. The Governing Council shall take all other measures necessary for the application of this Article.

Article 31
Foreign reserve assets held by national central banks
31.1. The national central banks shall be allowed to perform transactions in fulfilment of their obligations towards international organizations in accordance with Article 23.

31.2. All other operations in foreign reserve assets remaining with the national central banks after the transfers referred to in Article 30, and Member States' transactions with their foreign exchange working balances shall, above a certain limit to be established within the framework of Article 31.3, be subject to approval by the ECB in order to ensure consistency with the exchange rate and monetary policies of the Community.

31.3. The Governing Council shall issue guidelines with a view to facilitating such operations.

Article 32
Allocation of monetary income of national central banks
32.1. The income accruing to the national central banks in the performance of the ESCB's monetary policy function (hereinafter referred to as 'monetary income') shall be allocated at the end of each financial year in accordance with the provisions of this Article.

32.2. Subject to Article 32.3, the amount of each national central bank's monetary income shall be equal to its annual income derived from its assets held against notes in circulation and deposit liabilities to credit institutions. These assets shall be earmarked by national central banks in accordance with guidelines to be established by the Governing Council.

32.3. If, after the start of the third stage, the balance sheet structures of the national central banks do not, in the judgment of the Governing Council, permit the application of Article 32.2, the Governing Council, acting by a qualified majority, may decide that, by way of derogation from Article 32.2, monetary income shall be measured according to an alternative method for a period of not more than five years.

32.4. The amount of each national central bank's monetary income shall be reduced by an amount equivalent to any interest paid by that central bank on its deposit liabilities to credit institutions in accordance with Article 19.

The Governing Council may decide that national central banks shall be indemnified against costs incurred in connection with the issue of banknotes or in exceptional circumstances for specific losses arising from monetary policy operations undertaken for the ESCB. Indemnification shall be in a form deemed appropriate in the judgment of the Governing Council; these amounts may be offset against the national central banks' monetary income.

32.5. The sum of the national central banks' monetary income shall be allocated to the national central banks in proportion to their paid up shares in the capital of the ECB, subject to any decision taken by the Governing Council pursuant to Article 33.2.

32.6. The clearing and settlement of the balances arising from the allocation of monetary income shall be carried out by the ECB in accordance with guidelines established by the Governing Council.

32.7. The Governing Council shall take all other measures necessary for the application of this Article.

Article 33
Allocation of net profits and losses of the ECB
33.1. The net profit of the ECB shall be transferred in the following order:

(a)   an amount to be determined by the Governing Council, which may not exceed 20% of the net profit, shall be transferred to the general reserve fund subject to a limit equal to 100% of the capital;

(b)   the remaining net profit shall be distributed to the shareholders of the ECB in proportion to their paid-up shares.

33.2. In the event of a loss incurred by the ECB, the shortfall may be offset against the general reserve fund of the ECB and, if necessary, following a decision by the Governing Council, against the monetary income of the relevant financial year in proportion and up to the amounts allocated to the national central banks in accordance with Article 32.5.

CHAPTER VII

GENERAL PROVISIONS

Article 34
Legal acts
34.1. In accordance with Article 110 of this Treaty, the ECB shall:

– make regulations to the extent necessary to implement the tasks defined in Article 3.1, first indent, Articles 19.1, 22 or 25.2 and in cases which shall be laid down in the acts of the Council referred to in Article 42;

– take decisions necessary for carrying out the tasks entrusted to the ESCB under this Treaty and this Statute;

– make recommendations and deliver opinions.

34.2. A regulation shall have general application. It shall be binding in its entirety and directly applicable in all Member States.

Recommendations and opinions shall have no binding force.

A decision shall be binding in its entirety upon those to whom it is addressed.

Articles 253, 254 and 256 of this Treaty shall apply to regulations and decisions adopted by the ECB.

The ECB may decide to publish its decisions, recommendations and opinions.

34.3. Within the limits and under the conditions adopted by the Council under the procedure laid down in Article 42, the ECB shall be entitled to impose fines or periodic penalty payments on undertakings for failure to comply with obligations under its regulations and decisions.

Article 35
Judicial control and related matters
35.1. The acts or omissions of the ECB shall be open to review or interpretation by the Court of Justice in the cases and under the conditions laid down in this Treaty. The ECB may institute proceedings in the cases and under the conditions laid down in this Treaty.

35.2. Disputes between the ECB, on the one hand, and its creditors, debtors or any other person, on the other, shall be decided by the competent national courts, save where jurisdiction has been conferred upon the Court of Justice.

35.3. The ECB shall be subject to the liability regime provided for in Article 288 of this Treaty. The national central banks shall be liable according to their respective national laws.

35.4. The Court of Justice shall have jurisdiction to give judgment pursuant to any arbitration clause contained in a contract concluded by or on behalf of the ECB, whether that contract be governed by public or private law.

35.5. A decision of the ECB to bring an action before the Court of Justice shall be taken by the Governing Council.

35.6. The Court of Justice shall have jurisdiction in disputes concerning the fulfilment by a national central bank of obligations under this Statute. If the ECB considers that a national central bank has failed to fulfil an obligation under this Statute, it shall deliver a reasoned opinion on the matter after giving the national central bank concerned the opportunity to submit its observations. If the national central bank concerned does not comply with the opinion within the period laid down by the ECB, the latter may bring the matter before the Court of Justice.

Article 36
Staff
36.1. The Governing Council, on a proposal from the Executive Board, shall lay down the conditions of employment of the staff of the ECB.

36.2. The Court of Justice shall have jurisdiction in any dispute between the ECB and its servants within the limits and under the conditions laid down in the conditions of employment.

Article 37
Seat
Before the end of 1992, the decision as to where the seat of the ECB will be established shall be taken by common accord of the governments of the Member States at the level of Heads of State or Government.

Article 38
Professional secrecy
38.1. Members of the governing bodies and the staff of the ECB and the national central banks shall be required, even after their duties have ceased, not to disclose information of the kind covered by the obligation of professional secrecy.

38.2. Persons having access to data covered by Community legislation imposing an obligation of secrecy shall be subject to such legislation.

Article 39
Signatories
The ECB shall be legally committed to third parties by the President or by two members of the Executive Board or by the signatures of two members of the staff of the ECB who have been duly authorized by the President to sign on behalf of the ECB.

Article 40[3]
Privileges and immunities
The ECB shall enjoy in the territories of the Member States such privileges and immunities as are necessary for the performance of its tasks, under the conditions laid down in the Protocol on the privileges and immunities of the European Communities.

---

[3] As amended by Article 6, point III(4) of the Treaty of Amsterdam.

CHAPTER VIII

AMENDMENT OF THE STATUTE AND COMPLEMENTARY LEGISLATION

Article 41
Simplified amendment procedure
41.1. In accordance with Article 107(5) of this Treaty, Articles 5.1, 5.2, 5.3, 17, 18, 19.1, 22, 23, 24, 26, 32.2, 32.3, 32.4, 32.6, 33.1(a) and 36 of this Statute may be amended by the Council, acting either by a qualified majority on a recommendation from the ECB and after consulting the Commission, or unanimously on a proposal from the Commission and after consulting the ECB. In either case the assent of the European Parliament shall be required.

41.2. A recommendation made by the ECB under this Article shall require a unanimous decision by the Governing Council.

Article 42
Complementary legislation
In accordance with Article 107(6) of this Treaty, immediately after the decision on the date for the beginning of the third stage, the Council, acting by a qualified majority either on a proposal from the Commission and after consulting the European Parliament and the ECB or on a recommendation from the ECB and after consulting the European Parliament and the Commission, shall adopt the provisions referred to in Articles 4, 5.4, 19.2, 20, 28.1, 29.2, 30.4 and 34.3 of this Statute.

CHAPTER IX

TRANSITIONAL AND OTHER PROVISIONS FOR THE ESCB

Article 43
General provisions
43.1. A derogation as referred to in Article 122(1) of this Treaty shall entail that the following Articles of this Statute shall not confer any rights or impose any obligations on the Member State concerned: 3, 6, 9.2, 12.1, 14.3, 16, 18, 19, 20, 22, 23, 26.2, 27, 30, 31, 32, 33, 34, 50 and 52.

43.2. The central banks of Member States with a derogation as specified in Article 122(1) of this Treaty shall retain their powers in the field of monetary policy according to national law.

43.3. In accordance with Article 122(4) of this Treaty, 'Member States' shall be read as 'Member States without a derogation' in the following Articles of this Statute: 3, 11.2, 19, 34.2 and 50.

43.4. 'National central banks' shall be read as 'central banks of Member States without a derogation' in the following Articles of this Statute: 9.2, 10.1, 10.3, 12.1, 16, 17, 18, 22, 23, 27, 30, 31, 32, 33.2 and 52.

43.5. 'Shareholders' shall be read as 'central banks of Member States without a derogation' in Articles 10.3 and 33.1.

43.6. 'Subscribed capital of the ECB' shall be read as 'capital of the ECB subscribed by the central banks of Member States without a derogation' in Articles 10.3 and 30.2.

Article 44
Transitional tasks of the ECB
The ECB shall take over those tasks of the EMI which, because of the derogations of one or more Member States, still have to be performed in the third stage.

The ECB shall give advice in the preparations for the abrogation of the derogations specified in Article 122 of this Treaty.

Article 45
The General Council of the ECB
45.1. Without prejudice to Article 107(3) of this Treaty, the General Council shall be constituted as a third decision-making body of the ECB.

45.2. The General Council shall comprise the President and Vice-President of the ECB and the Governors of the national central banks. The other members of the Executive Board may participate, without having the right to vote, in meetings of the General Council.

45.3. The responsibilities of the General Council are listed in full in Article 47 of this Statute.

Article 46
Rules of Procedure of the General Council
46.1. The President or, in his absence, the Vice-President of the ECB shall chair the General Council of the ECB.

46.2. The President of the Council and a Member of the Commission may participate, without having the right to vote, in meetings of the General Council.

46.3. The President shall prepare the meetings of the General Council.

46.4. By way of derogation from Article 12.3, the General Council shall adopt its Rules of Procedure.

46.5. The Secretariat of the General Council shall be provided by the ECB.

Article 47
Responsibilities of the General Council
47.1. The General Council shall:

– perform the tasks referred to in Article 44;

– contribute to the advisory functions referred to in Articles 4 and 25.1.

47.2. The General Council shall contribute to:

– the collection of statistical information as referred to in Article 5;

– the reporting activities of the ECB as referred to in Article 15;

– the establishment of the necessary rules for the application of Article 26 as referred to in Article 26.4;

– the taking of all other measures necessary for the application of Article 29 as referred to in Article 29.4;

– the laying down of the conditions of employment of the staff of the ECB as referred to in Article 36.

47.3. The General Council shall contribute to the necessary preparations for irrevocably fixing the exchange rates of the currencies of Member States with a derogation against the currencies, or the single currency, of the Member States without a derogation, as referred to in Article 123(5) of this Treaty.

47.4. The General Council shall be informed by the President of the ECB of decisions of the Governing Council.

Article 48
Transitional provisions for the capital of the ECB
In accordance with Article 29.1 each national central bank shall be assigned a weighting in the key for subscription of the ECB's capital. By way of derogation from Article 28.3, central banks of Member States with a derogation shall not pay up their subscribed capital unless the General Council, acting by a majority representing at least two thirds of the subscribed capital of the ECB and at least half of the shareholders, decides that a minimal percentage has to be paid up as a contribution to the operational costs of the ECB.

Article 49
Deferred payment of capital, reserves and provisions of the ECB
49.1. The central bank of a Member State whose derogation has been abrogated shall pay up its subscribed share of the capital of the ECB to the same extent as the central banks of other Member States without a derogation, and shall transfer to the ECB foreign reserve assets in accordance with Article 30.1. The sum to be transferred shall be determined by multiplying the ECU value at current exchange rates of the foreign reserve assets which have already been transferred to the ECB in accordance with Article 30.1, by the ratio between the number of shares subscribed by the national central bank concerned and the number of shares already paid up by the other national central banks.

49.2. In addition to the payment to be made in accordance with Article 49.1, the central bank concerned shall contribute to the reserves of the ECB, to those provisions equivalent to reserves, and to the amount still to be appropriated to the reserves and provisions corresponding to the balance of the profit and loss account as at 31 December of the year prior to the abrogation of the derogation. The sum to be contributed shall be determined by multiplying the amount of the reserves, as defined above and as stated in the approved balance sheet of the ECB, by the ratio between the number of shares subscribed by the central bank concerned and the number of shares already paid up by the other central banks.

49.3.[4] Upon one or more countries becoming Member States and their respective national central banks becoming part of the ESCB, the subscribed capital of the ECB and the limit on the amount of foreign reserve assets that may be transferred to the ECB shall be automatically increased. The increase shall be determined by multiplying the respective amounts then prevailing by the ratio, within the expanded capital key, between the weighting of the entering national central banks concerned and the weighting of the national central banks already members of the ESCB. Each national central bank's weighting in the capital key shall be calculated by analogy with Article 29.1 and in compliance with Article 29.2. The reference periods to be used for the statistical data shall be identical to those applied for the latest quinquennial adjustment of the weightings under Article 29.3.

Article 50
Initial appointment of the members of the Executive Board
When the Executive Board of the ECB is being established, the President, the Vice-President and the other members of the Executive Board shall be appointed by common accord of the governments of the Member States at the level of Heads of State or Government, on a recommendation from the Council and after consulting the European Parliament and the Council of the EMI. The President of the Executive Board shall be appointed for eight years. By way of derogation from Article 11.2, the Vice-President shall be appointed for four years and the other members of the Executive Board for terms of office of between five and eight years. No term of office shall be renewable. The number of members of the Executive Board may be smaller than provided for in Article 11.1, but in no circumstance shall it be less than four.

Article 51
Derogation from Article 32
51.1. If, after the start of the third stage, the Governing Council decides that the application of Article 32 results in significant changes in national central banks' relative income positions, the amount of income to be allocated pursuant to Article 32 shall be reduced by a uniform percentage which shall not exceed 60% in the first financial year after the start of the third stage and which shall decrease by at least 12 percentage points in each subsequent financial year.

---

[4] As inserted by Article 17 of the Act concerning the conditions of Accession of the Czech Republic, the Republic of Estonia, the Republic of Cyprus, the Republic of Latvia, the Republic of Lithuania, the Republic of Hungary, the Republic of Malta, the Republic of Poland, the Republic of Slovenia and the Slovak Republic and the adjustments to the Treaties on which the European Union is founded.

51.2. Article 51.1 shall be applicable for not more than five financial years after the start of the third stage.

Article 52
Exchange of banknotes in Community currencies
Following the irrevocable fixing of exchange rates, the Governing Council shall take the necessary measures to ensure that banknotes denominated in currencies with irrevocably fixed exchange rates are exchanged by the national central banks at their respective par values.

Article 53
Applicability of the transitional provisions
If and as long as there are Member States with a derogation Articles 43 to 48 shall be applicable.

GLOSSARY

Accountability: the legal and political obligation of an independent institution to properly explain and justify its decisions to the citizens and their elected representatives, thereby making it responsible for fulfilling its objectives. The **European Central Bank (ECB)** is accountable to the European citizens and, more formally, to the **European Parliament**.

Bank for International Settlements (BIS): established on 17 May 1930 by an International Agreement concluded between Belgium, Germany, France, Italy, Japan, the United Kingdom and the United States, the BIS is the world's oldest international financial organisation. It fosters international monetary and financial cooperation and serves as a bank for central banks. In fulfilling its mandate, the BIS acts as: (i) a forum to promote discussion and facilitate decision-making processes among central banks and within the international financial community; (ii) a centre for economic and monetary research; (iii) a prime counterparty for central banks in their financial transactions; and (iv) an agent or trustee in connection with international financial operations. It is based in Basel and has representative offices in Hong Kong SAR and Mexico City.

Broad Economic Policy Guidelines (BEPGs): the Treaty obliges the Member States to coordinate their economic policies within the EU Council. The BEPGs constitute the main instrument of this coordination. They contain recommendations to policy-makers on macroeconomic and structural policies and provide a yardstick for ex post assessment in the context of multilateral surveillance within the EU Council. The EU Council, acting on a recommendation from the European Commission, formulates a draft of the BEPGs and reports its findings to the European Council. The EU Council then adopts a recommendation on the BEPGs based on the European Council's conclusions.

Central bank independence: legal provision which guarantees that a central bank can carry out its statutory tasks and duties without political interference. Article 108 of the **EC Treaty** establishes the principle of central bank independence for the **euro area**.

Collateral: assets pledged (e.g. by **credit institutions** with central banks) as a guarantee for the repayment of loans, as well as assets sold (e.g. to central banks by credit institutions) under **repurchase agreements**.

Committee of European Securities Regulators (CESR): a Committee, established by the **European Commission** in June 2001 in the light of the recommendation of the Report of the Committee of Wise Men on the Regulation of European Securities Markets, and composed of representatives from the national authorities regulating the securities markets. As the level 3 body of the revised European regulatory approach, it advises the European Commission on securities policy issues and helps to ensure a more consistent implementation of Community legislation in the Member States. It also improves coordination among European securities regulators.

Committee of Governors of the central banks of the Member States of the European Economic Community: a Committee created in May 1964 on the basis of Article 105(2) of the EEC Treaty to foster cooperation among central banks. In 1994 its tasks were taken over by the newly established **European Monetary Institute (EMI)** and the Committee was dissolved.

Committee on Monetary, Financial and Balance of Payments Statistics (CMFB): a Committee established by Council Decision 91/115/EEC of 25 February 1991 (OJ L 59, 6.3.1991, p. 19), as amended by Council Decision 96/174/EC of 26 February 1996 (OJ L 51, 1.3.1996, p. 48), bringing together statisticians from the national statistical institutes, **Eurostat**, the NCBs and the **ECB**. The CMFB advises the Commission on a range of statistical matters, in particular statistical aspects of the **excessive deficit procedure**, and promotes co-operation and co-ordination of statistical work at the European level.

Common operational systems: systems that have been established jointly by the ECB and the NCBs to make it easier to carry out decentralised operations. They encompass common information systems, applications and procedures and are organised according to a "hub and spoke" approach, with the hub located at the ECB.

Constitution for Europe: On 13 June 2003 the European Convention on the future of Europe adopted a draft Treaty establishing a Constitution for Europe that would supersede both the **EU Treaty** and the **EC Treaty**. The draft was submitted to the European Council meeting in Thessaloniki on 20 June 2003 and was under discussion in the Intergovernmental Conference (IGC) from September 2003 to June 2004. It was adopted by the EU Member States in June 2004 and is scheduled to be ratified by November 2006.

Convergence criteria: the criteria established in Article 121(1) of the **EC Treaty** (and developed further in Protocol No 21 annexed to the Treaty) as a basis for the assessment of whether a country may adopt the euro. They relate to performance with regard to **price stability**, the government financial position, exchange rates and long-term interest rates. They also cover the compatibility of national legislation, including the statutes of NCBs, with both the **Treaty** and the **Statute of the European System of Central Banks and of the European Central Bank**.

Corporate governance: procedures and processes according to which organisations are directed and controlled. The corporate governance structure specifies the distribution of rights and responsibilities among the different participants in the organisation – such as the board, managers, shareholders and other stakeholders – and lays down the rules and procedures for decision-making. In so doing, it also provides the structure within which the organisation's operational targets are set, and specifies the means of attaining those targets and of monitoring performance.

Correspondent central banking model (CCBM): a mechanism established by the **European System of Central Banks (ESCB)** to enable **counterparties** to obtain credit from the central bank of the country in which they are based using **collateral** held in another country. In the CCBM, an NCB acts as custodian for the other NCBs with regard to the securities held in its domestic **securities settlement system (SSS)**.

Court of Auditors: an institution of the **European Community** which carries out the audit in the European Community. One of its duties is to examine the operational efficiency of the management of the **ECB**.

Debt ratio: the subject of one of the fiscal criteria used to define the existence of an excessive deficit, as laid down in Article 104(2) of the **EC Treaty**. It is defined as the ratio of government debt to gross domestic product at current market prices, while government debt is defined in Protocol No 20 (on the **excessive deficit procedure**) as the total gross debt at nominal value outstanding at the end of the year and consolidated between and within the sectors of general government.

Deficit ratio: the subject of one of the fiscal criteria used to define the existence of an excessive deficit, as laid down in Article 104(2) of the **EC Treaty**. It is defined as the ratio of the planned or actual government deficit to gross domestic product at current market prices. The government deficit is defined in Protocol No 20 (on the **excessive deficit procedure**) as net borrowing of the general government.

Deposit facility: a **standing facility** of the **Eurosystem** which **counterparties** may use to make **overnight deposits**, which are remunerated at a pre-specified interest rate, at an NCB (see also **key ECB interest rates**).

EC Treaty: see **Treaty**.

ECOFIN Council: see **EU Council**.

Economic and Financial Committee (EFC): a consultative Community body set up at the start of Stage Three of **Economic and Monetary Union (EMU)**. The Member States, the **European Commission** and the **European Central Bank (ECB)** each appoint no more than two members of the Committee. Each Member State selects one member from among the senior officials of its national administration, and the second member from among the senior officials of its NCB. However, the NCB members only participate in EFC meetings when issues of their institution's particular expertise or competence are being discussed. Article 114(2) of the **EC Treaty** lists the EFC's tasks.

Economic and Monetary Union (EMU): was realised in three stages according to the procedures and timetable set out in the **EC Treaty**. Stage One of EMU started in July 1990 and ended on 31 December 1993. It was mainly characterised by the dismantling of all internal barriers to the free movement of capital within the EU. Stage Two of EMU began on 1 January 1994. It provided for, among other things, the establishment of the **European Monetary Institute (EMI)**, the prohibition of financing of the public sector by the central banks, the prohibition of privileged access to financial institutions by the public sector and the avoidance of excessive government deficits. Stage Three started on 1 January 1999 with the transfer of monetary competence to the **ECB** and the introduction of the **euro**. The cash changeover on 1 January 2002 completed the set-up of EMU.

Economic Policy Committee (EPC): a consultative Community body set up by a Council Decision 74/122/EEC of 18 February 1974 (OJ L 63, 5.3.1974, p. 21), composed of two representatives and two alternates from each of the Member States, the **European Commission** and the **ECB**. Its main tasks are to contribute to the ECOFIN Council's preparatory work in coordinating the economic policies of the Member States and the **European Community** and advise the **European Commission** and the **EU Council**. It cooperates closely with the **Economic and Financial Committee (EFC)** and focuses mainly on structural policies aimed at improving growth potential and employment in the Community.

ECU (European Currency Unit): prior to Stage Three of EMU, the ECU was a basket currency made up of the sum of fixed amounts of 12 of the 15 currencies of the EU Member States. The value of the ECU was calculated as a weighted average of the value of its component currencies. The ECU was replaced by the **euro** on a one-for-one basis on 1 January 1999.

EONIA (euro overnight index average): a measure of the effective interest rate prevailing in the euro interbank overnight market, based on transactions.

ERM (exchange rate mechanism): the exchange rate and intervention mechanism of the **European Monetary System (EMS)** provided for central rates of participating currencies against the **ECU**. These central rates were used to establish a grid of bilateral central rates between the participating currencies. Exchange rates were allowed to fluctuate within a band around the bilateral central rates. The central rates could be adjusted, subject to mutual agreement between all countries participating in the ERM. In 1999, at the start of **Stage Three** of **Economic and Monetary Union (EMU)**, the ERM was superseded by **ERM II**.

ERM II (exchange rate mechanism II): the exchange rate arrangement which provides a framework for exchange rate policy cooperation between the euro area countries and the EU Member States not participating in Stage Three of EMU.

ESCB committees: established by the **Governing Council** of the **ECB**, under Article 9 of the ECB's Rules of Procedure, to assist the work of the ECB's decision-making bodies.

EU Council (Council of the European Union): an institution of the European Community. It is made up of representatives of the governments of the Member States, normally the ministers responsible for the matters under consideration (therefore often referred to as the Council of Ministers). The EU Council meeting in the composition of the ministers of finance and economy is often referred to as the **ECOFIN Council**. In addition, the EU Council may meet in the composition of the Heads of State or Government for decisions specified in the **Treaty** (see also **European Council**).

EU Treaty: see **Treaty**.

EUREPO: the rate at which one prime bank offers funds in **euro** to another prime bank in exchange for collateral consisting exclusively of government bonds and bills issued by euro area countries. The EUREPO's calculation methodology is similar to that of the **EURIBOR**, but it is representative of rates in the secured markets (repo markets). The panel of banks is also different.

EURIBOR (euro interbank offered rate): the rate at which a prime bank is willing to lend funds in **euro** to another prime bank, computed daily for interbank deposits with a maturity of up to 12 months. Unlike the EUREPO, the EURIBOR reflects conditions in the unsecured market.

Euro: the name of the European single currency adopted by the **European Council** at its meeting in Madrid on 15 and 16 December 1995.

Euro area: the area encompassing those Member States in which the **euro** has been adopted as the single currency in accordance with the **Treaty** and in which a single monetary policy is conducted under the responsibility of the **ECB**. The euro area currently comprises Belgium, Germany, Greece, Spain, France, Ireland, Italy, Luxembourg, the Netherlands, Austria, Portugal and Finland.

Euro Banking Association (EBA): an organisation which provides a forum for exploring and debating all banking issues of interest to its members and, in particular, matters related to the use of the **euro** and the settlement of transactions in euro. At the end of 1998, the EBA established a clearing company (ABE Clearing S.A.S., Société par Actions Simplifiée à Capital Variable) to manage the new Euro Clearing System (EURO1) from 1 January 1999; EURO1 is the successor to the ECU Clearing and Settlement System.

Euro central rate: the official exchange rate of **ERM II** member currencies vis-à-vis the euro, around which the ERM II fluctuation margins are defined.

Eurogroup: informal grouping bringing together those members of the **ECOFIN Council** who represent the **euro area** countries. It meets on a regular basis (usually prior to meetings of the ECOFIN Council) to discuss issues connected with the euro area countries' shared responsibilities for the single currency. The **European Commission** and, when appropriate, the **ECB** are invited to take part in these meetings.

European Banking Committee (EBC): established in 2003 by Commission Decision 2004/10/EC of 5 November 2003 (OJ L 3, 7.1.2004, p. 36) as a level 2 committee to advise the **European Commission** on policy issues relating to banking activities; it superseded the Banking Advisory Committee. The **ECB** is represented in the field of banking and supervision in the Committee of European Banking Supervisors, which is a level 3 committee.

European Central Bank (ECB): the ECB lies at the centre of the **European System of Central Banks (ESCB)** and the **Eurosystem** and has legal personality under Community law. It ensures that the tasks conferred upon the Eurosystem and the ESCB are implemented either through its own activities or through those of the NCBs, in line with the Statute of the European System of Central Banks and of the European Central Bank. The ECB is governed by the **Governing Council** and **Executive Board**, and, as a third and temporary decision-making body, by the **General Council**.

European Commission: the institution of the **European Community** which ensures the application of the provisions of the **Treaty**. The Commission develops Community policies, proposes Community legislation and exercises powers in specific areas. In the area of economic policy, the Commission recommends **Broad Economic Policy Guidelines (BEPGs)** and reports to the **EU Council** on economic developments and policies. It monitors public finances within the framework of multilateral surveillance and submits reports to the EU Council. Until 1 May 2004 it consisted of 20 members: two nationals each from Germany, Spain, France, Italy and the United Kingdom, and one from each of the other Member States. Following a transition period after EU enlargement, the Commission will consist of 25 members, one national for each of the 25 Member States.

European Community: supranational organisation which was established by the **EEC Treaty** in 1958 as the European Economic Community (EEC). The EU Treaty extended the tasks of the EEC which was accordingly renamed the European Community in 1993. The main tasks of the European Community are to promote the harmonious, balanced and sustainable development of economic activity, a high level of employment and social protection, equality between men and women, sustainable and non-inflationary growth, a high degree of competitiveness and convergence of economic performance, a high level of protection and improvement of the quality of the environment, a high standard of living and quality of life, and social cohesion and solidarity among Member States. It fulfils these tasks, among other things, through the single market and EMU.

European Council: provides the **European Union** with the necessary impetus for its development and defines the general political guidelines thereof. It brings together the Heads of State or Government of the Member States and the President of the **European Commission** (see also **EU Council**).

European Court of Justice (ECJ): a **European Community** institution, based in Luxembourg, which i) ensures that the treaties are interpreted and applied correctly; and ii) decides on the validity and the meaning of Community law. The acts and omissions of the **ECB** are subject to review by the ECJ.

European Monetary Cooperation Fund (EMCF): a former Community body established under Regulation (EEC) No 907/73 of the Council of 3 April 1973 (OJ L 89, 5.4.1973, p. 2). At the start of Stage Two of **EMU**, the EMCF was dissolved and its tasks taken over by the **European Monetary Institute (EMI)**.

European Monetary Institute (EMI): a temporary institution established at the start of Stage Two of **Economic and Monetary Union (EMU)** on 1 January 1994. The two main tasks of the EMI were to strengthen central bank cooperation and monetary policy coordination and to make the preparations required for the establishment of the **European System of Central Banks (ESCB)**, for the conduct of the single monetary policy and for the creation of a single currency in Stage Three of EMU. It went into liquidation when the **ECB** was established on 1 June 1998.

European Monetary System (EMS): an exchange rate regime created in 1979 by a Resolution of the European Council of 5 December 1978. Its operating procedures were laid down in the Agreement of 13 March 1979 between the central banks of the Member States of the European Economic Community. The EMS provided a framework for close monetary and exchange rate policy cooperation between the Member States of the **European Community**. Its main components were the **ECU**, the exchange rate and intervention mechanism **(ERM)**, very short-term financing mechanisms and short and medium-term credit mechanisms. At the start of **Stage Three** of **EMU**, the EMS was superseded by **ERM II**.

European Parliament: a Community institution that comprises 732 representatives of the citizens of the Member States as of the parliamentary term 2004-2009. It contributes to the legislative process, although with different prerogatives according to the procedures through which EU law is to be enacted. In the framework of **Economic and Monetary Union (EMU)**, Parliament has mainly consultative powers. However, the **Treaty** establishes certain procedures for the democratic **accountability** of the **ECB** to Parliament (presentation of the Annual Report, general debate on monetary policy, testimonies before the competent parliamentary committees).

European System of Central Banks (ESCB): composed of the **ECB** and the NCBs of all 25 Member States, i.e. it includes, in addition to the members of the **Eurosystem**, the NCBs of the Member States that have not yet adopted the euro. The ESCB is governed by the **Governing Council** and the **Executive Board** of the ECB, and, as a third and temporary decision-making body of the ECB, by the **General Council**. The core tasks of the ESCB are carried out by the Eurosystem.

European Union (EU): established by the **Treaty on European Union (EU Treaty)**, often referred to as the "Maastricht Treaty", which was signed on February 1992 and entered into force on 1 November 1993. This Treaty has subsequently been amended by the "Treaty of Amsterdam", which was signed in Amsterdam on 2 October 1997 and entered into force on 1 May 1999, and most recently by the "Treaty of Nice", which was signed on 26 February 2001 and entered into force on 1 February 2003. The European Union (EU) rests on several organisations and arrangements with different legal natures that constitute the three supporting pillars. The first pillar comprises the **European Community** and the European Atomic Energy Community (Euratom), which both possess legal personality and are governed by separate Treaties. The second and third pillars are essentially intergovernmental arrangements on the common foreign and security policy, and police and judicial cooperation in criminal matters.

Eurostat: the Statistical Office of the European Communities. Eurostat is part of the **European Commission** and is responsible for the production of Community statistics.

Eurosystem: comprises the **ECB** and the NCBs of the Member States that have adopted the **euro** in Stage Three of **Economic and Monetary Union** (see also **euro area**). There are currently 12 NCBs in the Eurosystem. The Eurosystem is governed by the **Governing Council** and the **Executive Board** of the ECB.

Eurosystem staff projections: the results of exercises conducted by **Eurosystem** staff to project possible future macroeconomic developments in the **euro area** as part of the economic analysis.

Excessive deficit procedure: the provision defined in Article 104 of the **EC Treaty** and specified in Protocol No 20 (on the **excessive deficit procedure**) requires EU Member States to maintain budgetary discipline, defines criteria for a budgetary position to be considered an excessive deficit and sets out the steps to be taken following the observation that the criteria for the budget balance or government debt have not been fulfilled. This is supplemented by Council Regulation (EC) No 1467/97 of 7 July 1997 on speeding up and clarifying the implementation of the excessive deficit procedure, which is an element of the **Stability and Growth Pact**.

Executive Board: one of the decision-making bodies of the **ECB**. It comprises the President and Vice-President of the ECB and four other members appointed by common accord by the Heads of State or Government of the countries that have adopted the **euro**.

Fine-tuning operation: a non-regular **open market operation** executed by the **Eurosystem** mainly in order to deal with unexpected liquidity fluctuations in the market.

Foreign exchange swap: simultaneous spot and forward transactions exchanging one currency against another. The **Eurosystem** can execute **open market operations** in the form of foreign exchange swaps, where the NCBs (or the **ECB**) buy or sell **euro** spot against a foreign currency and, at the same time, sell or buy them back in a forward transaction.

General Council: one of the decision-making bodies of the **ECB**. It comprises the President and Vice-President of the ECB and the governors of all EU NCBs.

Governing Council: the supreme decision-making body of the **ECB**. It comprises all the members of the **Executive Board** of the ECB and the governors of the NCBs of the countries that have adopted the **euro**.

Harmonised Index of Consumer Prices (HICP): index of consumer prices whose statistical methodology has been harmonised across countries.

Interlinking mechanism: one of the components of the **TARGET** system. The term is used to designate the infrastructures and procedures which link domestic **RTGS systems** in order to enable the processing of cross-border payments within TARGET.

International Monetary Fund (IMF): an international monetary organisation which was established in 1944 under the Bretton Woods Agreement. It is based in Washington DC, and now has 184 member countries. Under the IMF Articles of Agreement, its main tasks are to foster global monetary cooperation, secure exchange rate stability, facilitate international trade and promote economic growth.

Key ECB interest rates: the interest rates set by the **Governing Council**, which reflect the monetary policy stance of the **ECB**. They are the **minimum bid rate** on the **main refinancing operations**, the interest rate on the **marginal lending facility** and the interest rate on the **deposit facility**.

Link between securities settlement systems: procedures and arrangements between **securities settlement systems (SSSs)** for the transfer of securities through a book-entry process. As an alternative to the **CCBM**, the **Eurosystem** uses eligible links for the cross-border mobilisation of **collateral**.

Longer-term refinancing operation: a monthly **open market operation**, conducted by the **Eurosystem**, with a usual maturity of three months. The operations are conducted as variable rate tenders with pre-announced allotment volumes.

Main refinancing operation: a weekly **open market operation** conducted by the **Eurosystem**. On 9 March 2004 the maturity of these operations was reduced from two weeks to one week, following a Governing Council decision of 2003. The operations are conducted as variable rate tenders with a pre-announced **minimum bid rate**.

Maintenance period: the period over which **credit institutions'** compliance with **reserve requirements** is calculated. Since 10 March 2004 the maintenance period has begun on the settlement day of the first **main refinancing operation** following the meeting of the **Governing Council** at which the monthly assessment of the monetary policy stance is pre-scheduled. The **ECB** publishes a calendar of the reserve maintenance periods at least three months before the start of the year.

Marginal lending facility: a **standing facility** of the **Eurosystem** which **counterparties** may use to receive credit from an NCB at a pre-specified **interest rate** against eligible assets (see **key ECB interest rates**).

Minimum bid rate: lower limit to the **interest rates** at which **counterparties** may submit bids in the variable rate tenders of the **main refinancing operations**. This is one of the **key ECB interest rates** reflecting the stance of monetary policy.

Monetary Committee: Committee established by Article 105(2) of the **EEC Treaty**; it was superseded by the **Economic and Financial Committee (EFC)** at the beginning of Stage Three of **EMU**.

MFIs (monetary financial institutions) : financial institutions forming the money-issuing sector of the **euro area**. They include the **ECB**, the NCBs of the euro area countries, and credit institutions and money market funds located in the euro area.

Monetary income: income accruing to the NCBs in the performance of the **Eurosystem**'s monetary policy function, derived from assets earmarked in accordance with guidelines established by the **Governing Council** and held against banknotes in circulation and deposit liabilities to credit institutions.

Monetary policy strategy: the general approach to the conduct of monetary policy. The monetary policy strategy of the **ECB** comprises a quantitative definition of the primary objective of **price stability** and an analytical framework based on two pillars – economic analysis and monetary analysis – which forms the basis of the **Governing Council**'s overall assessment of the risks to price stability and its monetary policy decisions. It also provides the framework for explaining monetary policy decisions to the public.

OLAF (European Anti-Fraud Office): the office of the **European Commission** which investigates fraud and other irregular action in the **European Community** in the case of a reasoned suspicion. In July 2003 the **European Court of Justice (ECJ)** ruled that OLAF's investigating powers also extend to the **ECB**.

Open market operation: an operation executed on the initiative of the central bank in the financial markets involving one of the following transactions: (i) buying or selling assets outright (spot or forward); (ii) buying or selling assets under a **repurchase agreement**; (iii) lending or borrowing against underlying assets as **collateral**; (iv) issuing central bank debt certificates; (v) accepting fixed-term deposits; or (vi) conducting **foreign exchange swaps** between domestic and foreign currencies.

Organisation for Economic Co-operation and Development (OECD): an intergovernmental organisation, established in 1950 and based in Paris. It currently has 30 member countries and links with 70 others. It provides a forum for its members to consult each other, to compare experiences and to cooperate in order to achieve the highest possible sustainable growth and improve economic and social well-being in line with the principles of a market economy.

Payment system: a set of instruments, banking procedures and, typically, interbank funds transfer systems that ensure the circulation of money. Payment systems require agreed technical standards and methods for transmitting payment messages between participants, an agreed settlement asset and a set of common operating procedures and rules covering, among other things, access criteria and pricing.

Price stability: the maintenance of price stability is the primary objective of the **Eurosystem**. The Governing Council defines price stability as a year-on-year increase of below 2% in the **Harmonised Index of Consumer Prices (HICP)** for the **euro area**. The Governing Council has also made it clear that, in the pursuit of price stability, it aims to maintain inflation rates below, but close to, 2% over the medium term.

Projections: see **Eurosystem staff projections**.

Quick tender: the tender procedure used by the **Eurosystem** for **fine-tuning operations**. Quick tenders are carried out within a time frame of one hour and are restricted to a limited set of **counterparties**.

Real-time gross settlement (RTGS) system : a settlement system in which processing and settlement take place on an order-by-order basis (without netting) in real time (continuously) (see also **TARGET**).

Reference value for monetary growth: in order to assess monetary developments, the **Governing Council** has announced a reference value for the broad monetary aggregate M3. This reference value refers to the rate of M3 growth that is deemed to be compatible with price stability over the medium term. The reference value is derived in a manner that is consistent with and serves the achievement of the **Governing Council**'s definition of **price stability** on the basis of medium-term assumptions regarding trend real GDP growth and the trend in the velocity of circulation of M3. Substantial or prolonged deviations of M3 growth from the reference value would, under normal circumstances, signal risks to price stability over the medium term. However, monetary policy does not react mechanically to deviations of M3 growth from the reference value.

Repurchase agreement: an agreement to sell an asset and to repurchase it at a specified price on a pre-determined future date or on demand. Such an agreement is similar to collateralised borrowing, except that in this case ownership of the securities is not retained by the seller. Repurchase transactions are included in M3 in cases where the seller is a monetary financial institution (MFI) and the counterparty is a non-MFI resident in the euro area.

Reserve base: the sum of the balance sheet items (in particular liabilities) which constitute the basis for calculating the **reserve requirement** of a **credit institution**.

Reserve ratio: a ratio defined by the central bank for each category of balance sheet items included in the **reserve base**. The ratios are used to calculate the **reserve requirement**.

Reserve requirement: the minimum amount of reserves a **credit institution** is required to hold with the **Eurosystem**. Compliance is determined on the basis of the average of the daily balances over a **maintenance period** of around one month.

Reverse transaction: an operation whereby the central bank buys or sells assets under a **repurchase agreement** or conducts credit operations against **collateral**.

Securities settlement system (SSS): a system which permits the holding and transfer of securities or other financial assets, either free of payment or against payment (delivery versus payment).

Settlement risk: a general term used to designate the risk that settlement in a transfer system will not take place as expected. This risk may comprise both credit and liquidity risk.

Stability and Growth Pact: consists of two **EU Council** Regulations, namely: (i) Regulation (EC) No 1466/97 of 7 July 1997 on the strengthening of the surveillance of budgetary positions and the surveillance and coordination of economic policies; and (ii) Regulation (EC) No 1467/97 of 7 July 1997 on speeding up and clarifying the implementation of the **excessive deficit procedure**, and of a **European Council** Resolution on the Stability and Growth Pact adopted at the Amsterdam summit on 17 June 1997. It is intended to serve as a means of safeguarding sound government finances in Stage Three of **EMU** in order to strengthen the conditions for price stability and for strong, sustainable growth conducive to employment creation. More specifically, budgetary positions close to balance or in surplus are required as the medium-term objective for Member States.

Stability programmes: medium-term government plans and assumptions provided by **euro area** countries regarding the development of key economic variables. They set out the medium-term objective of a budgetary position that is close to balance or in surplus, or the adjustment path towards this objective as referred to in the **Stability and Growth Pact**. Stability programmes must be updated annually. They are examined by the **European Commission** and the **Economic and Financial Committee (EFC)**, whose assessments serve as the basis for the examination by the **ECOFIN Council**.

Standard tender: a tender procedure used by the **Eurosystem** in its regular **open market operations**. Standard tenders are carried out within 24 hours. All counterparties fulfilling the general eligibility criteria are entitled to submit bids.

Standing facility: a central bank facility available to counterparties on their own initiative. The **Eurosystem** offers two overnight standing facilities: the **marginal lending facility** and the **deposit facility**.

Statute of the European System of Central Banks and of the European Central Bank (Statute of the ESCB): organic law of the **European System of Central Banks (ESCB)** and of the **European Central Bank (ECB)**, annexed as a Protocol to the **EC Treaty**.

TARGET (Trans-European Automated Real-time Gross settlement Express Transfer system): the **RTGS system** for the **euro**. It is a decentralised system consisting of 15 national RTGS systems, the ECB payment mechanism (EPM) and the interlinking mechanism.

TARGET2: the second generation of the **TARGET** system, which is being developed to increase financial integration within the **euro area**. The main objectives of TARGET2 will be: (i) to better meet customers' needs by providing harmonised interfaces; (ii) to guarantee cost effectiveness by introducing a single price structure for core services; and (iii) to pave the way for the future, including developments related to the enlargement of the **European Union** and the **Eurosystem**. In TARGET2, the NCBs will remain responsible for the accounts and business relations with credit institutions. It is expected that the new system will become operational in the second half of this decade.

Treaty: refers to the **Treaty establishing the European Community (EC Treaty)**. The Treaty was signed in Rome on 25 March 1957 (therefore often referred to as the "Treaty of Rome") and entered into force on 1 January 1958. It established the European Economic Community (EEC), which is now the **European Community**. The Treaty on European Union **(EU Treaty)**, which is often referred to as the "Maastricht Treaty", amended the EEC Treaty with a view to establishing the **European Community**.

BIBLIOGRAPHY

GENERAL LITERATURE

Official ECB publications

ECB (1999), *Annual Report 1998*, April 1999.

ECB (2000), *Annual Report 1999*, April 2000.

ECB (2001), *Annual Report 2000*, May 2001.

ECB (2002), *Annual Report 2001*, April 2002.

ECB (2003), *Annual Report 2002*, April 2003.

ECB (2004), *Annual Report 2003*, April 2004.

ECB (2002), *Compendium: collection of legal instruments, June 1998 – December 2001*, March 2002.

ECB (2002), *The European Central Bank* (public information brochure), September 2002.

Other publications

Papadia, F. and Santini, C. (1999), *La Banque centrale européenne*, Paris, 1999.

Raymond, R. (2001), *L'euro et l'unité de l'Europe*, Paris, 2001.

Scheller, H. K. (1999), *Das Europäische System der Zentralbanken*, in Glomb/Lauk (eds.), Euro Guide, Cologne, 1999.

Scheller, H. K. (2000), *Die Europäische Zentralbank*, Frankfurt am Main, 2000.

Von der Groeben, H., Thiesing, J. and Ehlermann, C.-D. (eds.), *Kommentar zum EU/EG-Vertrag*, 5th edition, Baden-Baden, 1997/1999.

Zilioli, C. and Selmayr, M. (2001), *The Law of the European Central Bank*, Oxford-Portland Oregon, 2001.

CHAPTER I

Official ECB publications

ECB (2000), *Convergence Report 2000*, May 2000.

ECB (2002), *Convergence Report 2002*, May 2002.

ECB (2001), *The economic policy framework in EMU*, Monthly Bulletin article, November 2001.

ECB (2003), *The relationship between monetary policy and fiscal policies in the euro area*, Monthly Bulletin article, February 2003.

Other publications

Andrews, D. (2003), *The Committee of Central Bank Governors as a source of rules*, Journal of European Public Policy 10:6, December 2003, pp. 956-973.

Baer, G. D. (1994), *The Committee of Governors as a forum for European central bank cooperation*, in Bakker, A. et al. (eds.), *Monetary Stability through International Cooperation: Essays in Honor of André Szász*, Amsterdam, 1994.

Berger, F. (2001), *12 into one: one money for Europe*, Frankfurt am Main, 2001.

Committee for the study of economic and monetary union (Delors Committee), *Report on economic and monetary union in the European Community*, 1989.

Committee of Governors of the central banks of the Member States of the European Economic Community (1990), *Introductory Report and Commentary on the Statute of the European System of Central Banks and the ECB*, November 1990.

Committee of Governors of the central banks of the Member States of the European Economic Community (1992), *Annual Report 1990/91*, April 1992.

Committee of Governors of the central banks of the Member States of the European Economic Community (1993), *Annual Report 1992*, April 1993.

European Commission (1995), *Green Paper on the Practical Arrangements for the Introduction of the Single Currency (COM(95) 33 final)*, Luxembourg, 31 May 1995.

EMI (1995), *Annual Report 1994*, April 1995.

EMI (1995), *The changeover to the single currency*, November 1995.

EMI (1996), *Role and functions of the European Monetary Institute*, February 1996.

EMI (1996), *Annual Report 1995*, April 1996.

EMI (1997), *The single monetary policy in Stage Three: specification of the operational framework*, January 1997.

EMI (1997), *Annual Report 1996*, April 1997.

EMI (1998), *Convergence Report: Report required by Article 109j of the Treaty establishing the European Community*, March 1998.

EMI (1998), *Annual Report 1997*, May 1998.

Scheller, H. K. (2001), *The Changeover to the Euro, in Caesar/Scharrer (eds.), European Economic and Monetary Union: Regional and Global Challenges, Baden-Baden*, 2001, pp. 243-263.

CHAPTER 2

Official ECB publications

ECB (1999), *The Eurosystem and the European System of Central Banks (ESCB)*, Monthly Bulletin article, January 1999.

ECB (1999), *The institutional framework of the European System of Central Banks*, Monthly Bulletin article, July 1999.

ECB (1999), *Legal instruments of the European Central Bank*, Monthly Bulletin article, November 1999.

ECB (2001), *Why price stability?*, June 2001.

ECB (2003), *The adjustment of voting modalities in the Governing Council*, Monthly Bulletin article, May 2003.

Other publications

Arrowsmith, J. A. A. (1996), *La non-participation à la phase 3: la vie à l'étage inférieur de l'UEM (Opting-out of stage 3: life in the lower tier of EMU)*, in Revue d'économie financière, No 36, 1-1996.

Caparello, M. (2003), *Internal audit in the central banking community*, in Courtis, N. and Mander, B. (eds.), *Accounting standards for central banks*, Central Banking Publications, London, 2003.

Duisenberg, W. F. (2001), *The European Central Bank, the Eurosystem and the European System of Central Banks*, speech delivered at the ceremony to inaugurate the new building of the Banque centrale du Luxembourg, Luxembourg, 18 May 2001.

Liebscher, K. (1998), *Die Rolle einer nationalen Zentralbank im ESZB am Beispiel der OeNB*, in 26. Volkswirtschaftliche Tagung der Oesterreichischen Nationalbank, May 1998.

Merriman, N. (2003), *Financial reporting in the Eurosystem*, in Courtis, N. and Mander, B. (eds.), *Accounting standards for central banks*, Central Banking Publications, London, 2003.

Padoa-Schioppa, T. (2000), *An institutional glossary of the Eurosystem*, article delivered at the conference on "The Constitution of the Eurosystem: the Views of the EP and the ECB", 8 March 2000.

Palmer, M. (2001), *The Banque centrale du Luxembourg in the European System of Central Banks*, Banque centrale du Luxembourg, May 2001.

Raymond, R. (1996), *Les Banques centrales nationales dans le système européen de banques centrales (National central banks within the European System of Central Banks)*, in Revue d'économie financière, No 36, 1-1996.

CHAPTER 3

Official ECB publications

ECB (1999), *The stability-oriented monetary policy strategy of the Eurosystem*, Monthly Bulletin article, January 1999.

ECB (1999), *TARGET and payments in euro*, Monthly Bulletin article, November 1999.

ECB (2000), *Foreign exchange reserves and operations of the Eurosystem*, Monthly Bulletin article, January 2000.

ECB (2000), *EMU and banking supervision*, Monthly Bulletin article, April 2000.

ECB (2001), *Eurosystem staff macroeconomic projection exercises for the euro area*, Monthly Bulletin article, June 2001.

ECB (2002), *Euro banknote preparations: from cash changeover to post-launch activities*, Monthly Bulletin article, January 2002.

ECB (2002), *The role of the Eurosystem in payment and clearing systems*, Monthly Bulletin article, April 2002.

ECB (2002), *The liquidity management of the ECB*, Monthly Bulletin article, May 2002.

ECB (2002), *Implications of the euro cash changeover on the development of banknotes and coins in circulation*, Monthly Bulletin article, May 2002.

ECB (2003), *The demand for currency in the euro area and the impact of the euro cash changeover*, Monthly Bulletin article, January 2003.

ECB (2003), *CLS – purpose, concept and implications*, Monthly Bulletin article, January 2003.

ECB (2003), *The outcome of the ECB's evaluation of its monetary policy strategy*, Monthly Bulletin article, June 2003.

ECB (2003), *Changes to the Eurosystem's operational framework for monetary policy*, Monthly Bulletin article, August 2003.

ECB (2000), *Statistical information collected and compiled by the ESCB*, May 2000.

ECB (2002), *Evaluation of the 2002 cash changeover*, April 2002.

ECB (2003), *EU banking sector stability*, February 2003.

ECB (2003), *ECB Statistics: a brief overview*, August 2003.

ECB (2003), *TARGET: the Trans-European Automated Real-time Gross settlement Express Transfer system – update 2003* (public information brochure), November 2003.

ECB (2004), *The monetary policy of the ECB (second edition)*, January 2004.

ECB (2004), *The implementation of monetary policy in the euro area: General documentation on Eurosystem monetary policy instruments and procedures*, February 2004.

Other publications

Domingo-Solans, E. (2003), *The importance of Eurostat for the monetary policy of the European Central Bank*, speech delivered at the academic meeting on the occasion of the 50th anniversary of the Statistical Office of the European Communities, Luxembourg, 16 May 2003.

Duisenberg, W. F. (2001), *The ECB's monetary policy strategy and the quantitative definition of price stability*, letter of the President of the ECB to the Chairperson of the Committee on Economic and Monetary Affairs, Mrs Christa Randzio-Plath, 13 December 2001.

Issing, O., Gaspar, V., Angeloni, I. and Tristani, O. (2001), *Monetary policy in the euro area: strategy and decision-making at the European Central Bank*, Cambridge University Press, Cambridge, 2001.

Issing, O. et al. (eds.) (2003), *Background Studies for the ECB's Evaluation of its Monetary Policy Strategy*, Frankfurt am Main, November 2003.

Trichet, J.-C. (2003), *The ECB's monetary strategy after the evaluation and clarification of May 2003*, speech delivered at the Center for Financial Studies' key event, Frankfurt am Main, 20 November 2003.

Trichet, J.-C. (2004), *Euro area statistics and their use for ECB policy-making*, speech delivered at the Second ECB Conference on Statistics, Frankfurt am Main, 22-23 April 2004.

CHAPTER 4

Official ECB publications

ECB (2000), *The ECB's relations with institutions and bodies of the European Community*, Monthly Bulletin article, October 2000.

ECB (2001), *The external communication of the European Central Bank*, Monthly Bulletin article, February 2001.

ECB (2002), *The accountability of the ECB*, Monthly Bulletin article, November 2002.

ECB (2002), *Transparency in the monetary policy of the ECB*, Monthly Bulletin article, November 2002.

Other publications

Noyer, C. (1999), *Politics and central banks*, speech held at Eesti Pank, Tallinn, 3 May 1999.

Zilioli, C. and Selmayr, M. (2000), *The European Central Bank: An Independent Specialised Organization of Community Law*, Common Market Law Review, 2000 – Volume 37, Issue 3, pp. 591-644.

CHAPTER 5

Official ECB publications

ECB (1999), *The international role of the euro*, Monthly Bulletin article, August 1999.

ECB (2001), *The ECB's relations with international organisations and fora*, Monthly Bulletin article, January 2001.

ECB (2002), *International supervisory co-operation*, Monthly Bulletin article, May 2002.

ECB (2002), *Review of the international role of the euro*, December 2002.

Other publications

Duisenberg, W. F. (2000), *The role of the ECB at the international level*, speech delivered at the Annual Meeting of the Institute for International Finance, Inc. (IIF), Prague, 23 September 2000.

Padoa-Schioppa, T. (1999), *The external representation of the euro area*, introductory statement at the Sub-Committee on Monetary Affairs of the European Parliament, Brussels, 17 March 1999.

Zilioli, C. and Selmayr, M. (1999), *The External Relations of the Euro Area: Legal Aspects*, Common Market Law Review, 1999 – Volume 36, Issue 2, pp. 273-349.

CHAPTER 6

Official ECB publications

ECB (2000), *ECB labour relationships and the social dialogue with regard to the ESCB*, ECB's Press Release of 5 October 2000.

ECB (2002), *Code of Conduct of the European Central Bank in accordance with Article 11.3 of the Rules of Procedure of the European Central Bank*, March 2001 (OJ C 76, 8.3.2001, p. 12).

ECB (2002), *Code of Conduct for the Members of the Governing Council*, 16 May 2002 (OJ C 123, 24.5.2002, p. 9).

ECB (2003), *The mission of the European Central Bank*, August 2003.

Other publications

Ricard, P. (2001), *Voyage au centre de la BCE*, Le Monde, 23 November 2001.

INDEX